W9-AFH-643

AVID
READER
PRESS

ALSO BY HARRISON SCOTT KEY

Congratulations, Who Are You Again?

The World's Largest Man

HOW TO

STAY

MARRIED

The Most Insane Love Story Ever Told

HARRISON SCOTT KEY

AVID READER PRESS

New York   London   Toronto   Sydney   New Delhi

AVID READER PRESS
An Imprint of Simon & Schuster, Inc.
1230 Avenue of the Americas
New York, NY 10020

First Avid Reader Press hardcover edition June 2023

AVID READER PRESS and colophon are trademarks of Simon & Schuster, Inc.

For information about special discounts for bulk purchases,
please contact Simon & Schuster Special Sales
at 1-866-506-1949 or business@simonandschuster.com.

The Simon & Schuster Speakers Bureau can bring authors to your live event.
For more information or to book an event contact the
Simon & Schuster Speakers Bureau at 1-866-248-3049
or visit our website at www.simonspeakers.com.

Interior design by Ruth Lee-Mui

Manufactured in the United States of America

1 3 5 7 9 10 8 6 4 2

Library of Congress Cataloging-in-Publication Data
Names: Key, Harrison Scott, author.
Title: How to stay married : the most insane love story ever told / Harrison Scott Key.
Description: First Avid Reader Press hardcover edition. |
New York : Avid Reader Press, 2023.
Identifiers: LCCN 2022059279 (print) | LCCN 2022059280 (ebook) |
ISBN 9781668015506 (hardcover) | ISBN 9781668015650 (paperback) |
ISBN 9781668015667 (ebook)
Subjects: LCSH: Key, Harrison Scott. | Authors, American—
21st century—Biography. | Marriage—Humor. | Christian life—Humor. |
Mississippi—Biography. | LCGFT: Autobiographies.
Classification: LCC PS3611.E966 Z46 2023 (print) | LCC PS3611.E966
(ebook) | DDC 813/.6 [B]—dc23/eng/20230327
LC record available at https://lccn.loc.gov/2022059279
LC ebook record available at https://lccn.loc.gov/2022059280

ISBN 978-1-6680-1550-6
ISBN 978-1-6680-1566-7 (ebook)

For my biological son, Gary,
who cannot read this, because he is a dog

A Note to Readers

Some have questioned my publishing this book, understandably worried that, in my attempt at healing, I might end up causing more hurt. I share that concern and have done my best to write with charity and discretion, altering names and details that might get one disinvited from a Rotary luncheon.

Writing this story is the second-hardest thing I have ever done in my life. Living through the events described here without committing a felony is the hardest. I would have preferred to write a less painful book. When everything went down, I was working on a novel about a Sasquatch who plays college football. My working title was *Big Man on Campus*. But I had to put that book on ice, which is probably for the best. Does Bigfoot speak English? Does he wear clothes to class? Fiction is hard.

Instead, I wrote this story, which is by turns confession, cautionary fable, true-crime romance, and paranormal nonfiction dystopian farce. Whatever you call it, it's our story, my wife's and mine. Others have their own. If they read this book, I hope they will find love in these pages. But sadly, no Sasquatches. Maybe next time.

"Angels can fly because they can take themselves lightly."

G. K. Chesterton, *Orthodoxy*

A CONVERSATION WITH THE BEAST

My wife and I sit on the worn leather sofa in my office, waiting for our therapist, Dr. Berman, to appear on the screen, as though we are in a Philip K. Dick rom-com. Lauren sits on the far side of the couch, as far as she can get and still technically be on this particular piece of furniture. I have little doubt that she would rather be swimming in a pod of famished orcas than sitting on this sofa with me. It is early afternoon. She holds a McDonald's Coke. I would like to be holding a bucket of wine, but this seems bad form for our first session of marriage counseling. She is here and I am here but we are not here together.

For many years, the sofa has served mostly as a place for the draping of lightly soiled garments, though I've been sleeping on it for six months. The sofa makes a fine bed, if you're looking to ponder your profoundest regrets while herniating a disc. I bought a weighted blanket, thinking this would help, because sleeplessness is always more fun when you feel like you're trapped under rubble.

Will I ever again share a soft bed with my wife? Perhaps Dr. Berman will have some insight.

When I was growing up, nobody I knew went to therapy because therapy was for weak people on TV with disposable income. My ancestors, I am told, were not weak. I come from a long line of frontiersmen and outdoorsmen, people who wore pelts and spent much of their time trying not to be mauled by bears. They spoke to God often, I assume, likely regarding the bears, but you wouldn't have caught my father at therapy. Pop knew that the best way to rid yourself of trauma was to bequeath it to your children. He was a generous man.

"Hello there!" Dr. Berman says, appearing on-screen, hirsute and massive, somewhere between a lumberjack and a rabbi. He's Jewish, I figure, which I like. We've tried a couple of Christian counselors in the distant past, nice men who frightened us off by quoting the sort of Scripture your MAGA aunt stitches onto pillows. I preferred a therapist who might quote Freud, or at least John Prine. I was excited to see what Dr. Berman had in store. Scream therapy? Hypnosis? Hand puppets? Things can get no weirder than they've been. The last year has been an absurdist nightmare.

After introductions, during which I make too many jokes and Lauren speaks like a skilled assassin who refuses to crack under threat of torture, Dr. Berman gets right to it:

"Can we table any talk of ending the marriage for at least six months?"

We both say, you know, sure.

Most people go to marriage counseling when they're at the precipice, but we've already gone over the precipice and discovered another precipice down below, from which we also fell, and another, then another, until all our bones were broken, our spines severed, our lungs punctured. We are highly experienced at falling off precipices.

By this point, I'm willing to try anything, even paying a stranger to ask questions neither of us wants to answer. By our second session, next week, he'll have us talking to each other with the aid of a small stuffed manatee called Dr. Beast, borrowed from one of my daughters. Sometimes it'll be a tiny panda and sometimes an enormous pickled cucumber with arms and legs called Mr. Pickle, but mostly it will be Dr. Beast. Every session, I go find a new animal from one of the girls' beds. I will soon have heard things you don't ever want to hear while staring at a stuffed sea mammal.

But we're not there yet. We've just begun.

"Who wants to start?" Dr. Berman asks.

I DON'T KNOW WHAT
YOU'VE HEARD

2021

I used to care what people thought of me. I could hide neither my physical nor my most obvious spiritual faults—the spectacular baldness, the heliotropic ears, the hillbilly teeth, my uncharitable spirit, an everlasting hunger for praise, the quiet condescension I project in the presence of men who cannot grow a beard—but I felt that if I could make you laugh, maybe you'd forgive me all this and love me anyway. And it worked.

The world showered me with affection in exchange for the laughter, on stages and podcasts, at parties and TSA screenings, and this genial parlor trick felt good, to know that others envied my life or at least found me hilarious, charming, and slightly mysterious, the mystery being how I could simultaneously look like a distended cadaver in a medical textbook and have such an attractive wife.

I am a needy man. My wit, I hoped, would enchant others, including my wife, and make the world and my home less resistant to my presence. If everyone loved me, good things would manifest. I would become wealthy. I would lose weight. My hair would grow back. The past would unhappen. But I no longer care to be loved. God loves me. That will have to do.

Because some stuff happened, and the stuff changed me. And it changed how others saw me, and how I saw others seeing me, and how I saw God seeing me. I have become the kind of man who sits in his driveway smoking cigarettes in his underwear while waving at moms from the school around the corner as they drive by and pretend not to see. They know. They know what happened. They've heard.

"Those poor kids," they say.

Our kids are fine. They'll be fine. I'm sure they'll be fine.

My wife and me, however. That's what this book is about.

"I thought you were going to get divorced" is one thing people said when they read my first book. I still get DMs like this. "I'm glad you didn't!"

"I was pretty sure you were going to cheat on your wife" is what people said when they read my second book. "I was so relieved you didn't!"

My wife, Lauren, is perhaps my greatest literary creation, this very real woman who served for so long as my foil, the deliverer of wincing punch lines to my foolishness. In most of what I have written about her, in books and essays you are welcome to google, I have chosen only her best lines, her finest comedy, and her choicest virtues: Her cast-iron love for the girls. Her ageless beauty, candor, and patience. Her gift for mothering all those around her. Her sense of humor, which is somehow both more wicked and more endearing than mine. Everybody who has read my work wants to be her friend. Maybe if I hadn't made her so likable and funny, maybe you wouldn't have been as surprised as I was by what happened.

What happened was, my wife for a billion years—the mother of our three daughters, a woman who's spent just about every Sunday of her life in a church—snuck off and found herself a boyfriend. Not cool. Her boyfriend, I mean. He has a decorative seashell collection and can't even grow a beard. I am not making this up.

This is why I smoke in my driveway and the nice moms look away—and why other moms, mostly single ones, now send me decontextualized Bible verses and memes involving sunrises and new beginnings, possibly with them. I am appreciative of the women who would like to spoon with me; really, I am, but I fear they may not wish to cuddle until after they hear the whole story. That is why I wrote this book. I wanted to strip away the façade I have worked so long to cultivate: in reality, in literature, in my imagination. My imagination is the real villain here. I did not write this book for revenge. Books cannot grant you vengeance against your wife's lover. That's what baseball bats are for.

No, I wrote this book to confess.

I am no stranger to confession. I've made a career of it. In books and stories and even a TEDx talk viewed, at last count, by 150,000 Russian bots, I've described my own vanity, ambition, ingratitude, incapacities, insecurities, failures. I've besmirched the names of the living and the dead, and I was allowed to do that so long as I made it hilarious and true. But some truths I have kept hidden, which shall remain hidden no more. I knew if I wrote a book about my marriage, I would also be compelled to write about all the garbage unearthed in my own heart by the marriage. If this book is a hit job, my pride is the true target.

Mrs. Pulaski, my high school English teacher, taught me a great lesson about truth. On the first day of school in the tenth grade, when she introduced herself, she said something that stuck with me. After writing her name on the board, she said, "On some days, I might look different to you all because I have a condition that causes me to bloat."

Mrs. Pulaski was a fantastic teacher, especially cherished in the small public school in Star, Mississippi, where many of the students could hardly read and those who could often refused to on religious grounds. With authority and feeling she taught us how to pull apart a sentence and name its parts and instantiate its meaning. I remember Mrs. Pulaski's lessons well, and you know what else I remember? That thing she said about bloating. Why did she tell us that? Because all through high school, that's all we thought about.

"Is she bloating today?" we wondered.

"No, she looks the same."

"No, she's totally bloating."

Why was she bloating? Was she dying? You don't just go telling a roomful of hormone-ravaged clods that you have a condition that causes transmutation: they will eat you alive. But we did not. Why did we love her? She was sparing with praise, spent most of her time explaining how terrible our writing was, how pitifully bereft our minds were of original thoughts, and how these facts, in the aggregate, represented the imminent decline of world civilization and thus caused further bloating. No, we loved her not because she came in with threats or swagger or charm, but because she presented us with the thing that would set us free.

So I confess it to you now, the Truth.

My wife had this affair with a man who had been my friend. I want to tell you all about it: all the secret befores, all the dreadful afters, including the part where I cried so hard at work they sent me home with a frozen chicken pot pie.

Men never talk about being betrayed. I want to. I feel I must. I have many deep convictions, and one of them is that suffering can and should be monetized. But before I can walk you through my hilarious nightmare, I have to confess something else, which is that I, like my dear wife, am a Christian. It will be important to understand this bewildering fact about me because my weirdo religious faith shapes everything in this story: what I believed and no longer believe and sometimes still do believe about marriage, family, truth, community, home, evil, love, forgiveness, miracles, and all the rest. If you're reading this, there's a good chance that no matter what you believe about organized religion, your concepts of love and marriage have been shaped by monotheism, and I cannot reckon the facts of this story without also reckoning with the faith that has warped me into the hideous, broken, beloved creature that I am.

What do I believe, exactly? I believe there is a thing called God. I believe happy endings are real. I believe the Bible is both a comic novel and the oddest and most accurate accounting of human psychology ever assembled. For some of you, I know this is weird stuff. And it is. It is very weird to subject yourself to an ancient religion that dares you to live according to a collection of primitive writings featuring more murder and foreskin content than is perhaps advisable for young children, the central theme of its stories being that everyone should imitate the strange behaviors of a divine hayseed born in a Palestinian cowshed to an eighth grader who just woke up one day pregnant.

You probably believe some crazy things, too. I know a respected scholar who believes electromagnetic energy can cleanse her breast milk of impurities, but I don't tell her I think she's nuts, because Jesus says I have to feel compassion for crazy people. I'm sure she thinks I'm nuts because I believe the Christmas story really happened. I've known many teenage mothers who are virgins. They're called Baptists. So, yeah, I believe the miracles. Miracles are easy to believe when you need one yourself. I've needed several, lately.

I've needed miracles because my wife's affair sent me to hell. It sent her to hell, too. Did we come back? I don't know. The book just started. Let's see where it goes.

My pagan friends sometimes ask me, Why didn't I burn my wife's things in the yard and walk away? Why haven't I moved on to a religion that seems more fun and relaxing, with fewer restrictions on, for example, ritual murder? Fair questions. Pray for me. It will have to be you who does the praying. I go to God asking for help, and in a second or two I'm wondering why Amazon makes it so difficult to return gifts. Maybe this is why my wife left. I get distracted.

This book is about my marriage, but it's about far more than that. It's also about my spiritual journey through the wastelands of being and my seeking, and being alternately sought by, and quite often being urgently embarrassed of and thus running desperately away from, the thing we call God. So, throughout this story, I find myself wandering back to those moments in my past where I wrestled with the reigning Heavyweight Champion of the Universe or those who pretend to speak on his behalf. Why have I shared the details of my spiritual journey in a book about my marriage? Because the wounds and scars I have on my heart from those battles have a lot to do with how this marriage story ends.

Chapter 2

WHAT'S IN THE BOX

2017

L auren was born a child of the church in Yazoo City, Missis-sippi, and was raised in Birmingham, Alabama; her mother a zealous homeschooler of three, no small thing in the 1980s, when homeschoolers were freakish, cave-dwelling cryptids made to hide under the furniture and read *The Pilgrim's Progress* by kerosene lantern to evade county truancy officers. To be a homeschooler back then was hardly different from being in a well-read militia.

Lauren's father, I'll call him Jeff, was an ordained minister in the Presbyterian Church in America, until he quit one day—nobody ever said why, though I have a few guesses—and jettisoned himself into the mission field of automotive sales, with occasional forays into restaurant management. Jeff changed jobs a lot, and Lauren's family lived perpetually on the brink of ruin. Lauren likes to talk about being fed wheat germ and dry oatmeal for dessert. Her mother, Trudy, with a degree in elementary education, might have gotten a teaching job for cash and stability, but her commitment to being a homeschooling mom of three trumped all.

In high school, Lauren participated in a mission trip to the former Soviet Bloc, where she danced for the Kazaks. Ballet for Jesus. I am sure they loved her, with her Ukrainian locks and Estonian skin and Eurasian eyes. When she returned to the United States, she studied at a Christian college called Belhaven—where we would meet—and continued to perform pas de deux for the Lord, dancing, for example, with the Mississippi Mass Choir and a Christian ballet company led by the man who played Little Ricky in *I Love Lucy*. Christians are everywhere, man. It's a cult.

We wed when she was twenty-five and I was twenty-seven. Our early days of marriage were as gangly as everybody else's, though they were sweet days, too. We had so few real obligations, no children, few friends. We watched TV and got fat. We loved to laugh and were considered by many the funniest people they knew. Comedy was our love language. Many a night we'd watch *Lost* and share a blanket, and I'd lay my head in her lap affectionately, just the two of us, relishing the hope and tranquility of our new marriage while Lauren remarked on the immensity of my skull.

"If I was just a head, would you still love me?" I'd ask, looking up.

"Maybe."

"You could carry me around in a bowling ball bag."

"That actually sounds nice." She would kiss my forehead and cover my enormous head with the blanket.

It felt so good to have finally found a partner who could insult me and be so sweet about it. Something about the comedy felt almost divine, a check on pride, a way to prevent either of us from taking ourselves too seriously.

For a brief time in our first year of marriage, we tried to jog together, waging warfare against the dark forces of marital obesity. She wanted me to slow down, but I never would. Our workouts ended suddenly one hot afternoon when she fell behind, collapsed, wet her pants, and was scooped into the arms of an attractive man playing tennis nearby who'd seen her fall.

"Does anybody know this woman?" the hot tennis star asked as I jogged up.

"I've had sex with her, if that's what you mean," I said.

Lauren, limp but fine, looked into this other man's eyes and probably thought, "Hmm, handsome *and* kind."

I spent mornings trying to write a book, and we spent nights trying to make a baby. We made three people before I made a single book. By the time she was thirty-two and I was thirty-five, we had three girls, whom I'll call Coco, Pippi, and Ruth Bader Ginsburg, because I can if I want. Lauren stayed at home with the children when they were little, something she'd long dreamed of doing. We made it work. When Coco, our oldest, was five, we homeschooled her for a few months, just to say we tried. Lauren continued to teach ballet even when great with child, the shape of her belly always suggesting she might give birth to a large toaster oven. But it was a girl, every time.

She has taught ballet to each of our three daughters. They know all the French words and just enough technique to mock the sad feet of gymnasts, which makes me happy. I have tried to give our children a love for music and stories and just enough wildness to give them joy, and Lauren has given our children a love for form and grace and quiet nights at home. She is a lovely dancer and a patient teacher, in addition to being prodigiously gifted at keeping secrets.

When you hear about one of your friend's marriages breaking up, it's always like "No way! Really? What happened?" I'd find myself going back over all the interactions with the couple in question, to see if I'd missed any clues to the crack-up: a misplaced wedding band, a veiled threat through a pinched smile.

"They're getting divorced," Lauren would say.

"Who?" And she'd tell me who, and I'd be like, "I had no idea."

I possess the EQ of a freshwater mollusk and am an easy man to hide things from, if hiding is your thing. I was always far more surprised by these breakups than Lauren. Bad news pinged through Savannah's cell towers often. This happened again and again, with other couples. We'd see a couple out at a party, and later Lauren would say, "They hate each other."

Or "They're about to separate."

Or "She's an alcoholic. They're probably divorcing."

My question was always "Wait. What?"

For so long, I was just a giant head in a bowling ball bag. She kept me in there a lot, when she didn't want me to see things.

The day she unzipped the bag and pulled my head out and told me the truth seems a lifetime ago, in a land only remembered now in dreams. It was a Monday. Early October. Warm. That week, I was reading a book on the history of architecture by Witold Rybczynski, which I would never finish. The old me started dying that day—all of me, even my reading habits.

Three days before, on a Friday, we'd gone out to dinner, the whole family. I'd been thinking a lot about my failures as a father and a husband, how dark the days had been for so long, how they didn't feel so dark anymore. I was grateful.

Early on in our marriage, Lauren made it clear that she wanted to stay at home with the girls, to swab them with Huggies baby wipes and launder onesies and fill the pantry with bread and eggs and Pepperidge Farm Goldfish crackers. I think part of her must've wanted to relive her own childhood, before her dad left. My own mother spoke often of her regret at leaving me at home when I was a month old, to go back to her middle school teaching job. I never saw myself as the primary breadwinner with a wife and baby at home. I'd spent my twenties running fast and far from the perils of nuclear domesticity, but suddenly at the dawn of this twenty-first century and the imminence of my thirtieth birthday, the vintage idea of male breadwinning felt almost radical. I wanted to make a book and she wanted to make a home and it felt right. It felt good. It felt highly countercultural. And the arrangement worked, until it no longer worked.

My work evolved. Demands increased. I became the chair of a department. I took on additional assignments to earn more money to pay for more things, while simultaneously devoting myself early in the mornings to the realization of my dream to become an author. My writing shoved a wedge between Lauren and me. I got distracted. No surprises there.

Her work evolved, too. The children grew. They pulverized Goldfish and Oreos and endless bricks of Nature Valley granola bars and flung the powdered garbage into every nook of every cushion. Her cleaning was endless: of babies, bedclothes, bath towels. My work was endless: papers to grade, performance reports to file, sentences to revise. My writing demanded more from me than my wife was prepared to allow me to give, especially when she started working full-time outside the home, as the fine arts director at a local private school.

I got distracted, she got bitter: accused me often of selfishness. Writing, I tried to explain, demands it. The entirety of my second book had, in its way, endeavored to explain this fact, but by the time Lauren dropped the bomb, her bitterness had already done its work, devouring our marriage in secret, though I had no idea. I hoped we were better now, stronger, more aware of each other. That's why I was grateful that night at the Mexican restaurant three days before she told me of her affair.

We ordered tacos and sat there destroying mounds of tortilla chips, the kids happy. I remember sharing all this with Lauren at the table, casually, how I felt like I'd grown up, the rewards of time and experience. I thanked her for loving me through it all. Our partnership had bought us a fine new home, really a whole new life. The future felt bright as new sun in the trees. But it was not a sun. It was a radiating mushroom cloud.

In retrospect, knowing what she knew, that she had already begun an affair, when she heard me speak all this gratitude, she must have wanted to die.

"I feel like I've been inside a tunnel for a long, long time," I said. "I feel like I'm finally on the other side."

She didn't say much, naturally, which I was used to. That was Friday. On Monday, around ten o'clock that morning, when I was about to teach a class, she sent me an email:

"Tonight, after the girls go to bed, can we talk?"

So opaque, so vague, so awful.

"Sure, of course," I replied. "About what?"

"Life."

It must be hard living with an idiot. You have to spell everything out. I might hold more degrees than your average chemist, but my wife was always the intelligent one in this marriage, three steps ahead. She possesses the intuition of Florence Nightingale and the organizational intelligence of a field general. When it comes to her interior life, she gives nothing away. You want to know how I feel? Just ask. You'll wish you hadn't. Ask me how things are going, and thirty minutes later you're just hoping for an aneurysm so I'll stop.

I have to be funny just so people won't run away when they see me coming, and many still do. Lauren, though. If she played professional poker, I wouldn't have to write these books just to pay for the children's braces. She gives you so few words. I have to study them like a paleobotanist trying to divine an entire ecosystem from a shard of petrified conifer.

After class, I skipped lunch and walked, puzzling through that word: *life*.

Good God, it could be anything. Had I done something wrong? I'd been drinking a little too much, nothing wild, but I'd grown accustomed to pouring comically deep glasses of red wine and falling asleep in the living room. She might confront me with an indictment of alcoholism. Back at the office, I took an online diagnostic. According to the internet, I was no alcoholic. Perhaps she had emotions to confess: unhappiness, melancholy, depression. Her lower back had been giving her trouble. She had migraines. Maybe she wanted to quit her job and stay at home again, maybe have another baby? Who knew? Not me.

She might suspect me of having an affair. Was I? I was not. I had to think about it for a second. I worked at a university lush with sensual, smart, creative women and traveled the country to sign books and sit in hotel bars with authors and agents and hot freethinking bookstore managers who seemed like they had bedrooms full of witchy candles and fragrant oils. I'd had more than one unpublished poetess hand me her phone number across the signing table. I've always enjoyed many friendships with women who were painters, writers, editors, photographers. I had seen none of them naked among the flicker of witchy candles, though I had often imagined it.

Perhaps my wife had some addiction to confess. Pills? No, her migraines were too frequent and unpredictable to add more pills to the mix. Gambling? Not her style. Porn? It could be porn. Women consuming porn, it happens more and more, they say. In the first year or two of our marriage, I'd gotten into the habit of looking at pornographic images at work, like some kind of drooling idiot. I'd look at a naked photograph or two and delete my search history and shut off the machine and feel dirty and sad and worthless, but I kept doing it, for months.

"I have something to tell you," I'd said to her one night after dinner, after another guilt episode. We faced each other on the sofa in the tiny living room of our little duplex. She looked wan. "I look at pornography on the internet every day, but I've stopped."

"Okay," she said, relieved.

"I feel like telling you will make it easier to stop."

So now maybe that's what she was about to do? Confess a thing to make it easier to stop? Maybe it was all in my head. Maybe she just wanted to tell me that she'd been offered an amazing new job across the country and could we consider moving? It could be anything. Whatever it was, I knew, even then, before I knew, that the greatest battle of my life was upon me. The dark flaming thing you think you see out of the corner of your eye, I saw it. I knew it was something big, lurking unseen for so long, preparing to be seen, to be revealed, the veil torn, the thing revealed. Fire. Shadow. Apocalypse.

Eventually the workday ended and I went home and we cooked dinner and put the girls to bed and found ourselves in the living room alone.

"Well," I said. I turned off the TV.

She sat on the near side of the couch, closest to the big overstuffed chair where I sat. All our laughter, our lifetime of comedy and loving insults, seemed light-years in the past.

"I want a divorce," she said.

No prologue, no preamble, no sound check. She opened the show with a killer number. When she said it, all the other possibilities, alcoholism or pills or porn, all seemed so petty, so small. How could this woman—my wife, the superhero mother of three, the mom new moms called when their own babies refused to latch or sleep, the Baby Whisperer, VBS teacher, Children's Church curriculum coordinator, this sweet homeschooled ballerina for Jesus—commit such profound emotional violence against her family? I felt like a man falling through a deep, wide hole in the earth, untethered, approaching death with terrific speed.

"Why?"

"I'm in love with somebody else."

She said they wanted to marry, that they'd been in love for years. All I could say, the only words my brain could conjure, were the ones it always conjured when my emotional intellect came up wanting.

"Wait. What?"

My wife presented me with a little box, and in the box was my very own confused and severed head, removed from my body before I even knew it was happening.

Chapter 3

WHERE THE
DRAGONS ARE

1975–87

As a sheltered homeschooling child in suburban Birmingham, Alabama, Lauren was spared the more degenerate vicissitudes of contemporary American life, depriving her of the rich masterworks of Van Halen and the *Gremlins* franchise. She and her two siblings were occasionally allowed to view smut, such as *Back to the Future*, when edited for network broadcast. In her home, MTV was a tormentor's paradise where effeminate men held their guitars in their crotches like enormous electrified penises and everybody had AIDS. The family listened only to contemporary Christian music— Twila Paris, Amy Grant, Michael W. Smith—with all that swelling, operatic vibrato and the slow, tortured piano of daytime drama. It is music that would turn anyone psychotic. Ballet was her life in those days. Homeschooling afforded her and her sister the freedom to dance and rehearse for hours every day.

Where my wife had been cosseted away from the world, my parents did the opposite, sending me out into the demonic provinces of Satan himself in the public schools of rural Mississippi, where I heard tales of sexual degradation that prompted one to consult books of anatomy. By the sixth grade, I knew every curse word and had seen more violence than one finds in the book of Judges.

My family lived far out on a piney, weedy pasture rife with buckthorn and cattle, roamed by coyotes on lunatic nights, but twice on Sundays and once on Wednesdays we drove to town to the Skyway Hills Church of Christ, a nineteenth-century sect that preached a Mississippi frontier faith. Our church was a throwback to another time, before electric guitars or math. We had Black deacons with great booming voices and Brylcreemed white elders and women who spurned makeup and wore long flowing skirts because God was God and sin was sin and ladies' pants belonged in hell. Adultery and fornication were decried often from the pulpit, in addition to ladies' pants, which my mother wore in defiance.

"God couldn't care less what I buy at Penney's," she said. "We're not Pentecostal."

You could find neither pianos nor pipe organs in our sanctuary, nor tambourines, nor choirs, all of which were considered unholy. Christmas carols could scarcely be found in our hymnal, with all their pagan compromise. Easter was celebrated, but the more learned among us suggested the bunnies and eggs had a secret affiliation to vernal equinoxes and sex cults. Our branch's founder was Alexander Campbell (b. 1788), of county Antrim, Ireland, a bellicose reformer, and so they called us Campbellites, which sounded more like a military-grade polymer developed by Dow Chemical.

Our spare little branch of this ancient religion had been skinned back to nothing from the overwrought Protestant theologies of the Reformation that complicated faith with systematic theologies and liturgies authored by men with too much education. We practiced the Occam's razor hermeneutic: if they didn't practice it in the first century AD of the New Testament, we didn't practice it in the twentieth century AD of the American South, which is why you'd find neither infant baptism nor Romish creeds nor U.S. flags in our church, for we could find no records of baptized babies nor of popes in the Bible, nor could we even locate any mention of the Second Amendment, hard as we strained to find it. You could be anybody you wanted in the parking lot, where modernity raged like tongues of fire, but inside the sanctuary, it was the first century, practically a historical reenactment, like those orchestras that only play period instruments. Noble and a little weird.

The general thrust of every Church of Christ sermon was that this terrestrial life was fleeting. One was here but for the blink of an eye, then all of us would fly away to mansions over the hilltop or hell below. Jesus was how you got to the mansions.

Some churches, they sign you up for the faith before you even have a chance to think it through, but in our church, it was DIY Jesus. You had to compare your life to the various rules and guidelines of the handbook, discern exactly how you'd effed things up, and then, once you were fully aware of your effedness, step forward during the altar call in front of everybody and politely request to be dunked. If you didn't want to, well, fine. Burn in hell if you want. It's a free country.

In retrospect, I find myself appreciative of the bald candor of this message. It's easy to mock this belief in a real Satan and a real God, you go ahead. I could hardly believe it myself. Most Sundays we sat behind a lady whose ex-husband had raped and beaten her almost to death with a scissor jack when he found out she was pregnant with his own child. Sermons on hell can scarcely offend someone who's already seen the Devil.

•   •   •

By seventh grade, I still wasn't baptized, because the idea of walking down front and having a congregation of bighearted salt-of-the-earth freaks watch me get plunged into a dunk tank seemed a little dramatic, and I had no interest in drama that did not involve my performing cartoon impressions. Declaring your fealty to the Prince of Peace by a metaphorical drowning seemed off-brand for a young man whose spiritual gift was laughing like Woody Woodpecker.

The whole cosmic story of human history, which I heard from the pulpit and in the Bible, sounded comically weird. God seemed, if not wholly imaginary, then at least elusive. Satan, however, followed me around like a duck hungry for bread, daring me to flaunt community pool regulations or eat all the ice cream before anyone else got home. If I was out in the yard doing chores and came across a copperhead that needed killing, I could count on Satan to come calling.

"Leave it," the Devil would say.

"I should kill it," I'd tell the Dark Lord. I didn't want the dogs getting hurt.

"If you leave it, God will send you to hell. You will love it there."

These imagined conversations were funny to me. I'd kill the snake, like a good boy, and Satan would vanish for a time and then come sliding back soon enough, daring me not to eat all the Pringles. Sometimes, the Devil came into my bedroom and watched me sleep, like a pervert, breathing his hot evil breath on me. I felt it. Imagined I felt it. Felt ridiculous for imagining I felt it. Was it true? Was any of this true? Was evil inside me, as Brother Dale, our preacher, said?

I don't know if my future wife ever felt like evil was inside her. I never haven't felt darkness in me. I talked too much in class and agreed to dares and got paddled at school more than anybody on the honor roll probably should. At home, I used gunpowder and gasoline and film canisters to make small bombs to incinerate mounds of bovine excrement in the pasture, even though I'd specifically been asked by my mother not to make bombs of any kind.

"You boys thought about joining the church?" Pop asked one night. I had just turned twelve, and Bird, my older brother, was fifteen.

"Everybody at that church is crazy," Bird said. If Satan lived in anybody, he probably lived in Bird. He'd already been expelled for gambling and had a C in math.

"I've thought about it, I guess," I said.

"Well, think some more about it," Pop said.

"Pray about it," Mom said.

"How can we pray if we ain't even Christians?" Bird said.

All I had to do to be exempted from burning in pools of magma while being raped by demons in hell for a trillion years was admit in front of our church family that these same demons lived in me and then ask for them to be removed via the holy rinse cycle. Did I truly have to believe this wild story?

I loved the people of God. Our pews held more diversity than I have ever seen in prettier churches. We welcomed gypsies and scalawags. The odd tattoo peeked out from this or that weathered forearm. There were motherless children brought to church on a bus and men who smelled of turpentine and chewing tobacco and others with thick black motor grease under their nails. Heaven would look like this, they said, peopled by grotesques of all kinds.

I loved the monthly fellowship luncheons, with mountains of fried chicken and biscuits soft and deep as hotel pillows and gravy good enough to drink. I loved the community of it all, the hymnody and the delicious fatty foods and the cute girls from town, smelling of Electric Youth and Teen Spirit, and all the unending praise by nice church ladies who led us through Bible stories and asked me to read them aloud in class and praised my gift for pronunciation. Say what you want, but there are worse ways for a child to spend weekends than misinterpreting ancient texts. Sunday school was a thrilling seminar in literary analysis, where young children recited poetry and wrestled with the deepest questions ever posed by the human mind.

Any given Sunday, you might find yourself wondering how snakes could talk and seas could part and men could walk on water or how someone could be eaten by a whale and not merely survive but be carried hundreds of nautical miles inside the beast and not require medical attention. It was easy to believe that King David slew a lion and a bear at the same time, but what to make of Samson's slaying a thousand men with the jawbone of an ass, which seems like it would break after slaying just one or two?

"Are unicorns real?" I asked my parents on the way home from church one day.

"They might be," Pop said.

"Unicorns are not real," Mom said.

"It says here God is strong as a unicorn," I said, my finger in the book of Numbers.

What questions the Bible did not address could be answered by a convenient wall of brochures, free to the curious: pamphlets on baptism and drunkenness and lust and the wickedness of amplified music and Charles Darwin. The earth, these pamphlets explained, was but four thousand years old. Men had not evolved from gorillas, no matter what the wicked cabals of biologists had to say about it. The existence of dinosaur bones could not be denied, it was true, they were there for anybody to see, but this was easy to explain, for these were the "behemoths" of Scripture. One salacious tract suggested dragons were real, or at least possible, given that the teeth of primordial cattle and other leviathans were "flintlike" and that these creatures had gastrointestinal expurgations that were quite obviously gaseous, which could be ignited with a mere spark, causing fire to belch from their mouths.

"Look!" I said to Mom, handing her the tract.

"Lord have mercy, Son. I can't think about dragons right now."

How thrilling to wrestle every week with unicorns and dragons and terror and eternity and the love of God for all the wretched of the earth! Sometimes I didn't even care if it was true or not. Fascinating is what it was.

"He'll make a fine preacher one day," they said in my direction, though I found most preaching repetitive, which is perhaps why I snuck novels into church, tucking them into my KJV to hide the crime from my parents. Back then, I had a taste for science fantasy stories where humanoid aliens made love to brave earthlings in distant galaxies, which I knew might upset Jesus, if he was real, though it could hardly be called a sin, as all this reading greatly improved my vocabulary with words and phrases like *orifice* and *erogenous tentacle*.

"Put that away," Mom would say.

"Boy," Pop whispered, placing a hand big as a bear trap on my neck and squeezing until I required chiropractic intervention. I'd tuck away my pulp novel for the Bible itself, diving in for as long as the sermon would let me. The older I got, the stranger this book seemed. Noah's groin is practically the protagonist of Genesis 9. You could hardly get out of the Pentateuch without feeling like you'd swapped galactic porn for Bronze Age boudoir drama.

Sometimes, I'd find myself listening to the sermon and overcome by a desire to stand up right there in the middle of the sanctuary and just say something that would freak everyone out, like, "Hey, look at this erogenous tentacle!"

I had begun to worry I was a child of perdition, unsure if the hell

I gaped into was real or lived only in my imagination, a projection of my malformed conscience, some ancient story conjured by ancestors to make me behave. If I could just see the Devil with my own eyes, or one of those fire-breathing cows, maybe then I could believe.

I finally saw the truth one Sunday, at a Baptist church of all places, Rock Hill Baptist, a short walk from our house out in the country. My parents weren't feeling well that morning, so I gamboled over to this sanctuary to lean on the everlasting arms for an hour or two before lunch. This is how good a Christian I used to be. I'd go to a church that wasn't even ours, which my own church considered full of blasphemers and defilers. I'd begun to feel like a blasphemer myself.

I arrived at Sunday school first and sat alone, reading my Bible. I'd always been so enthralled by its ghosts and prostitutes and pillars of fire, but still could not see what any of that had to do with me. Brother Dale often preached about the blind receiving their sight and the lame walking and the lepers being cleansed and the deaf hearing and the wretched of the earth being raised up, but all that seemed in the past. Why should one become a disciple of the Lord God Almighty in such mediocre times as ours? What was there to preach for, besides school bonds and improved highways? We had no wars at a convenient distance. Terrifying holy angels no longer appeared in clouds of smoke. Cows no longer breathed fire.

Other young people, friends from school, trickled into the classroom. Right before class, through the door came our teacher— and with her she brought something more real and fearsome than a dragon: a poor little blind boy with no cane.

"Good morning, children," the teacher said. "This is Willy."

"Hi," Willy squeaked.

I cannot tell you the morning's lesson, for I was consumed by a deeply Christlike compassion for this poor child of God. What blessings had I, to live in such luxury with two working eyes? It's like he stepped right out of the Bible, this child. Time flew, as always happens when I am feeling exceptionally righteous, and before long, class was over.

"Can someone help Willy get to the sanctuary?" the teacher asked the class.

"Yes, ma'am," I said, volunteering. Jesus, if he was real, would want it.

"Thank you," Willy said in my general direction.

I could feel the seed of charity growing inside my disbelieving little heart. Willy clutched my arm as we navigated our way toward the sanctuary through forests of thick forearms and the squeak of Sunday shoes on polished linoleum. How did Willy spend his days? I wondered. I spent mine with axes and footballs and knives and rifles. You can't give a rifle to a blind boy.

"What do you like to do?" I asked as we walked down one hallway, then another.

"I like horses. I like riding them."

I pictured Willy riding a horse across a green pasture, perhaps into a ravine. It seemed unsafe. I liked helping people, especially when others noticed me helping. *Laying up treasures in heaven* is what my grandmother would've called it, when good people do good things because God is watching and remembering. Such an act of service elevates you to a higher spiritual plane, which can make it difficult to lead the visually impaired, who in fact dwell on the earthly plane, where many three-dimensional objects exist, whether you see them or not, and that's when I heard the crash. Poor Willy, clutching his face and crumpled now in a heap at my feet, had, in the midst of my holy reverie, slammed into a floor-mounted drinking fountain.

"Oh gosh," I said, looking down at Willy, doubled over and bleeding from the face.

"It's okay," poor Willy said, through a blood-soaked grimace. More responsible churchgoers rushed in to help the boy, lifted him from the floor, brought tissues for his nose. I stood there stunned, humiliated, hot coals heaped upon my head. I tell you, no matter how many treasures you've got locked away in the First National Bank of Canaan's Land, you do a thing like that, it feels like all the good gets washed away. God put that fountain there, I knew it, I knew it in my heart, and I hadn't noticed because I'd been noticing everyone noticing me.

"I'm so sorry," I said.

Something had ruptured, come unmoored deep inside me, the demon of pride let loose and made visible. Willy had broken his nose, and I had fractured my enduring belief in the unsullied purity of my intentions. It would take me years to understand this, but the understanding began in that church hallway, that a good person is a temporary and imaginary creature, as make-believe as unicorns and fire-breathing cows, because the best of us are often the worst, full of proud and viperous snakes, believing ourselves gods. The dragons did not just live in history and myth. They lived inside me.

"I think we should get baptized," I said to Bird not long after, while working in the yard.

"Might as well get it over with," he said.

Bird and I got dunked a few days later in an empty church, Brother Dale and Pop and Mom the only ones present. I liked it this way. Fewer witnesses to see me pledge devotion to a being I had never seen, the swearing of a loyalty oath to a benevolent leprechaun who may or may not heal blind children. Did I believe? At the time, I still believed in Sasquatch, and I'd never seen one of those, either.

After Brother Dale sent me into the water, questions crowded my head, which I have never really stopped asking. What parts of me had died? What remained? This seems to be the way of things. You make promises and don't even know what it is you promised. My long internship at Jesus Enterprises, LLC, had begun.

I couldn't have told you the first thing about the war that was to come. I often think of Willy on his horse, his nose slightly misshapen due to my spiritual blindness. Blindness has characterized my own pilgrim's progress from the very beginning. Blind is how I felt the day my wife told me she was in love with someone else. Blind to the dragon in me, and the one in my home, a dragon that looked just like a man. A man who had been a friend.

Chapter 4

THE UNFORTUNATE FACT OF THIS MYSTERIOUS MAN

2017

I admired the naturalist minimalism of the moment my wife laid it on me. The lines were so simple, so elegant, as if written for a pair of actors and delivered via quietly controlled performances. No tears, no raging. Perfectly Pinteresque restraint.

"I want a divorce."

"Why?"

"I'm in love with somebody else."

I wanted the truth, but not, you know, that truth. I wanted kinder truth, truth I could work with, or at least a courteous lie. A lie would have been nice. I might have preferred "I don't think I want to be married anymore."

Or "This isn't working."

Or "I've changed."

Or "You've changed."

I could stomach that. I could solve that.

But "I'm in love with somebody else"?

I'm pretty sure my eyes crossed a little. I may have involuntarily moaned. My heart turned into a bagel and formed a singularity of inverted surprise with unreality at its chewy center. You had to give it to Lauren. She did not share her feelings often or well, but when she did, she dropped bombs. If she was in love with someone else, that meant she'd long ago fallen out of love with me, long ago went wandering, long ago got naked with someone new.

Holyyyyyyyyyy

Shiiiiiiiiiiiiiiiiiiiiiiiiiiit.

The fabric of space and time rent until I gaped through the gauzy slit at the dark hot heart of the universe. This was the day my reality dissolved. Time frayed, space smeared, Lauren's face blurred out in a streak.

Who?

Who?

Who?

A newsfeed of faces raced across this strange new galaxy. Maybe it was someone from the classical school where she worked? I could not see my wife committing adultery with anyone who read Latin for fun, but then she'd married me, hadn't she? Maybe it was somebody from church. Maybe one of her doctors? The baby doctor? The internist? The migraine specialist would understand her suffering. The radiologist would understand her mammaries. She'd begun working out at the YMCA a few months earlier. Dear God, had she fallen for someone with abs? In earth time, mere milliseconds passed, but I was in outer space now.

A neighbor, perhaps? Mentally, I ransacked the homes of everyone on our street. Was it Paul, always in his yard? The young federal agent across the street, with his young wife and their young baby? I couldn't even remember their names. What about the husband a few doors down?

"He's very good-looking," Lauren had once said of him.

He had a pool. Only pool on the block. Had this attractive man made love to my wife in his pool?

My mind roved every corner of every party, every dinner, every home in Savannah where we'd ever been invited since moving here a decade before. I ran backward all the way to the beginning, when we'd moved ourselves to the marshy tidewater majesty of this little town, a tiny shoebox of a house with a serviceable porch and a bathroom the size of an airplane toilet. The house sat on a short street with enough old trees to seem quaint, and we'd bought it with zero down and all the optimism we could afford.

There was Jimmy on the corner, who only really came outside to ask us for money or set garbage on fire in his yard. There was the couple to our immediate right, Chad and Lane, our closest friends. It was Chad, the good-hearted neighbor who liked to fish, to whom I'd given most of my father's fishing tackle when Pop died. Chad's wife, Lane, a pediatric nurse, frequently babysat our girls. There was the couple across the street, Jason and Allie, the newlyweds with outside cats always lazing in the street. She worked in a lab. He managed restaurants. Was it Jason? Jason liked gin. Lauren liked gin. There was the divorced father of three, Kevin, kindly and talkative, who painted our dining room. There was the bachelor who grew kale in his backyard and hardly spoke, except to give everyone kale.

Lauren loved kale.

We all knew one another, borrowed sugar and eggs, hosted the occasional block party, Halloween party, cookouts. I wouldn't have called any of these people my best friends because I didn't really have best friends, not then. I was too busy with writing and small children and twelve-hour workdays and a rusting crucible of unrealized dreams to let anyone else in. Maybe I would have friends one day. This, too, was a dream.

Those neighbors were no longer our neighbors. We'd moved away three years ago, though we still kept up with a few of those friends on social. Who was it? Who was my wife in love with? Which of these two or three dozen men had my wife fallen for? Trysts, hidden assignations, secret plans made in the dark, a bomb constructed in private to lay waste to my family? Who'd helped her build this bomb?

"Chad," she said.

I wish I could tell you his real name, which is somehow even dumber than Chad. Apologies to all the Chads of the world. They don't deserve this. Nobody does.

Chapter 5

NOTES ON CHAD

2007–17

To start very generally: Chad is a man. He does not represent all Chads, or even all men.

We've all been dumped for Chads.

The thing about Chads is, we want to hate them. If you get dumped for an attractive Chad, you must reduce him to vanity. A rich Chad must be assumed vacuous. Your wife leaves you for a brainy Chad, you have to believe he's a pedantic dullard. If he's a jock, then you must suppose he's a date rapist who oils his delts.

This inborn desire to reduce Chads to less than human is troubling, but can be helpful in times of great distress, such as, for example, when being told that your wife is in love with one to whom you'd given all your dead father's fishing rods in an anguished gesture of kindness. Perhaps this penchant for dismissing the humanity of Chads is a survival mechanism, a vestigial psychic anti-inflammatory designed to keep the human heart from rending in two and the ego from dissolving into a froth of rage and self-loathing. Because when you first learn of the Chad in your own life, your immediate reaction is to compare.

Is he richer than me?

Smarter?

Funnier?

Kinder?

More caring?

A better listener?

More beautiful in a hot tub?

These are the questions your partner's betrayal compels in you. They are nonsense questions, helpful to nobody, but you will ask them, because the first thing that happens when you discover your partner is cheating on you with a Chad is, you will go insane.

In addition to going insane, you will feel pain that transcends all prior experience. Pain without precedent. Pain that burns away the sky. The pain did not make me cry, not yet. It did not make me rage and break things, not yet. What the pain did was detach my brain from my spinal column and kick it like a football into new galaxies. Everything I knew had to be unknown. Everything I did not know had to be learned. You never realize how much you know until you learn all of it was wrong.

Chad had been a friend, my first real friend in Savannah. Who was this man? There is the hypothetical Chad, the abstract Chad, the potential Chad, lurking at the edges of every marriage—neighbor, colleague, family friend—and there is the real Chad, the specific Chad, the Chad who has seen your wife naked. We must try to understand him.

My particular Chad is not an evil man, though he committed acts that, without reserve, I call evil. If this word, *evil*, makes you uncomfortable, then welcome to the party. I don't like sounding like a CPAC campaign ad any more than you do.

I am not sure Chad believes in evil. I am not sure Chad believes in anything except, perhaps, the viability of Kid Rock as a political thinker. "I'd vote for him," Chad once told me, though to be fair, he was high at the time. But I am getting ahead of myself.

I met him in the winter of 2007, right after we moved to town. I'd just bought three young crepe myrtles for the new yard. That day, as I stood with a shovel, surveying the young trees in their new holes for compositional balance, a man approached me with his big white dog. The dog barked over and over.

"Hush!" was the first thing the man said.

But the dog kept on barking. Sometimes I think the dog was trying to warn me. "Run! Flee from this wicked place!" the dog was saying. "You and all whom you love will surely die here!"

It didn't seem like a wicked place, and the dog's owner didn't seem like a wicked man.

"You must be my new neighbor," I said.

"Welcome to the hood," the man said, in a slight drawl.

"I'm Harrison." I extended a hand.

"I'm Chad."

We got to talking, and I learned that he hailed from deep in the Georgia interior and had been living in Savannah a few years now. I wouldn't have called him a redneck exactly, but after more than a decade spinning my wheels in the desperate urbanity of American higher education, where all the Chicagoans in my Foucault seminar looked at me funny when I told stories about how as a boy I'd sometimes had to kill livestock with a woodworking tool, I found it refreshing to know, just by the sound of his voice, that my new neighbor probably didn't know who Foucault was. I liked him, or wanted to like him, instantly, though as I would learn, there was little else about this man to grab onto. He was vanilla ice cream, without the vanilla. A cipher.

He appeared intensely ordinary in every way, as if every element of his appearance were designed to make you forget he was even there. His hair was neither blond nor brown, his build neither heavy nor spry, his manner of dress supremely normcore—jeans and one of those North Face fleeces they shoot from air cannons at SEC football games—and a face so excessively unremarkable that even now, after seven years as neighbors and so many moments conjuring his countenance in private that I could imagine melting it with a welding torch, I can scarcely find words sufficient to describe the man's visage. If he went missing and the police asked me to describe him for the APB, I'd have said, "He's white. He may have eyes and a nose."

Sometimes, I wonder, if, in that moment, when we stood in my new yard, if God had instructed me to beat this man to death with my shovel, to prevent the future betrayal, what would I have done? I would have laughed. Chad did not look capable of destroying a marriage. It had been a lifetime since Willy the Horse Boy taught me the perils of spiritual blindness, but I had learned nothing. Of course, there was nothing much to see. How could I have known everything that would come to pass between this Chad and my wife? What I didn't know and couldn't see is that underneath the abjectly uninteresting façade of this man beat the heart of the world's greatest romantic. The man was a fucking poet of love, and nobody knew but Lauren.

Over the years, I was a good neighbor to this guy. I let him borrow my chain saw. I listened to him complain about the rising cost of Michelob Ultra. I didn't ridicule his love for Kid Rock, at least not in front of him. In summer, I found no call to mock Chad's cargo shorts. I could have. But I didn't. Not then, not now. People who like Kid Rock also like cargo shorts. This is an immutable law of nature.

I wish I could tell you that Chad was a convicted pederast who trafficked children out the back of a Chuck E. Cheese or that he had many prominent moles, but the truth is, he was a quiet, hard-working IT professional who repaired software for small businesses and only had one prominent mole. He enjoyed yardwork and fishing and throwing the baseball with his young son and occasionally smoking a little reefer in his garage when the kids weren't around. He was several inches shorter than me, but I never held this against him, and clearly neither did Lauren. His only real crime, at least up until the moment he did his best to destroy his family and mine, was that he was rather dull.

He spent most of his free time in the yard. I never said a word about the continual electric scream of his leaf blower because my religion says to let those things go. Saturday mornings, I would come home from writing at the café and there he'd be, frightening off all the birds.

"Yard looks good," I'd say.

"Thanks!" he'd say.

Weekend afternoons, we'd stand there with a beer and discuss sod placement. We didn't have much else to say. I would have preferred a more interesting neighbor, somebody with an eclectic taste in films or books, or at least someone with a pair of Jet Skis and a basic grasp of irony. I'd have been fine with a conspiracy theorist or a flat-earther. I can work with delusion. But Chad didn't even have the courtesy to be strange. He was just there.

"Love your neighbor as you love yourself," Jesus tells me.

And I tried, in my feeble and distracted way, to love Chad. I asked him about his former life in rural Georgia and what led him to choose a career in IT, but hardly got anything in return. Speaking with him in the yard about the absurdities of contemporary American life felt like trying to discuss the novels of Gabriel García Márquez with a cadaver. Most people don't care about magical realism. Which is fine. Most of us on this planet don't have enough money to choose our neighbors. You get what you get.

At least our kids got along. Our wives were close. We cooked out in the backyard and remarked on the heat. I'd stand there and watch Chad put away a dozen wings and never once hazarded the notion that my wife might in secret be burning for this man. A Spotify algorithm had more charm. He had whatever the opposite of a personality is.

That sounds ugly.

I don't want to be ugly here.

I could tell you he seemed about as deep as bro country and possessed all the charm of an unsalted potato, but this would be a literary description powered by resentment. Truth is, he seemed a decent father, a good neighbor. We were friends, or at least friendly.

His wife, Lane, was one of those funny nurses with a tattoo who always had a glass of wine and loved telling stories of health-care grift and medical incompetence. She was more talkative, more outgoing, curious, always asking me questions about my work at the university, about my writing, about the girls. She and Lauren were best friends. She always made a tomato pie and American-flag cakes on the Fourth and told the girls how cute they looked. She laughed fully and often. Chad didn't laugh much. For many years, I believed his vacuity was merely a natural introversion, but now I know this belief was wrong. I tried to be his friend. He tried hard not to be mine.

If there's a Chad in your life, then you can bet you're that Chad's

Chad, too. He's likely reduced your humanity long before you ever reduced his. It's the only way he can go full Chad on you, with your wife, in secret. He's got to believe you're a cruel spouse, derelict, vain, vacuous, pedantic, whatever. You can bet Chad hates you. Maybe that's why he never had much to say to me. It's hard to be vulnerable with the husband of the woman you covertly dream of marrying. Maybe he had to make himself hate me. I am told he occasionally referred to me, over the many years of their clandestine romance, as a "big, fat walrus."

Fair enough. For years, I was very big and quite fat. Like a walrus, I have whiskers and have been known to emit guttural barks at people until they throw food at me. And like these gregarious sea mammals, I, too, can be violent when provoked. The 1918 memoir by Donald Baxter MacMillan, *Four Years in the White North*, detailing the Crocker Land Expedition of 1913–17, describes a walrus attacking a boat and killing all aboard. One can only assume the boat was full of Chads. What can I say? I am the walrus.

"Him," I said to Lauren the night she confessed. "Him. Really?"

I had so many questions.

About him, and me, and us, and why.

Why?

Why?

Why?

A few weeks earlier, he'd sat right there in our living room to watch a college football game. I'd fed him pork and the best baked beans in town.

"I love these beans," I said. "I hate beans, and I love these beans."

"Mm, yeah." He loaded hog into his face so he wouldn't have to say more.

"How's the new job?"

"Good," he said, toward the wall.

"Did you sell your truck?"

"Yeah," he said, toward the unseen floor joists.

I have to assume he was looking so intently at the walls and floors and fixtures of my home because he knew them well, had seen them often when I was not at home, and had thought long and hard about what it might be like to call this home his own, because he believed he would soon be living here, as soon as he could convince Lauren to drop the bomb.

Chapter 6

THE TRUTH WILL
SET YOU FREE TO
LOSE YOUR MIND

2017

When you hear the most shocking news of your life, what do you do? Do you weep? Laugh? Go for a drive? A run? A gun? What I did was stare across the room at a beach ball, a toy left on the floor, ever so slightly deflated, with a pinprick hole never to be repaired. Its days of play were over. So were ours.

"So, it's Chad," I said, staring at the ball.

Lauren sat on the couch, quiet, having said her piece, setting a lighted match to every good thing in my life, and waited for me to react. Would I explode, threaten her with legal vengeance, take the wooden Louisville Slugger from my office and pay Chad a visit? They hadn't been our neighbors in years, though he lived but minutes away.

I stood and took the deflated beach ball in my hands. I think better on my feet, with something to hold. Reality now felt as weird and useless as this ball, filled with expended breath, so easily destroyed.

"When did this start?" I said.

"A long time ago."

She did not look like my wife anymore. She spoke like an indifferent alien droid who did not necessarily wish to destroy life on earth but had been programmed to do so.

"I need to know when all this started," I said.

Here's what I did know: During those many years as a neighbor, Chad worked from home much of the time. Lauren worked from home, too, as primary caregiver to daughters. On hundreds of afternoons, I'd return from work to find them both in the yard, he with a water hose and a beer, she with a juice box. Lauren must have found it refreshing to chat with someone who did not wish to discuss the state of contemporary nonfiction. I had nothing to fear from this man. I'm not the jealous type. I am, however, an idiot. I'd gotten some things wrong about Chad, about Lauren, maybe even about me. I needed facts, which I extracted from Lauren with a pair of reductionist tongs during that first hateful night of this new tribulation.

FACT NO. 1

On many of those weekday afternoons when I was off doing foolish, irresponsible things, such as working to provide for my family, Chad entered my home in secret and helped my wife with chores.

"He would take out the trash," she said.

"Why in God's name would you let another man into our home?"

FACT NO. 2

In those days, as I would soon learn, but had been too ignorant to see, my wife was incredibly sad and lonely. Her heart had become a slaughterhouse of death and pain, having experienced deep psychological wounds in childhood and beyond: poverty, homelessness, the tragic and untimely death of her mother, abandonment by the one man who should've loved her more fiercely than any other—her father, Jeff—the ordained minister who, when Lauren was in high school, ran off with a Christian Scientist and became a whole other person, an excommunicated car salesman who listened to Plácido Domingo and hung paintings of naked women in his bathroom. Had his desertion years before planted the seed of abandonment in her? Perhaps Lauren was not in possession of the tools to express her pain.

FACT NO. 3

If only there were someone she could talk to.

FACT NO. 4

Cue the sound of a leaf blower.

FACT NO. 5

Oldest story on the planet.

FACT NO. 6

"But when did the affair start?"

"We were just friends for a long time."

"When did you become more than friends?"

"It just happened."

FACT NO. 7

After three years as neighbors, they got close. There was flirting. There were feelings.

FACT NO. 8

Everybody has feelings. I have feelings all the time. Rage feelings. Crowbar feelings.

FACT NO. 9

At some point, she hardly remembered when, she'd written Chad an email, declaring her feelings and suggesting that perhaps the feelings were not good to have and that perhaps they should not talk so much in the driveway anymore, owing to the feelings, which, once confessed, could hardly be unfelt, especially when the one expressing those feelings lets you in her house when the babies are napping.

FACT NO. 10

All this time, we're married. We're raising a family. We're having lots of decent sex, during which I am thinking about sex and she is thinking about a man in cargo shorts. Later, I chat about gravel with this man. Sundays after church, Lauren and the girls often went outside to play and throw the ball with Chad while I locked myself away in an office, to wrestle with my past, come to terms with my own traumas and make them as hilarious as possible. I wrote funny stories about my family. I published these stories. People read them. They commented about how funny my wife was, our hilarious marriage, how it was all so "real."

FACT NO. 11

"But when did the affair start?" I asked again and again the night she confessed.

She wouldn't say. She couldn't. Didn't hardly know how.

FACT NO. 12

They pined in secret for years, he for her, she for him, but nothing happened, she said. Only if pining in secret is nothing.

FACT NO. 13

After seven years as neighbors, Chad got a job in North Carolina and his family moved away, and not long after, we moved to a better neighborhood, and I was happy to be gone from that neighborhood for reasons I could not then fully explain.

FACT NO. 14

Chad and his family moved back to Savannah three years later because, I assumed, he missed living near the ocean. I did not realize the thing he missed was my wife.

FACT NO. 15

Once again, our families spent time together. They now lived about fifteen minutes away. She wanted to see them? Fine. I do not like being paranoid. Our children loved his son. His wife loved our girls. Our families had been friends for so long. What was I going to say? I don't want them to come with us to the pool because he eyeballs your ass when he thinks I'm not looking? She'd gaslight me, tell me I was crazy. I let it go. It's not like I knew he was texting my wife about how pretty the moon looked.

FACT NO. 16

In late summer, a few months after they moved back, I left the country for a couple of weeks, for work. If there's any advice I could give those feeling distant from their spouses, it would be to never leave the country for work, especially if your wife's been pining in secret for a man who loves helping other people's wives with chores and describing harvest moons via text.

FACT NO. 17

The day I left for France, Lane invited Lauren and the girls to come over to their new house for dinner. My family ate, played, came back home. That night, according to my wife, Chad texted her and told her he wanted to tell her something in person. The next night, while the children were upstairs asleep, he came into my home and let it all out like a mewling kitten. He wanted her, wanted to be with her, forever, had for years. It must have worked, because Lauren said some version of the same.

"But why?" I still didn't get it.

"He's helpful."

The implication: I was not helpful. Which, okay, fair enough. I had already come clean on this point a hundred times over, just in case she hadn't heard me the first time. I did my penance. I got rehabilitated. I laid it all out there and flayed myself on the altar of my failure to scrub toilets or fold laundry because I was out in the world beating back the dragons of debt with two jobs that made it possible for Lauren to stay home with the girls. I wasn't out doing hot yoga with MILFs. I did not scrub toilets, okay, but I did cook more meals than any other husband I knew and paid every bill and cut the grass myself so we could afford the car payment. Dear Lord, wasn't that enough? Hadn't I given her everything that was mine to give? What more could I have done? These were frightening questions I was not yet capable of asking myself. My marriage, freshly murdered, the body still warm, lay upon the hard earth. We had a crime to solve, and I had no interest in being a person of interest. No, I told myself. This was not about me. I was a good man, on paper. Wasn't I?

One thing I've learned is that once you make the mercenary move of letting yourself fall in love with someone outside your marriage, you must compel yourself, unconsciously or not, to interpret all available data to support that move. I could've purchased my wife a new flying car and she'd have told herself I was foolish with money. I could've moved us out to a pasture for a happy life of homesteading with chickens and goats and she'd have said the goats were unkind to the children. The thing was done. Nothing I could do would ever be enough. Not now.

FACT NO. 18

Their love had been ratified in August. It was now October. They had a lawyer.

FACT NO. 19 OR POSSIBLY LIE NO. 3,382

"When did you first have sex?" I said.

"We haven't."

"You're lying."

"We really haven't."

How do you elect to burn down your life and everything good in it when you haven't even consummated the flame? How do you so freely choose to destroy the man who had collaborated with you to create three perfectly miraculous human beings whose very existence would come crashing down in minutes, hours, years, altering the story of their lives and forever changing their personalities, when you haven't even had sexy time with the guy?

"I don't know," Lauren said.

"Me neither."

I wanted to believe her, but did not believe her. I wanted to know everything, and yet, with all these facts in my hands, I knew nothing. If this ever happens to you, be prepared not to know things. You will never feel as ignorant as you do after you know. Questions only lead to more questions. The answers will never satisfy, though you need them, desperately. You need answers like a beach ball needs air.

I wanted every plot point, every line of dialogue. It was time for revision. The story I'd been telling myself about my life was bogus. The wise and tenderhearted mother, the fiercely funny wife, all of it was an elaborate fairy tale. It's weird to stare at a woman you've been staring at for years and see something new, hidden there all along, waiting for you to see it, if you would only look. But the woman in front of me had few answers to give.

"It's late," she said. It was a school night. We both had to work the next day.

"I'm not done."

"We can talk more tomorrow."

She looked spent. She could remember no more, speak no more, having provided the merest outlines of the affair, an unfinished Wikipedia entry at best. If I wanted to fill in every blank, then I'd need to do my own remembering.

Chapter 7

LAUREN'S FIRST LIE

2002

How far back do you have to remember to learn how you got here? Where had the wrong turn been taken? Or at least the first wrong turn, which precipitated a series of increasingly ruinous turns to follow, which had carried us thousands of miles into the bush of this hateful wilderness where you get robbed at gunpoint by your own wife and neighbor, who want to take your home, your children, and your sanity?

I should never have bought that house.

I should never have moved us to Savannah.

I should never have gotten married in the first place.

I tried to remember any red flags from the earliest days of our courtship. Who was she, back then, and who was I?

I have always loved women and longed to be loved by them. All of them. The romances of youth were never not a terrific delight, electrifying: risk, reward, flirtation, dalliance with failure, confirmation of love, *yes/no/maybe*, held hands, gentle kisses and exploratory dental varnishing, the phone calls, dates, proms, fogged windows, hidden places revealed, borders crossed, love stolen, love given, what thrilling sin! But age complicates love. Lovers want. Lovers need. Lovers fail. Lovers leave.

In the decade between puberty and young adulthood, I had a few serious girlfriends and several dozen unserious ones, which I preferred. The serious ones asked too much of me, I felt, though the truth is, we were vampires all, sucking what we needed from one another and moving on to the next victim. I dated many Good Christian Girls who allowed me to see them naked, or mostly naked, in exchange for my attending Bible studies with them, a reasonable offer, though when they pulled out their crucifixes, I often hissed and fled back to the coffin of my solitude.

By my midtwenties, in a PhD program for playwrights, I was interested in wooing only a dissertation committee of genial pagan scholars whose experience with world religions was restricted largely to architectural tours of churches. I knew marriage could happen, like gallstones or the death of a beloved pet. I did feel that the whole concept was probably a good idea, generally, imperfect but sturdy, like a Craftsman socket wrench, something good to have around the house. But like most young vampires, I wanted only to take, never to give.

My parents had three divorces between them but managed to stay married to each other, despite a surfeit of differences: Mom was a college-educated schoolteacher who preferred the indoor entertainments of books and movies and the wriest humor, where Pop was a dropout with a farmer's tan whose favorite books were brochures on experimental fishing lures. You could not have designed a keener pair of opposites. They fought about the things most couples fight about—money, time, how many fishing rods one required to experience the love of God, how much football their bookish youngest son ought to be made to play—but I never sensed any lingering apathy or contempt between the pair. Their marriage was imperfect but sturdy.

As a young adult, like my father before me, I had a weakness for restaurant hostesses and could find something to love about almost anyone who greeted me at a Chili's. In grad school, I preferred pagans to the godly: the pixie-cut cutie with the dream-catcher tramp stamp ("I'm not a Christian, but I love that you are"), the med student who disrobed me and placed her head on my stomach ("I'm listening for fluids and gases"), the server at the Corner Diner who smoked more weed than a California wildfire ("Can't we just get high like a regular couple?"). I liked them all, but after a date or three, no matter how sweet and smart and sensual they could be on a futon, I always walked away. By then I was already writing every day, devoting every spare hour outside class to my truest love. Her name was Literature. She saw me, I wrote her. We fought like lovers do, followed by passionate revisions on the kitchen floor. "Being your slave, what should I do but tend / Upon the hours and times of your desire?" Shakespeare writes in Sonnet 57. "I have no precious time at all to spend, / Nor services to do, till you require."

By my final year of grad school, I'd come to believe aloneness might be my calling, the default setting of an operating system betrothed to language. I knew, even then, that this devotion might become unhealthy, cutting me off from others. It already had. No love could rival the high. I had become an addict: low and hollowed out and sick of body and soul. I'd lost something like fifty pounds in two years. Suddenly, I could try on jeans without requiring a complex system of pulleys. Women began to show more interest than they ever had, due to my not being morbidly obese. I got eyeballed at the grocery store, in bars, on campus, in a way I never had.

"I love that you love to write," they said, over beers as they stared into my eyes, and I stared through theirs and out the backs of their heads, already in bed with the next sentence, which I might fondle the next morning, if I didn't sleep over. I began dressing differently, in tighter jeans and shorter shorts and those low, loose V-necks where you could see one of my nipples, seductively. I'd never had a body like this. To my family, I looked like a double in those movies where everybody smokes meth.

"Are you on drugs?" Mom asked, on my rare visits home. "Do you do grass?"

"I've never looked hotter."

"You look peaked." She handed me a sandwich.

I was heartsick for something whose name I did not know. Writing was no lover. She could never provide what a body and heart need most of all. I had slowly come to believe it was just Jesus and me, walking along the beach of my destiny together, when in truth I was up to my nose in the surf while the Lord sat in the life-guard chair like, "You idiot."

This was the condition of my heart when I fell radically in love with the woman who would one day fall radically out of love with me.

She was the most exquisite creature who'd ever agreed to be in the same car with me, an Elizabeth Arden ad come to life, backlit by divine luminosity, blond and absolutely royal, otherworldly, cheek-bones high and timeless as the cliffs of Dover, with Corinthian pos-ture and a smile so perfect you felt she had been discovered by a scouting agent in a remote colony of highly skilled orthodontists.

I've told how we met many times, in books and stories, and

I'm not sure how much to tell you now, other than to say that we actually first met in my freshman year of college, when she was still fifteen years old, which she doesn't remember, but I do, because when you meet a homeschooler who looks like Grace Kelly, you feel like you've been lied to about what homeschoolers look like. We met again when we were eighteen and twenty-one, and somehow she was more gorgeous than before, so why bother, the system is rigged and I couldn't pull on my socks without blacking out, and anyway, I was still a vampire of love. We met again when she was twenty-three and I was twenty-six, which means I was now malnourished and, for a brief window and in certain light, at my least unattractive, historically. A solemn and urgent desire had already begun to stir in my heart that a romance with words, no matter how unrequited and undying, could not sate my most human desires.

Lauren waited tables at the Greek restaurant near the place we'd both gone to college, and I was home from grad school visiting friends and remembered her and she remembered me and I turned on the charm and she squinched her mouth in that flirty disappointed way, and I knew we would be getting married. I can't say why I suddenly felt capable of marriage, the way you wake up one day and start ordering salad for lunch. One moment, words mattered most of all, and the next moment, they dimmed in the light of this very real woman. I felt my vampiric tendencies wane a little. My heart warmed. I busted up my coffin for scrap lumber.

We found ourselves on an empty back porch one cold night over the holidays and talked until we heard birdsong. Her holy radiance came from somewhere deep beyond physical beauty, the place where old secrets and ancient pain burn like fire. This made her sad and it made her attractive and it made her funny. She was very funny.

That night, I told her about the dirge of emptiness that plagued me like a solitary bagpiper on a distant hill, and she told me how her father had left her poor homeschooling mom ten years before. "He's a stranger now," she said. "I miss him. I miss my dad."

Trudy, her mother, dispossessed of a marriage a decade hence, had been diagnosed with breast cancer within a year of her divorce, when everything came crashing down for all of them, Lauren and her little brother and older sister. The good news was, after a thousand surgeries and specialists and chemo and radiation and a double mastectomy, Trudy had been free of cancer for several years, and now lived in Yazoo, an hour north of Jackson, where she built a new life.

"The best thing about cancer is, you never have to pay late fees at Blockbuster," Lauren said. "It's the cancer trump card. Late fees, missing work, everybody gives you a pass. You can keep the *Runaway Bride* as long as you want if your mom is dying."

Her mom was better now, but Lauren, not so much. She had, she said, medicated her grief at her father's abandonment with an endless series of boyfriends and lackluster rebounds, which never lasted. She was now dating a guy with frosted tips who ran a Sunglass Hut. She said he was nice.

"Are you going to marry him?"

She took a drag and paused. "No."

Six months later, back home for summer break, we found each other at a wedding.

"How's the Sunglass Hut?" I said.

"We broke up."

Within days, we were spouting desperate *I love you*s like toddlers who'd just learned how to say *chicken nuggets*. I said it first, and I never say it first. It struck me, even then, that I might just be another rebound. I occurred to me years later, on the night she confessed her affair, that perhaps she had been a vampire, too.

• • • •

We spent that first summer in each other's arms, and when fall came, I returned to grad school in the Midwest, determined to be the longest rebound in romantic history. My writing of plays and essays and monologues was no longer a love affair. This old mistress became, instead, what she should've been all along: mode of being, rather than being itself. I gave words to Lauren like flowers, and she to me. We wrote letters, read them aloud over the phone. If anything bound us together enough to want to marry, it was our words and their desperate ache for love and comedy. I've kept these ridiculous letters and emails all this time, and it's hard to tell where the romance stops and the comedy starts.

"I love questionnaires, but I love you more," I wrote.

"My foot touched yours last night and I had chills," she wrote.

"I love you even though you seem like you're always dying of an aneurysm," I wrote.

She shared with me her anxieties, about tumors she may or may not have found in the shower, and how she hated her father and couldn't summon the courage to tell him this when he called every six months, hated that she hated him and somehow loved him, hated him for leaving them with a mother whose body had been colonized by tumors like the imaginary ones Lauren found in the shower. We let each other in. I'd never done this before. I'd finally lost my emotional virginity. I was a vampire no more, it seemed. We had no option but to marry. She was too gorgeous, too broken, too funny to let go. There had to be a catch.

Just like my parents, we were perfectly unmatched: her love of room service and mine of ramen, her country club teeth and my cavities. In college, I'd assumed she came from money, due to the teeth, though it's possible a compassionate orthodontist cut her family a deal out of mercy. They'd had so little money.

All through college, when Lauren had nothing to do with me, she'd almost exclusively dated guys with what I felt was an unhealthy interest in Pearl Jam and not reading. She had no interest in bluegrass or debating the merits of Bertrand Russell's *Why I Am Not a Christian*. Mind-blowing David Mamet scenes did not blow her mind. The rump-shaking encore of "Harlem / Cold Baloney" on *Live at Carnegie Hall* by Bill Withers had little observable effect on the movement of her rump. She cared more for sweet coffee and quiet afternoons and plates of hummus and fat babies. I'd never met a woman who cared so little about music or art or books. I found her indifference intoxicating, an antidote to my excesses. I'm sure she found me exotic, too, with my premature baldness and lack of Eddie Vedder body art. Dayton, an old college friend, said we were like two fish who should not be in the same tank.

"There's something you should know about me," she said one night on the phone, after we'd been dating for a few months. My stomach sank. This was it: the catch. "I've been lying to you."

"About what?" I said. She had not really broken it off with Sunglass Hut. She was cheating on him with me, or something. Whatever it was, this was the end.

"I'm not really blond. I dye my hair."

Less than a year later, we were married.

Chapter 8

LOVE IS A JOKE

2003–17

Marriage is a partnership, the ministers and officiants of weddings tell us, a dance, duet, sun and moon, rain and shine, gin and tonic, Ali and Foreman, the Rumble in the Jungle, and everybody wins, or nobody: some couples die in the ring of brain trauma and broken hearts. My long marriage to Lauren always felt more like vaudeville, Abbott and Costello, Nichols and May, *Dumb and Dumber*. Our comedy only got better the longer we were together, evidence, I suppose, that we were both depressed much of the time but fun at parties.

From the first, our marriage was all laughter, at TV ads for medical procedures and at redneck baby names and at suggestive sermon analogies, like the time we heard a man preach on marital love and the need to cultivate his wife's "garden."

"Did he just say that out loud?" I whispered to Lauren in the pew.

"I guess her hedge needed trimming," she whispered back.

We got to giggling and couldn't stop because we are despicably vile children, our minds flocking like a pair of adolescent humming-birds to the vulgar at the first mention of horticulture. This giggling animated our marriage. We laughed at all the same things, incontinence and genital humor and ghoulish unibrowed infants who couldn't even help it. We especially enjoyed those social media posts by earnest married couples who so rapturously expressed their marital love.

"I married my best friend!" these couples so often declare, underneath a photo of themselves in matching Ravenclaw scarves. Sometimes the lovers are on a beach, splayed casually on a picturesque dune in coordinating jorts and white oxfords. "Not only is this amazing man my husband," the wife declares, "but he is also my soulmate and my best friend!!"

"Gross." I'd show the phone to my wife. "Look."

"Maybe they're insane," Lauren would say.

At some point, I started seeing this nauseating sentiment everywhere, from Oscar speeches to the newsfeeds of common folk. Sometime in the first decade of the twenty-first century, all of a sudden everybody wanted everybody else to know that their marriage not only included sexual intercourse and a joint checking account but also rapturous friendship and the forced wearing of Mario and Luigi costumes on Halloween. These always seemed to me like people with too much free time and zero children who probably did CrossFit together and screamed encouragement to each other during sex. Quite often, these amorous couples posted pics of themselves practically making out in public, which seems, I don't know, bizarre, two married people doing that.

"Try not to barf." I'd turn my laptop around. "Look how in love they are."

"Sad," Lauren would say.

This stunning woman, to whom I'd now been married nearly a decade and a half, was not my best friend. You would not be seeing any Facebook photos of us doing that thing where the wife stands on a slab of driftwood and drapes her arms around the goateed husband's neck as he dreams of cheese fountains. I mean, sure, in the early years she pretended to like novels and canoeing, despite her fear of drowning, and I faked enjoying *The Sound of Music*. Who cared? The hills were alive with the sound of our baby making.

The brownshirts of familiarity always turn up. Pretty soon, whenever she declared her desire to watch *The Music Man* in bed, I'd be overcome with the sudden urge to sleep on the roof. Whenever I wanted to read aloud some wry Charles Portis passage from *The Dog of the South*, she'd turn on the loudest household appliances. Lauren had begun looking at me the way you look into a sack of fast food when the order's wrong and you're already two miles down the road.

The polarity of our personalities, once so intoxicating, had grown merely toxic. She'd always loved the diligence I took to prepare food—how, for example, I reanimated leftover pizza in a cast-iron skillet or cooled fresh brownies in the fridge to ensure a clean cut with the knife. After a few years of marriage, I'd turn on the stove to work my magic on cold pizza and she'd turn it right off again and throw the pizza into the microwave.

"It'll be rubbery and dead," I'd say.

"Who cares? I'm hungry."

She'd slice up the brownies right out of the oven, mauling the surface with a butter knife.

"You're destroying the brownies," I'd say.

"*Who cares.*"

Her playful resistance to human touch—cuddling, holding hands, sweet embraces in the kitchen—which had once been an oddly endearing quirk, now seemed vaguely malevolent.

"Touch me again and I'll slap you," she'd say.

"Kinky," I'd say.

But really, I only found it cruel.

Her aversion to many forms of merrymaking (loud music, pig roasts, second-line parades), another cute eccentricity, now seemed a fatal flaw. I have always loved parties: art show parties, football-watching parties, Christmas parties, wakes, feasts. What Lauren likes is leaving parties and going home and putting on pajamas and crawling into bed and disappearing into sleep, where parties cannot find her. I tried to tell myself that our being contraries was a good thing, a quality that inspired healthy balance, but suddenly we seemed like people who belonged in different marriages.

But it was fine! It's fine! We were happy enough in our marriage, which consisted largely of insulting one another's music and making sex for minutes at a time. Long before I knew of her love for Chad, I knew of her loathing of me. We did what all loving married couples do, growing haggard and sad and quietly seething with contempt. We were rotting from the inside out. Our vampiric selves had not been banished after all, just sated for a time.

The more I made audiences laugh at book festivals, the more she refused to crack a smile. She was keeping me humble, okay, that's fine, but after a while, I wondered, "What's up with this woman? Is it marriage fatigue? Some undisclosed childhood trauma manifesting as joylessness?" I shook it off. The summer of our fourteenth anniversary, we hardly touched, though life was generally great. I'd just recorded my first audiobook, and my writing had gone so well for so long that I hardly remembered my anguish at those distant creative blocks surmounted years before. I'd come home from work and put my arm around her and lean in for a tender kiss, and she'd pull away like I smelled of Funyuns.

"Come on," I'd say.

"Your beard. It's prickly."

I'd had a beard for a quarter century by then. How was it now suddenly prickly? I trimmed the beard and used mouthwash, but still she winced, her arms limp at her sides, not returning the embrace. I'd have had more luck making out with an abused rescue beagle.

Maybe it was her back. Something got dislodged in her spine that year and consigned her to a special chair most nights, to reduce the spasms. Problems with vertebrae will ruin anybody's comedy act. Sex had grown scarce and tepid, as a result of the back issue and her obvious disgust at my presence. We'd make out every few weeks, but it felt increasingly like some unrehearsed magic show act in which the lady in the box might want you to go ahead and saw her in half.

Quirks become customs, customs become habits, habits become punishable by death. My adolescent love of blasting Run-DMC tapes as I got ready for school became the habit of rattling wall décor with exasperating Phish solos as I got ready to teach, and Phish, as many American wives of a certain kind of white boy know, is a leading cause of divorce.

"Can you turn that down!" Lauren would scream through the sound of a hair dryer as I danced naked through the bedroom.

"Just wait," I'd scream back. *"They're about to lay down the funk."*

Later, on a family trip, when I played another concert album, Lauren laid down the funk of judgment, seizing control of the volume knob with a look that said she wanted to throw both the car stereo console and me out onto the interstate.

"You liked Phish when we dated," I said, sulking now. "You loved this music."

"I was lying."

She suddenly seemed contemptuous of everything I adored:

music, morning sex, reading in bed, doing anything in bed but sleeping as far apart from each other as possible without requiring a change of address. In those days I saw more of her back than her front. I was too much a fool not to turn down the music and stop the tickling. Who didn't want to be tickled? A good tickle should lead to playful wrestling, which leads to playful lovemaking, no? I had internalized this truism. I'd seen my father tickle my mother in the kitchen, and she loved it, and hated it, and it always ended with a dance, an embrace, a kiss. But tickling Lauren only ended in my daubing my wounds with peroxide, in a bid, if not for love, then for pity from the children.

"If you tickle me again, I will hurt you," she said. Then I would tickle her again, and, to my surprise, she would choose violence: wooden spoons, fists, forks. All I wanted was touch, which eluded me, unless you count the forks. This dance of contempt spiraled until I stopped touching her altogether, which is, I suppose, what she wanted. Why would I attempt to seduce a woman who poked holes in my forearms with kitchen utensils as if I were a baked potato? Her clandestine reunion with Chad would soon commence, a virus ready to enter her weakened body. I don't know. Maybe he didn't tickle her. Maybe he did whatever she told him to.

I used to think only the deviant or unlucky—addicts, swingers, abusers, drunks—got to the tortured point in marriage where divorce obtains. Nobody ever told me that every marriage comes to this cataract in the river many times over, that every marriage goes over the falls. The two of you go tumbling across the smooth mossy rocks of time, and down you go and some couples die and some don't, but everybody goes toppling. I'd witnessed many weddings, Jewish ones and Christian ones and freethinking barefoot ones, and never heard a single officiant explain the crucible of suffering that

awaits every married couple. They say things like, "You'll have ups
and downs," and we smile as if to say, "Yes, yes, the road shall be up
and down and the river of life indeed rocky." I've never heard an
officiant say, "Kenneth, Belinda, you will both grow extraordinarily
comfortable with daily fantasies about the other being thrown from
a speedboat and the body never recovered."

One day, you wake to find yourself standing on opposite sides
of the river, when mere seconds ago you'd been in the same inner
tube having a grand old time. Whenever Lauren was slighted by a
girlfriend, I should've taken her side, but instead found myself playing devil's advocate.

"I mean, she does have a point," I'd say, making the common
mistake of thinking my wife wanted my opinion, when all I really
did was make clear that I was not in her corner. I was no best friend.
A best friend invites vulnerability, letting you be naked, emotionally, without fear of judgment, but this quality does not come easy
to two funny people who've been making love and budgets and grocery lists for half their lives, taking turns as the gag man while the
other plays it straight, arms crossed, like the time I lost an important
tooth and had to go without it for several months, for reasons the
periodontist failed to explain. Every time I'd try to make out with
Lauren, she'd turn away.

"You look like a hillbilly," she'd say. "I can't."

Naturally, I'd get butthurt and hurl myself out of the bed, nursing wounds in the living room until I could return the favor, as
when, days later, she came bounding into my office to explain she'd
lost ten pounds.

"From which part?" I said, studying her body.

"Jerk."

I hadn't meant it to come out like that, but it was funny. Isn't
that why she loved me?

• • •

At its best, comedy provides a check on power and pride, keeps you realistic about how good you don't look in those jeans, and I do believe that our shared love of laughter kept us both humble. But, man. Funny people sure can make a marriage lonesome. I began to worry that my wife and I were just ordinary assholes, doing twenty-five to life for crimes of the heart. I avoided her in the house—little eye contact, zero touching—so obvious was her disgust, while she chose to share news of her aneurysms with others, anybody who'd listen and not always mock. Chad, for example. He was out there, a text away.

I think most divorces are merely a failure of imagination: you lose the capacity to conceive of a happy future. The two of you are like a wet pair of matches, hardly able to get the fire back. Why keep trying? The world is full of dry matches. All you need is a new one.

Lauren and I had come to that place many times, every slight raked into a sad little pile of hurt, which is probably why we both laughed with such obvious scorn whenever our acquaintances euphorically declared their marital friendship on the internet. We laughed because we privately coveted those friendships and had begun believing that genuine affection was no longer possible in this particular marriage. But it was fine. Only a few more decades of this pathetic business and we'd be dead. Can't wait!

In the months before Lauren confessed the agonizing truth, it would not have been uncommon to find me, any given night, trapped inside a box of wine while she was somewhere else in the house, strapped to a heating pad, lost in her phone, reading up on clots, and quietly texting a man about whatever dumb thing just happened on *Survivor*. They texted for years, and I never knew. I assumed she was over there in her chair coordinating rides to ballet.

All I knew is that my marriage had grown about as fun as a skin graft. Christ is the bridegroom, Saint John tells us, the church his bride. In most Christian homes, you grow up in the constant shadow of this entirely weird metaphor, just another frustrating example when the Bible seems less like a story and more like a book of indecipherable Jedi koans.

If marriage was supposed to be like the love of Jesus for the church, then it's also like a great big dish of leftovers that you're obligated to finish, no matter how long it takes, the casserole growing inexplicably wet and pruned, and still you have to eat. It's like a local haunted house fundraiser you can't leave, worse by the minute, everybody screaming and doors slamming and chain saws screeching, a fever dream of pretend decapitations. It's like wanting to return a pair of pants you've already worn and washed and lost the receipt to and now you have to wear the pants every day for the rest of your life, even while swimming. It's like sinking underwater in those pants that once felt so good on your body. It's like an underwater breathing contest with somebody else wearing the same pants, and the first one who goes up for air is the loser and the winner dies.

A buddy of mine at work went through a divorce a few years back, and I asked him, straight up, "What was it like? Did you feel relief?"

"No," he said. "Don't ever do it. Don't do it. It's like death. It's like something dies and the thing that dies is you."

Death is what it felt like when she told me everything a few months later, all the disgusting facts of the betrayal, all those times he snuck into the house to watch her sweep the kitchen floor and to hold the dustpan and not, for example, make a joke.

Chapter 9

THE DARKNESS HE
CALLED NIGHT

2017

That first night—Night Zero, for all that was to follow would be dated from the singularity of that moment—she slept in the guest room, and I threw my disbelieving body across a bed that would never again be ours, a bed she'd shared with another man, a bed I now wanted to douse in gasoline and burn. I used to love that bed.

How banal the products of entertainment make infidelity seem! How many TV and movie scenes of perfidious love had I passively observed over the years, endless pairs of amorous toads shredding garments to get at each other's gonads. Infidelity colors all of popular music and world literature, from blues to the Bible, like descriptions of battles from some ancient, eternal war in which I had woken to discover myself a combatant. I lay there in the dark, the idiot, the fool, blind, betrayed, and worked my way through all the stages of heartache: astonishment, followed by Ambien and incredibly specific hallucinations of assault and battery. I would not murder Chad, no, although this thought entered playfully into my mind. Murder would amplify the evil into a mushroom cloud of all-consuming hellfire. Breaking his short little legs might only make Lauren love him more.

The thought of living alone made me sad. I would have more time for body sculpting and books, but might be too sad for the fiction of self-improvement. Then again, sex with strangers could improve one's mood tremendously. I'd grown comfortable with the idea of sex with this woman and only this woman for the rest of my life, like when you only bring one pair of shoes on a weekend trip. Bold choice, make it work. But now the idea of sex with literally anyone I could legally convince to have with me, this opened up exciting avenues in my mind. I made a mental list of all the women I would probably make out with, which ended up being most of them, which seemed unwise.

And, dear God, do you know what happens to children of divorce? Some kids turn out okay, I guess, but how do you know anybody's really okay, and if the kids are, how much therapy had it taken to restore the okayness? They say the youth are resilient, can bounce back from just about anything, toss them into a volcano, it's fine, and yet I know plenty of children from broken homes who never got over it. These kids, who's to say: maybe the trials of family trauma strengthen them with internal resolve to be better, or maybe they become college students with a documented need for a mental wellness ferret.

I foresaw a grievous future for us all, our children growing into adults who would never stop self-medicating the pain of their mother's abandonment with whatever drug was closest to hand: sex, booze, inconvenient piercings, careers in multilevel marketing. Our girls would hate Lauren and pack this hate into the Crock-Pots of their hearts and serve it up one day in their own relationships. I felt sick.

In the coming days, I would crawl into the panic room of

research databases such as JSTOR to see what the experts had to say about the future of my family, where I learned that infidelity occurs in one of every four marriages, which seems high, or did, and that children who suffer through the unfaithful marriages of their parents are more likely to inflict the selfsame hurt on their own unions. They say a man should protect his family, but how do you do that when you share a bathroom with the predator? I felt genuine and justified violence in my heart and hands, but the rage dissolved as quickly as a prescription sleep aid, leaving me with a quiet, exhausted grief. In our vows, I'd promised to love her in sickness and health, and my funny, loving wife suddenly seemed very sick. She did not seem like a woman in love with another man so much as a woman on the edge of a bridge and ready to jump, skittish as a wounded animal. Have you read *Medea*? She seemed like Medea, filled with a savage cold fire, so desperately hurt by others that now she wanted to hurt everybody.

Lauren didn't know what she was doing, hadn't thought it through. Did she not understand that my attorney, should I acquire one, could stipulate in a divorce agreement that she not be allowed custody of the children if cohabitating, for example, with a married man? Chad was still married, too. Could she wait a year or more, living alone, only seeing her children on visits? Didn't she understand that nobody in her family would support this decision? Lauren adores her people: her sister and brother, all those dear aunts and uncles and cousins and nephews and nieces. Lauren's love for her family is a wondrous thing to behold. She would live next door to all of them, if she could, and so would I. I text my wife's cousins. Lauren's uncle has mailed me books on or by Elizabeth Bishop, Marjorie Rawlings, Sun Ra, V. S. Naipaul, Peter Matthiessen. These people share recipes with us. We send memes. They would not be welcoming Chad into their homes for this or any Thanksgiving.

Whatever Happily Ever After my wife imagined was a fantasy. Did she not realize any of this?

The poet Rilke said no feeling is final, but when you've just realized your life has been a lie, you come to see that no thought is final, either. My heart clouded with impossibility. I strained my feeble mind to understand what was happening, but could not see my way forward. Lauren had seemed so sure of herself when she announced this news—cold, but sure. Maybe she knew what God knew, that in addition to being an idiot, I am a terrible human being, at least as corrupt as her, full of vile, vainglorious, petty snakes, though I did not yet have much interest in cataloging my snakes. I suppose I could've climbed out of bed and gone outside and shaken my fist at God for this ruinous turn of events, but what would that solve? Blaming God is like blaming Walt Disney for your inability to have fun at the Magic Kingdom. Whatever had gone wrong in my marriage, I felt sure it was as much my fault as hers. What had I done? I didn't want to think about it.

My career had bought us a home, zeroed out our college debt, paid off the car, and granted us more financial security than either of our families had ever known, but the years of work compelled an emotional abandonment of the woman I'd vowed to love and honor. It didn't matter that I was now a little less blind and much more present. It was too little too late.

Our boat had gone over the falls and busted up into a million fragments of heartache. My hilarious comedy of a marriage turned out to be the biggest joke of all. That night in the dark, God dragged me through the emptiest valley of the shadow of death, the lowest altitude of my life. I needed to pray, but how do you pray to a God who had allowed the joke of this marriage? What do you even say? I crawled out of bed and onto the floor.

"God," I said, into the dark. "Help."

I didn't even know what to ask for help with. I just said it again. "Help me."

The world had been unmade. My reality was a fiction.

"Help me know what is real."

Was God listening? Was he a fiction, too? If God was just as unreal as my marriage, then what to make of the virtues of love and justice and mercy, which emanated from the character and person of God, according to the teachings of my religion? What did I believe, precisely, about God, anyway? Whatever future lay ahead for my family, I knew, would be determined by my answer to that question.

Chapter 10

A BRIEF HISTORY
OF DOUBT

1993

I'd believed and disbelieved in God many times over the years. Seasons of faith followed by seasons of doubt, a lifelong biofeedback loop of knowing and not knowing. I sometimes believed love was a law of the universe, like gravity. Sometimes I believed love a human invention, like flying reindeer. A nice idea. Could be fun. But probably made up. It's not a happy notion to grapple with, the idea of the animating power of your religion being a myth.

The first time I wrestled with doubt, I was seventeen years old. It all started the spring I graduated from high school, when Pop called me into the living room with news.

"Come in here," Pop said. "I got to ask you something."

"Sir?"

Mom sat on the couch, her *Reader's Digest* closed, lips cinched like a purse.

"Did you bring a book to church last week?" He reached beside his chair to reveal a swollen, tattered copy of *A Brief History of Time*, by Stephen Hawking, the bestseller about the mysterious origins and eventual collapse of a godless void.

"They said you was talking about this in Sunday school," Pop said.

"Maybe. It's a very interesting book."

"Do you believe in evolution?"

"That book is not about evolution."

"What did you say in Sunday school?" Mom said.

I'd told everyone in class that human history would probably not end with Jesus' triumphant return but rather with a state of maximum entropy being achieved and the resultant heat death of the universe. But how do you say this to your parents?

"Do you believe we all are just monkeys?" Pop said.

"No," I lied.

"Shirley MacLaine wrote a book about reincarnation," Mom said. "I found it fascinating."

"Ain't nobody in this family a monkey," Pop said.

"I just loved her in *Terms of Endearment*," Mom said.

"That book is all physics." I pointed to Hawking's book. "I wrote a paper on it."

"If I die and come back," Mom said, "I want a housekeeper."

After a God-soaked childhood, I found the water leaking out of my faith in more holes than I had fingers. I'd been taught, for example, that dancing was wrong, as it might lead to mass impregnations. In defense of this position, Mr. Sammons, one of our Sunday school teachers, cited the book of Matthew, where a young woman seduces King Herod with a sexy dance, such that Herod promises to give her anything and what she asks for is the head of John the Baptist on a plate. Which, okay. Sexy dancing leads to murder.

"What about King David?" I asked, citing his aggressive dancing in the second book of Samuel, all that leaping and shouting.

"That's not dancing," Mr. Sammons said. "That's just being very excited."

Our church had precepts against pants and instrumental music and lady deacons and alcohol of any kind, even though Paul in the book of Romans clearly addresses a deaconess named Phoebe, and it says right there in the book of Luke that Jesus had no qualms about manifesting enough cabernet to shoot a *Godfather* wedding scene.

"What about the miracle at the wedding feast?" I asked Sammons. "Why would he do a miracle like that if wine is wrong?"

"That was grape juice," Mr. Sammons said.

He launched into a tortured description of ancient methods of fermentation and the lexicology of *wine* and the particular refreshing deliciousness of Welch's. It wasn't the nonsense that did me in: it was my community's absolute inability to address the questions with anything approaching a healthy Socratic disposition of free thought. I didn't want answers so much as evidence that my people had the ability to ask, for example, why anyone not heavily medicated would serve grape juice at a wedding.

I had harder questions: If God was both omnipotent and omniloving, why would he allow a deacon at our church, Mr. Shirley, a husband and father who helped coach our baseball team for two summers, have an affair and leave his wife and son, one of my good friends, never to be seen again? This question of the apparent cruelty of a God who lets it happen is not original, I know, every Goth kid in your high school had the same question, but when you grow up in a system of belief that presumes to explain every jot and tittle of existence, and then you find a bag of tittles and jots in a chest buried underneath the church, you wonder why nobody told you about them. I found myself reading just about any book that promised the kinds of answers my church wouldn't give me, books such as Hawking's. I suppose word got out that the Key boy had been asking too many questions, because a few days later Pop announced at dinner that I had been chosen by the church for a special honor:

"Preacher asked if you would give a sermon."

Maybe they felt all my questions could be reined in by such an assignment. Maybe they meant to humble me. It does happen sometimes in country churches and small churches, rogue youth being invited to preach a short lesson before the congregation, especially when the salaried prophets need a vacation and there're no funds to pay a pro.

"It'll be Sunday night after next," Pop said. "You best prepare."

How do you tell your parents, who dutifully carried you to church three times a week and invited you into an ancient rite that in the aggregate had created inestimable goodness in the world and given rise to the greatest cities and civilizations and art and ideas ever known in human history, that you had begun to doubt all of it?

"It's just—I have questions," I said.

"About what?"

"About how we all got here."

"I ask myself that every day," Mom said.

Possessing all the necessary virtues of a future Church of Christ preacher, including testicles and a love of my own voice, I had no choice but to give the sermon. I'd heard thousands of sermons in my young life, maybe too many. I have always felt pity for people who did this for a living. You try writing and delivering a new TED talk or two every week for ten or twenty or thirty years, based on a book nobody reads, baring your inmost thoughts for a crowd of friendlies who've heard it all before and strangers who'd rather be washing a cat.

For the next two weeks, I prepared my homily, wrestling with demons who might not exist and seeking inspiration from a God who might not be listening. At the Brandon Public Library, I checked out books on public speaking, looking for guidance, if not from God, at least from enthusiastic pagan experts, who recommended that I ease my nerves by picturing everyone naked, which seemed unwise, just based on the indifference to physical fitness among those in our church.

So, I decided to preach about heaven. Who knows why. Maybe because I no longer believed in it. Maybe I could convince myself the brilliant Hawking was wrong. I threw myself into the Bible, and what I found was so opaque and fantastical that I felt like a man writing a defense of Santa's elves.

A week later, during the Sunday evening service, I stood at the pulpit and surveyed in awful wonder the soft curious faces of the congregation as they looked up at me from too far away. I did not want to be here. This is a chronic theme of my life, obediently agreeing to be somewhere and upon arrival very much wishing my head would miraculously burst into flames so that I could be hauled away by medical professionals.

I set down my notes gingerly and cleared my throat and removed my wristwatch and placed it beside my Bible the way I'd seen preachers do all my life, a gesture to show everyone that while I might be a spirit-filled mouthpiece for El Shaddai about to rain down on them blistering tongues of prophetic truth straight from the factory floor of eternity, I knew all these nice people had Sunday leftovers waiting for them in a CorningWare casserole dish somewhere. I looked around the room and saw only heads bobbing on the surface of reality, a congregation of turtles, smiling. My hands shook a little. I grew cold. I looked out at my parents, Pop stoic, Mom smiling.

I began my sermon by reading aloud from the book of Revelation, with its vivid descriptions of paradise: those golden streets and gates of pearl and skyscrapers of glass and many rainbows and gemlike fountains and a massive throne for Jesus and innumerable angels in festal gathering and so many bright sparkling lights that you didn't need a sun or a moon because all the light came from God and the light shone on all the dead people who were no longer dead but alive and spoke many languages and walked around giddy from all the light and all the endless buffets of foods. My sermon had one central thesis: "Wow, heaven is probably pretty cool, though we have no way of knowing!"

It was June, the sun still bright and hot but falling over the trees, the frosted windows to my left orange in the last fiery blasts of day, the windows to the right already painted a wash of blue. "Blah blah blah," I said into the microphone. This is not what I said, but it is not much different, either. I made so little sense that members of the congregation must have assumed I'd finally succumbed to all those football-induced head traumas. Desperate, I tried to picture everyone naked, but that's not always advisable when the average age of your audience is somewhere between "Guadalcanal veteran" and "life alert bracelet." It didn't feel right, undressing all these elderly God-fearing saints with my mind while simultaneously trying to preach about the paradisiacal delights of heaven, which they would all be entering soon. I wanted God to be real, just so he could send me to hell and be done with it. As I concluded, I said a prayer, the way all preachers do, and I prayed a second silent prayer that Jesus would take the image of all the naked people out of my brain forever.

When I finished the sermon, whole pews of churchgoers appeared to be dead. My father had a pained look. Mom sort of looked above and just beyond my head: hurt, pathetic, but brave, the sort of expression she typically reserved for TV specials on malnourished children she longed to sponsor. I sang the closing hymn along with everyone else but felt no peace, saw only dullness and death beyond the rim of time. I knew so little—about anything: heaven, science, reality—but I did know this: in one instant, my faith collapsed like a supernova. I could no longer summon the will to believe any of this nonsense.

I would have to leave the church and the good people who'd fed me the most delicious fried chicken and the Word of God, including the parts that nourished you to nourish others, to mow the lawns of the indigent and to carry communion trays of unleavened bread and grape juice to the homes of the destitute. They had taught me to love the fatherless and feed the motherless and set aside money to carry on that work, when they hardly had any money to spare. These people were doing their best to show me how to live as nobly as they knew how, even if they couldn't admit to not having all the answers, even the easy ones. They had given me a Bible the week I got baptized, to carry with me all my days to be a lamp for my feet and a light to my path, and they had given me a home that could be my home forever, if I would only accept the limits of my knowledge and take what remained on faith.

I was on a new road now, a road that has never not been paved over with unanswerable questions—a road that would lead me in its winding way to the woman I would marry. That very year, Lauren, only fifteen, was learning to doubt everything, too. Her father sat her down, next to her siblings on the couch, to explain that he was going away forever. He had been a pastor, but now he was an adulterer.

That summer, I left that church and never returned. The undeniable possibility of a godless void was the most terrifying thought I have ever welcomed into my mind, until the moment, twenty-four years later, when I woke in a dark bedroom and felt a void vaster than anything conjured by the mind of a physicist.

Chapter 11

GOATS AND MONKEYS

2017

My bed was empty and my heart was empty and the clock said 5:00 a.m.

They say that when you get news of a partner's infidelity, the ancient lizard part of the brain takes over. The predatory response systems fire up, the way they do during house fires and tornadoes. Fight, flight, or freeze?

Fight: Call an attorney. Threaten. Remind my wife of everything she was about to lose: her children, family, stability, income, everything. Burn all her bras and panties in the yard. Take an ax handle to the south side and hit a home run with a Hobbit's skull.

Flight: Pack my things? Leave? Cry in a motel room? Find a carriage house somewhere and start over? Let her have the girls? Finish those children's books, finally, no longer being required to kill cockroaches for the children who would hate me forever for leaving them?

Freeze: Do nothing? Go to work? Like nothing happened?

Confuse her? Freak her out a little? Bring her a Pop-Tart? Ask how she slept?

I stood up in the empty bedroom and walked to my office, past the guest room where Lauren must have been awake half the night, texting her tiny boyfriend. I took my laptop and went to a coffee shop that opened early. I had something more urgent than writing to do.

At the café, I opened my machine and got to work, changed every password, every username, moved all the cash. I couldn't see my wife emptying out the accounts and taking off for the Yukon, but neither could I have seen her falling in love with someone like Chad. Anything was possible. I no longer knew my wife. She could still use her debit cards, but she could no longer walk away with the tens of thousands of rainy-day dollars we'd saved over the years. I might be made by law to give her half of it, eventually. But not today. I moved my direct deposit, too.

She'd be fired from the school if it got out that she'd left her family for a married man. Actions have consequences. Even witch's covens and farmer's markets have guidelines. I'd have to scrape together tens of thousands of dollars in tuition, immediately. The rain for those dollars.

Once the money was safe, I felt better. I breathed.

"Where are you?" she texted.

"Hell," I replied. "It's fun. You should come."

Now what? Should I go somewhere and pray? Sharpen my machete? Don sackcloth? Offer a sacrifice? What would Abraham do? He seemed good in a fight. What about Jesus? Would he offer to wash Lauren's feet? Curse the trees in the front yard, forbidding them ever to bear fruit? I did what I always do. I opened a blank document. I typed, "A story about a man who finds out his wife is cheating."

•   •   •   •

In grad school, I took a course called Deconstructing *Othello*, where the professor, a celebrated playwright, invited us to approach the play like an alien spacecraft found in some New Mexican desert. We dismantled the plot down to the line, the word, the breaths of syllables, to learn how the thing flew. We would steal its technology and master its machinations. How does Shakespeare tighten the screw of tension as the play builds toward its tragic climax, where a good and honorable Venetian officer is fooled into believing his sweet wife is unfaithful and, enraged and anguished, snuffs her out with a downy pillow?

For the final assignment, we were asked to write our own version of *Othello*, using all we had learned. Some of us reimagined the play taking place in a women's prison, others as a classic spaghetti western. I thought it would be funny to make the tragedy a comedy. I called it *Goats and Monkeys*, a title stolen from one of Othello's lines, when he imagines Desdemona and Cassio making love like animals in some kind of weird barnyard where monkeys have access to goats. I would give my play a happy ending, where Iago reveals the whole thing was a prank. I don't know, I was an idiot. I still didn't understand how to make a story work. I was a child. I wrote my play and it turned out more sad than funny.

But seventeen years later, I was no child. It would not be a play but a novel. In this version, it would be no prank. In my book, the plot would be turned upside down. The wife would be obviously having the affair. The husband would refuse to believe it. Maybe it seems silly that on the morning after discovering my wife's infidelity, I started writing a novel about it. Writing has always been my method of discovering what's actually going on in my life. To write a story about a woman having an affair would require me to understand her motivation. I think this was God's way of saying, "You have to understand your wife."

I called the wife Rachel. My wife's middle name.

I called the husband Scott. Mine.

Rachel would be beautiful. Like my wife.

Scott would be black. Like Othello.

Why was Rachel cheating on Scott? Hmm. I made some notes. Attachment issues? Fear of abandonment, which led her to abandon others before she could be abandoned? Perhaps Scott was a terrible ass? An alcoholic? Hideous naked? A pathologically writing-obsessed egoist? Hmm, interesting!

I believe now, looking back, that this strange and untimely urge, to write about us, or to write about a couple like us, was the first step toward goodness in this dreadful and dark season. Writing held wisdom if I could only heed it. If I could understand my wife, perhaps I could forgive her. Even if she carried out her plan to marry Chad, forgiveness still seemed desirable. We would be enmeshed in each other's lives forever because of the children and would have a thousand decisions to make together regarding money, schedules, college, weddings. Forgiveness would make all that so much less unpleasant, wouldn't it?

I had forgiven plenty in my life. I'd forgiven friends for small betrayals, students for plagiarism, my father for hitting me continually with a belt, such that I could not walk. Hadn't writing my first book been one long, hilarious, heartbreaking attempt to forgive him?

I had asked for forgiveness, too, of the same friends whom I likewise betrayed, of teachers and administrators for the breaking of policies, of God for treating my body like a plaything with women and alcohol, of employers for cutting corners, of my wife for my having shown more love to art than to her? Hadn't writing my second book been one long, hilarious, heartbreaking plea for forgiveness from her?

"Are you coming home?" Lauren texted, again. Why did she care?

I had to be at work soon. How could I work? How could I teach? I had a lecture to give in a few hours on literary humor. The topic: "Making Sad Things Funny."

Back at home, Coco, Pippi, and Ginsburg were readying themselves for school and soon out the door. Lauren had called in sick. She sat on the bed.

"Well," I said.

"Well."

She and Chad wanted to live in the house, she said. They would buy me out.

"I'm not sure you can afford it," I said. He made a modest living as it was, and she was soon to be unemployed.

"We'll make it work," she said.

"This seems like a big house for two people."

"You're not taking the girls."

"I'm not 'taking' anything. They're our children."

"Yeah, well."

"It seems like you're the only one who doesn't want to be in this family," I said.

Forgiveness seemed a noble but terribly remote concern, crowded out by more urgent realities. We would have to share custody. Two dumb houses, two pathetic Christmases, a thousand new toothbrushes. Our children would become sad little pack mules. Every new revelation came at the speed of light. I knew I needed a little help from God to figure things out, but I hadn't spoken with God in years, though I'd been in and out of churches for decades, mostly out of duty and to lessen the crushing weight of guilt whenever I let myself be elsewhere. I had so often wanted to believe God imaginary, but suddenly I wanted him to be very real, so I could ask him a few questions.

Chapter 12

THE GRAVITRON OF GOD

2007–10

Twelve hours after learning my wife was in love with another man, I hopped on my bike and headed downtown, looking for answers. I suppose my truck would've made more sense, but something felt right about being on the bike, a metaphor for the naked exposure of this new reality, for Lauren had ripped the skin right off the bones of being.

I found this exposure oddly thrilling. I love the sensation summoned by crisis: hurricanes, tornado warnings, kitchen fires, car accidents, live audiences waiting to be entertained, former neighbors waiting to be bludgeoned to death with a gardening tool—these awake in me a heroic fearlessness I do not feel most days. Whatever came next, I knew, would demand impossible strength, which lived inside me, waiting for its moment. Maybe that's my ego talking. If so, thanks, ego! At least you haven't abandoned me, too!

I pedaled myself to church, which would be empty on this

Tuesday morning, which was ideal. I wanted to sit alone in the great marbled echo chamber of the sanctuary and pray.

When we first moved to Savannah ten years before, Lauren and I knew we needed something heavy to anchor us in this new place, which is why I'd quieted my distrust of the starchier garments of religion and we'd started looking for a church home.

Sure, okay, I became an atheist in late adolescence, but only half-heartedly. I was as bad at nonbelieving as believing. In the decade between losing my faith at seventeen and finding a marriage at twenty-seven, I'd limped back into new churches, different churches, hoping to find a few answers about how to live a good and useful life. Maybe God was imaginary, but if ten years in higher education taught me anything, it's that everything can be doubted, even your doubts. Besides, the birth of children has a way of compelling you to feel around for solidity, something real to which you can lash your new family amid the squall. We had a baby by then, Coco, and felt this baby deserved exposure to religious trauma that would one day cause her to run screaming from religion until she had a baby, too. Church suddenly made a weird kind of sense.

Our first year in the city we visited a small church near the house, but there were too few young couples and hardly a baby in sight but ours. Lauren stayed at home with Coco. I'd come home from the college and find her quietly sad at the kitchen table.

"How was your day?" I'd ask.

"I organized the Tupperware drawer." She'd stare out the window. "I washed baby vomit out of my hair."

She seemed vaguely miserable. She needed friends. The nice thing about church is, if you move to a new city and find a good one, you've got instant access to dozens of friend prospects who are kind and funny and who may also believe Jesus held a concealed-carry permit. You never quite know whom you're going to find there. Once, we visited a midsize nondenominational church where, during the hymns, most people raised their hands as if being beamed into alien spacecraft. It was a little odd. The hymns were so earnestly sung that you felt all of us were auditioning for *American Idol*.

"Everybody was nice," Lauren said, after.

"I never know what to do with my hands," I said.

I remember the day we decided to visit Independent Presbyterian Church, a storied downtown congregation with the tallest steeple in town. I used to hate the idea of great big churches. But then one afternoon, following a short drive over the Savannah River, we drove back over the high bridge as I surveyed the wonder of this new and very old city far below, the stone and iron and timber of other centuries pushing up through the jungle of green, steeples of every American stripe and one higher than the others, the Presbyterian steeple, and I no longer cared much about the problem of big churches. I wanted the ancient dirt. I wanted my wife to find some friends. Maybe that steeple could be our steeple. I longed to learn what the building knew and to sit on pews rubbed raw by the dead.

"I think we should try that big church." I pointed. "The big Presbyterian one."

"I bet they have a good nursery," Lauren said.

What strikes you most about the Independent Presbyterian Church is how small the place makes you feel, every architectural gesture gently reminding visitors that God owns a quarry. On approach, the immense white ornamented façade draws you in with a delicious promise, upheld by eight massive Doric columns of granite, an engraving under the portico pressing down on all who enter with the mighty weight of its history:

FOUNDED 1755

A BRANCH OF THE CHURCH OF SCOTLAND

JEHOVAE

PATRI FILIO SPIRITIQUE SANCTO

Bound up the wide low steps of this stone fortress and look higher, and what you see is the vertiginous steeple that summoned you here, the sponsored Instagram post of its day, all twenty-two stories of it, and a great big clock fit for God's own wrist, and you grow dizzy just trying to reach the top of this steeple with your eyes, where sits not a cross but a weathervane, reminding you that old churches served as the way-finding apps of earlier centuries, locators in space and time, like a great pin in the earth you could see from pagan hillsides.

I had to smile on those first few Sunday mornings at Independent, walking up the steps with Lauren and Coco as a family of what sounded like Germans halted to gape at the immensity of this massive Puritan temple. I had never belonged to a church that tourists wanted to photograph. In the Mississippi of my youth, they only photographed churches during arson investigations. The church of my boyhood looked more like a small dry goods warehouse for the storage of used mattresses, the architecture upsetting by design, as if to make you look away and toward heaven for something better. But this. Striding through the immense mahogany doors, tall enough for a mountain troll, felt like stepping into perfect power.

The interior of the church doubles down on the façade, with high Corinthian columns upholding the massive suspended wooden dome, all in white, suggesting a beautifully made wedding cake that might end up eating you. On the way home after our first visit, Lauren and I agreed we should go back.

"Everybody was nice," she said.

"I know. It was weird."

After church every Sunday, around noon, when the tourist trolleys and Huns stood outside the sanctuary to photograph the steeple and all the well-dressed American zealots emerging onto the lawn in their pearls and seersucker, we smiled, proud as we were to be living inside a historical reenactment of What America Was Probably Never Really Like.

We loved so much about this big old boring church. The beauty and history, of course, the everlastingness of it all. I'd sit in the sanctuary, bathed in tides of sound from the massive organ, and marvel at its age: 1755. I tried to wrap my head around the fact that this church had been granted a charter by King George II. Once a year, one of the berobed ministers climbed the high pulpit and read aloud the charter, with visitors learning that the king permitted this new church to be founded and to operate under the empire's protection in exchange for "one peppercorn a year." Jesus instructs us to be salt, but I guess George had other plans.

During this ritual, a small glass jar is revealed, filled with peppercorns—more than 250 grainy black nuggets by the time we'd joined—and a new peppercorn is added. Everyone smiles a little at the silliness of the rite, but not everybody. Many sat straighter in their pews. Some wept. I wanted to laugh, but for a church to stick around that long had to count for something. When they founded this congregation, Catherine the Great was in her twenties. Goethe was six years old. Crispus Attucks and Kant and Voltaire walked the earth. The last emperor of the Holy Roman Empire, heir to Charlemagne, hadn't even been born yet and neither had Mozart. You had to admire it. The world was better with great big old pretty churches in it, I told myself. We were honored to be there and felt we had stumbled upon something important that must be preserved. We wanted to be in that jar, too.

The church had much to recommend it. On Sunday nights in summer, the congregation repaired to an idyllic property called Point Pleasant, out on one of Savannah's many residential islands, where, after an evening service in a large chapel overlooking the marsh, a big meal was served and everyone walked the property while children hunted fiddler crabs and played on a swing that pushed out over the water. Others walked the pier toward the deepwater dock. Some swam in the pool. We loved the pool. I'd change Coco into her suit and hold her in the water while Lauren enjoyed a break from the baby and made new friends. This is why we'd come.

The Point Pleasant property, they said, had been donated to the church long before by some frail and godly widow, to sanctify the people of God with refreshment. Here was generational wealth on display in all its edifying goodness, and all were welcome. The big pancake breakfast and egg hunt every Easter, the family carnival with hot dogs and bounce houses every Halloween, all of it gave us something to do, to belong to. The Christmas program alone, where our tiny cherubs sang of lowing cattle as candles burned in the alcoves was something out of a fairy tale.

Back downtown on Sunday mornings, sitting inside that old, polished, Corinthian-columned sanctuary with checkerboard marble flooring and the Bach preludes was enough to make your head spin with the grand story of Christendom across the centuries. It was the Gravitron of God, the hymns and the ritual and the people in their finery and the robes and the ancient creeds and the sermons delivered from way up in a vertiginous mahogany pulpit that made every word feel like a proclamation directly from the mouth of the Great I Am. I loved that a U.S. president had been married in this church and that babies who had been baptized here had been buried here a century later. I didn't mind that I found some of the congregants silly, with their talking-points conservatism and the suggestion in Sunday school one morning that Hillary Clinton might be a Wiccan high priestess. Someone had read this on the internet. I found it edifying to worship with the deranged, especially when they let you swim in their pool.

In those first years at the church, I never connected with anyone enough to call the person a friend, but Lauren did, and that was plenty. I wasn't quite sure whom I was supposed to be. The bow tie and eyeglasses and PhD ensured I was welcome. When we formally joined, we were announced as "Dr. and Mrs. Harrison Scott Key," and everyone nodded approvingly. Presbyterians love a PhD, which hearkens back to a happier time when Christians ran all the best schools. But so often I felt like a man in costume. The rebellious wildcat inside me wanted to howl and tear down solemnity wherever I saw it. I had begun to write stories by then, whence I did my best to shape the wildcat's howl into a kind of exuberant literature that might make others laugh, and so much of this exuberance felt unfit for the staid customs of Independent. But I loved the church. I wanted to love the church. There were many friendly people: a pair of affable dentists who asked me for book recommendations and a wetland scientist who took me duck hunting and an irrepressibly upbeat aerospace engineer and a physician who started carrying a pistol on his leg after a spate of church shootings. They were kind to me, but I couldn't shake the increasing sensation that everyone's appearance, including mine, masked something dark that could not be allowed out of its cage.

My enthusiasm for Sundays waned after a couple of years. I could scarcely abide waking up early on my one real off day for the privilege of sitting in a folding chair while someone who exclusively reads Navy SEAL biographies attempted to explain the beauty of the Psalms. It was painful.

"Perk up," Lauren said, every Sunday morning on the way downtown. She'd found her people, the Young Wives of the Young Babies, but I still felt like a visitor. Our marriage was already falling apart and I had no idea.

I began drugging myself on Sundays just to make it through the wastelands of Sunday school. Having recently enjoyed three root canals, I was in possession of a drawerful of opioids that I saved for the Lord's day. Hearing someone rail against rap was always more pleasant while drugged. I'd sit there and think, "This isn't so bad." Even then, a decade before the revelation of the affair, my heart knew something was wrong, not just at this church, but at home, too.

Eventually, the pills ran out, and I felt it might be good to find a church that didn't make you need to get high just to not hate it. I longed to spend the day drinking bottomless mimosas like my pagan friends, but, no: I stood in my kitchen, dressed in Brooks Brothers I'd found on eBay, preparing to fellowship with people who, if I saw them in a liquor store, might not actually speak to me. I pined for deliverance from this feeling that I did not belong. I prayed for faith, and perseverance, and something good for lunch, as our growing brood of daughters screamed at my wife for having the audacity to insist they wear clean panties into the house of God.

"It's time," I'd say. "We need to leave now if we want good parking."

"Ugh," Lauren said. She'd begun to dread church as much as I did. She had her friends, but she, too, seemed to feel a distance from others in the pews. I couldn't quite say why.

Sometimes we drove the girls to Sunday school and strolled a block over to drink espresso and eat scones and enjoy not being endlessly bombarded with humorless disputations of Scripture. It felt wrong. It felt right. It was pleasant to sit with Lauren at Gallery Espresso. I would do a little reading and she would scroll her feeds.

Sometimes we talked, mostly we didn't. Lauren seemed to have secrets even then. I knew she went to church out of duty. I knew she wanted stability for our girls, so they could find good and decent friends from good and decent families. We both loved casting ourselves as fairy-tale characters peopling the enchanted village, but increasingly the fairy tale had begun to peel away from the reality of our lives.

Lauren still grieved her mother's death and her father's cruel abandonment. She did not speak of this grief, but it was in there, working its ruin. I had my own nameless melancholy. Life had grown dull and gray. Church clothes made me unhappy. I was, by then, a big, fat walrus. My writing was garbage. The idea of death had a certain appeal. I needed help, long before I would need even more help.

Most churches, at least the old ones, talk a lot about "spiritual disciplines," those habits of being that strengthen faith and make a better you: reading the Psalms every morning, acts of charity and generosity, fasting, prayer. Fasting seemed cruel for a man whose only happiness in those days was Cuban pork, and we had so little money that generosity seemed feeble. But prayer didn't require money. Even the morbidly obese, such as me, could pray.

Presbyterians love to pray, arms outstretched from the roof of the world, great wizardly sleeves of those Genevan robes, eyes wrenched closed, the rhetoric as high as the pulpits, stuffed with well-worn clauses, *lordoflords* and *trueandlivinggod* and *thykingdomcome*.

One of my issues with our grand old Waspy church is how they claimed to love prayer, but seemed, at least in the presence of others, too emotionally frigid to pray with the desperate specificity of, say, Jesus, who once begged God not to let him be tortured and murdered. Most Presbyterian petitions, by contrast, ran to the abstract: "Our Father in heaven, you are the Absolute Person, the Never-Changing One, the I-Am-Who-I-Am, First and Last, Ever-Blessed Impassable God, invincible, holy, perfect, absolute, boundless, changeless, stainless, relentless, breathless, sleeveless, strapless, majestic, merciful, perpetual, plenipotentiary, radiant, sacred, sovereign, a meat lover's supreme, with extra cheese. You are God. Abba. Father. Yahweh. Elohim. Jehovah. Adonai. Lord of Hosts. Ancient of Days. King of Kings and also of Leon."

The sequence of vocabulary words always unleashed themselves into the void of the sanctuary like a thousand rabid fruit bats looking for somewhere to land. At first, I was highly impressed by these nineteenth-century orations, the hierarchy of clauses and subordinate clauses, but week by week I became quietly enraged at this incomprehensible appeal to divinity. Even in smaller groups, like Sunday school, which often began with a short prayer led by the teacher, you'd be hard-pressed to hear genuine expressions of specific human suffering.

"Are there any prayer requests?" the teacher would ask.

Sometimes, a hand would go up, but it was always a prayer request for somebody's great-aunt who needed a hip replacement, a biopsy, a cornea transplant. We could not bear to hear about the suffering of the people in the room, Good Lord, no: too real. We never prayed for our marriages, our children, our interior lives. The fable of our being respectable taxpayers would be shattered by anything real. I needed prayers. Even then, long before I knew of my wife's growing crush on our neighbor, I knew she was unhappy. She'd already suggested her taking the girls and going away for an unsaid length of days. Sometimes, I'd raise my hand during the prayer requests and say something verging on confessional.

"I've been a little listless lately," I'd say. "Everything seems to have lost its color."

Everybody would shuffle. Lauren would stiffen. I didn't say why I was sad. I didn't want to make everyone go pale. I didn't want to say, "My wife said she wanted to move out."

Growing up, I was taught to say my prayers at bedtime: *If I die before I wake, I pray the Lord my soul to take.* You have to admire a religion that has the balls to remind children they might die in the night. Back in Mississippi, we prayed plenty, but not in the high-flown abstractions of Calvinism. Our Church of Christ prayers were desperate and specific. Anyone might be asked to pray aloud, and you were expected to riff, improvise, draw together themes of the sermon and items mentioned in the bulletin, deaths, births, divorces, influenza, a deacon crushed by a pulpwood truck. My father gave the most inventive prayers. None of us will soon forget the time Pop prayed for a woman who'd just had a hysterectomy.

"And we pray for Juanita's speedy recovery," he said, with great reverence. "And we hope it brings her many pleasures."

Ask my mother. He said this. He really said this.

As ridiculous as my father's public prayers could be, they were no match for the madness of praying wrought by social media, where distant high school acquaintances, people I hadn't seen in years, would cryptically announce some malady of body or spirit and demand my petitions.

"Unspoken prayer request," they'd say.

"Prayers comin' your way!" everybody piped in.

"Praying now, girl!"

It just seems to cheapen the whole act of divine petition. I am sorry your cousin's stepmom's little teacup poodle has an anal fungus. But I am not going to lift up Tiny's name in prayer. I don't even *know* Tiny. I don't even know your cousin. I don't really even know you.

Writer Anne Lamott once said that there are only two prayers:

"Thank you, thank you, thank you" and "Help me, help me, help me." To that list, I would add "Stop it, stop it, stop it" and "Die, Tiny, die."

In those days, I needed prayer as much as any number of small cancerous dogs. I was grateful for my job at the university but couldn't see three or five or ten years down the road where it might lead. Would writing my stories always feel like a second job that demanded everything and paid nothing? Would being a father ever feel natural? Would my marriage ever feel exciting again? Why did my wife keep asking me if I was having an affair? I resigned myself to a marriage as flat as root beer in the sun.

One Sunday, it was announced that the church would be hosting a men's prayer breakfast, a custom with roots in the Old Testament, when the Israelites were instructed to make a sacrifice every morning, in preparation for the day's smitings. Generally, I don't go in for prayer breakfasts, leery of any event that seeks to put two perfectly fine concepts together and ruin both, like chicken and spaghetti. But I was trying to grow. Maybe a hearty breakfast would help.

It was a halcyon March morning that day long ago as I pulled up to the Savannah Golf Club, the oldest in America, they say, carved out of coastal pastures sometime right after the American Revolution, muskets beaten into five irons. The breakfast was part of our church's Missions Conference, an annual event where they bring missionaries from distant pagan lands like Kenya and the University of Georgia for us to hear harrowing tales of degradation and to offer thanksgiving to the Lord for letting us live in a city that everyone wants to visit and nobody manages to leave. The theme of the conference was "Declaring the Mystery of Christ," which seemed odd, as Presbyterians generally don't like mystery. They don't like not knowing things, and they don't like God not knowing things, which is why they love the idea of predestination.

I walked through the clubhouse and wandered for a bit, a desert pilgrim in the sprawling complex, feeling my way down carpeted hallways and across darkened ballroom dance floors where, in the gloaming, there appeared pictures of happy leprechauns pinned to the wall, in preparation for the city's annual celebration of alcohol poisoning. Off in the distance, I heard the delicate murmur of Protestants.

The dining room was a surprise. I had been expecting rich mahoganies, mantels of Georgia granite, pocket doors of rare curly pine, a roomful of mink-oiled club chairs that once proudly bore the heft of statesmen and generals, but the low-ceilinged hall dripped with the deadly pallor of fluorescence, walls of drab eggshell white, and the sort of dark green carpeting best suited to camouflaging blood and vomit in the hallways of Holiday Inns. I sat down at an empty table near the front and was joined by two or three acquaintances.

Everything was hushed, without even the merest provocation of feeling, which, as any Calvinist knows, can lead to all sorts of disturbing behaviors, like laughter and eating candy. We shuffled the length of the buffet, scooped eggs and hash and wicked piles of flaccid pork the color of a lung onto heavy industrial china. The place smelled of Sterno.

"Morning."

"Morning."

"A lovely spread, this."

"Quite."

I'd experienced more joy at the burial of a puppy. We chewed obediently as speakers slouched toward the podium, fine and intelligent people, doctors of divinity, speakers of Greek, readers of Hebrew, and I was eager to hear their imaginative extrapolations of the glorious inscrutability of Christological mystery, but they spoke more like undertakers respectfully suggesting a closed casket.

"Speak the mystery of Christ," Saint Paul says, and "walk in wisdom toward them that are without, redeeming the time."

I heard no time-redeeming talk that morning. I heard only theological dissertations on the second law of thermodynamics and the unwinding spool of the world, this notion that everything is always worse than it was and never as bad as it's going to be soon if we don't mow our lawns more diligently and teach our children about the need to eliminate the capital gains tax. And also, that we are all extremely, utterly, horribly depraved human beings, all of us. This note about depravity is the "Stairway to Heaven" of a certain strain of turgid evangelical, who can be counted on to play it in every gathering of God's people.

I like the idea of human depravity—really, it explains so much—but it's not a breakfast-friendly doctrine. Is this what I'd come here for? To hear a slew of joyless men masquerading as nineteenth-century rhetoricians declaim the world's degeneracy from a podium flanked by vistas of eighteenth-century Lowcountry grandeur on a swath of land that cannot be walked except by private invitation? I'd have thought somebody might get up there and at least thank Jesus for inventing economies of scale. I closed my eyes and prayed for patience.

What do other churches do at prayer breakfasts? I found one example on YouTube, where all the praying had musical accompaniment, including a nice little lady tucked into a corner behind an electric piano and a man in a black leather blazer sitting at one of the tables wearing a saxophone. Sometimes he played, sometimes he ate. Another man sang his prayers, which made them more interesting, but not as interesting as the large wooden crucifix he played like a percussion instrument. It was my kind of prayer breakfast, loud and loose and holy. None were trying to hide their pain, though it was hard to tell what they were praying for, exactly. It sounded as if one lady with a microphone said, "O God, we ask you to have your baby. O God, go behind these prison walls today. O, touch my nose and bacon."

There was joy in it, if not a little chaos. You might even call it funky, if prayer can be such a thing. And then, that morning at the prayer breakfast among Caucasians, as the too-sober speaking was over and the praying was about to begin, things really did get funky.

Hugh, the oldest of our church's three or four ministers, stepped up to the lectern. Hugh was a spry old Yank and liable to say anything. He reminded me of my father, being the only pastor I've ever heard use the phrase *rectal procedure* in a sermon. What came out of his mouth in the ballroom shocked me.

"The praying shall commence, brothers, if everyone could take a knee."

Kneeling, an illicit flirtation of body with spirit, is supposed to be an affront to good Presbyterians, who typically prefer a safety-first worship environment: hands to yourself, no sudden movements. I'd never seen any proclivity to popish kneeling at this church, so it was quite astonishing to see all these dreary men descend to the floor. Before I could even disappear the last plug of sausage from its fatty puddle, the place looked like a classroom in an earthquake drill, chairs in disarray, everybody hiding under tables.

I pushed back my chair as Hugh, hiding on the floor behind the lectern, invited us to take various prayer assignations. Roger would pray for this, Eddie for that, et cetera. Voices called out from under the furniture, as though trapped under rubble. I sank to the floor, to this unpadded carpet, and wished I'd worn sweatpants. I had just eaten enough delicious breakfast meat to fill a schooner, and now my khakis conformed to my gut with the devotion of a Danskin leotard.

I bowed down to God the Maker in my tight pants, eyes closed, and remembered my seasonal vertigo, which causes me to fall over unless my body is lashed to a post. To right myself, I grabbed the chair, setting my elbows down on its cushion, hooking my hands into the curlicue struts of its back, a perfectly comfortable position. It looked as though I were now making love to the furniture.

I'd been to Episcopalian churches where they knelt so much it'd make a man keep Dramamine handy. Looking around, I saw two or three older men incapable of kneeling who'd thrown themselves prostrate over their plates. I thought some of them might be sleeping. I thought one or two might be dead. Being dead would have been an improvement.

Could I have quieted my mind in that moment, gripping a chair at that ridiculous prayer breakfast, and prayed for God to insert himself into the tragicomic machine of my life to stop the sadness? No. It would have been impossible. I would've collapsed in uncontrollable sobs on the floor, confirming everyone's unspoken belief that I was out of my mind. I couldn't do it.

Over the years, I've not prayed much for money or love, but often asked God to keep me or loved ones alive. I've prayed often for my children, that they would not be terrible human beings or die in some sad specific way, such as on a paddleboat. I've prayed for my wife more than just about anyone else, because God says to pray for your enemies, and marriage can sometimes be a war of attrition and one of siege, sometimes cold, occasionally hot. But at the prayer breakfast, I could not pray the prayers I needed to pray, even though I knew Lauren was already drifting away from me. I hoped God could hear those prayers trying to break free of my heart, tight as a gorilla fist. Maybe that's all prayer is: wanting to pray and hoping God sees you wanting. And that's when I let go.

I didn't break into heaving sobs. I didn't tear at my raiment like Jacob at the death of his son or weep like Jesus in the Garden of Gethsemane on the night before his murder. Instead, I gave up every pretense of trying not to pray, and in a sudden and unexpected resignation of will, I climbed down from my chair, and as I settled back into crisscross applesauce, my right kneecap made a sound like a heavy glass paperweight falling onto a factory floor. I wanted to roll and scream, but instead, I prayed for the ability to learn to walk again. This I could pray. This could be a way into my own heart.

Next, I threw myself into Child's Pose, known to physicians as the fetal position and yoga instructors as the Best Position for the Obese Adjacent. It almost worked, too, although the pressure on my knee was so great that I catapulted myself onto all fours, like one of those women on TV who have their babies on the bathroom floor. As I started rocking, praying silently that the praying would end, which would definitely make me less sad, my pants burst along a critical buttock seam.

"Help me, Jesus," I said, and then the praying was over.

We stood, and I pulled myself to an upright position. Congregations of bones could be heard cracking, returning to their appropriate offices within the body. Boys who had come with their fathers yawned, stretched. The elders, laid across their plates like the victims of stroke, rose from the dead. We barely spoke as we filed out.

Say what you want about puritanical believers like those at Independent, but they had surprised me. I'd believed them much too solemn, though it was I who still lacked the courage to look unblinking at the darkness in me. Or maybe that was the point. Maybe God has to break all your favorite bones just to loosen you up enough to ask for help. Help would be necessary in the years ahead, for the broken, spewing, bilious, raging, hurting tides of the world had been unleashed already, in secret, set in motion by God or fate—and heading right for my family. I only saw my pain through a glass darkly. I found my car in the parking lot and plunged the key into its body and felt it roar to life. When would I roar again with life? The prayer breakfast had been apocalyptic in the truest sense, exposing my need for divine aid and new pants and perhaps an aggressive diet that did not require biscuits when I spoke to God.

"How was it?" Lauren asked all those years ago, as I hobbled up the steps into our home.

"God tore a hole in my pants."

Years later, as I hobbled up the steps of the church on a Tuesday morning, hoping to sit and pray for an hour, it was clear that God had torn the clothes right off my body.

I tried the two colossal mahogany doors, and they were, in a subtle gesture, locked. I yanked at them a couple of times for dramatic effect: the jilted and desperate husband, finally compelled by tragedy to desperately want to be inside this church for the first time in a long time, only to be denied entry. I sat on the steps.

The weather was nice, warm even for October, but with enough stirring in the air to suggest autumn had boarded its flight and would soon be arriving. A few midweek tourists photographed the church façade as I contemplated things. It occurred to me that perhaps I had been the cause of Lauren's affair. I'd been depressed for years. The evidence was all there: my clinical overeating, my overwhelming melancholy during the week, my irritability on Sundays, the hydrocodone I parceled out like reward pellets just to make it through church.

Maybe I didn't need to pray. Maybe I needed to go talk to a pastor.

From where I sat on the steps of the grand old church, I looked across the lane at the administration building, another imposing granite structure. There would be men inside, some of the very men who'd led that prayer breakfast. I am a silly man on most days, and what I needed right then was the counsel of serious men who might tell me what to do. I stood up. I walked across the lane. This door, too, was locked. I knocked.

Chapter 13

EXILE FROM THE
MAGIC KINGDOM

2017

A few minutes later, I was led to the office of the senior pastor, who, I was told, would be in shortly. This man was handsome, as men of God go, supremely Harrison Ford–ish, with stony Welsh blood, tall and imposing in his thick, heavy black gown: Han Solo's head on Darth Vader's body. He'd played baseball at the University of Southern California and worked this fact into every other sermon, but his vibe was all Puritan, his preaching style in the long and proud Reformed tradition, stern and joyless and vaguely disappointed, like a history teacher passing out an exam on which he knows everyone cheated. I will call him the Reverend Doctor Hairshirt.

In his preaching, Hairshirt did not raise his arms or his voice in prophetic howls of indignation. His dominant emotion was amazement, not at God's goodness or the majesty of creation, but at the fact that more people had not come to church. Incredulity was his love language. Even when he had wondrous insights to share, of divine love and the gift of eternal life through Jesus, say, he expressed these miraculous revelations with the grace of an oncologist announcing that the chemo hadn't worked. He smiled little from the pulpit unless discussing Beethoven's Seventh Symphony or, in moments of pure exaltation, the University of Southern California.

I loved Hairshirt's churlishness. It was hip, in its way. It was also boring. I was not asking to be entertained, but did long to be engaged. In most old mainline churches, sermons live in the head, right at the tiptop of the skull, all exposition and proposition. It gets old quick, even if it's true. I've been powerfully moved by many a sermon over the years, challenged in my thinking, sure, usually when there's a story. Stories always make you wake up. But Hairshirt repeated his abstractions through inverted rhetorical forms that made me feel insane: "Jesus is God and man. A man and God. God, and also a man. What is he? Two things. And I will tell you what they are. God and man. Man and God. Let me say it again. . . ."

"We got it!" I wanted to stand and scream.

But then I'd look around and see everyone scrawling in their journals, even my wife. What were they writing? Grocery lists? Meal ideas? I looked at Lauren's notes:

Poppy seed chicken
Taco soup
Goldfish
Fabric softener
Baby wipes

Every Sunday, Hairshirt's preaching tilted toward the windmill of contemporary society with every breath. The enemy was Now. Now was bad. Now would strip your family naked and turn your sons into rutting lizards and your daughters into childless foot models.

Now would make your husband breed with poker machines and your wife do the Electric Slide. Now would raise your taxes and take your guns, and guns were important because your sons needed alternatives to the imaginary guns of video games, which melted their brains and could make them do terrible things, such as go looking for your guns.

The antidote to Now was Then, back when violence was not celebrated, except when it was being done to people who had behaved undemocratically. In the music of Then, the people really crooned. They didn't talk about lust and sex, though when they did, they didn't get so grossly specific about it. Everybody knows that sex talk belongs in medical textbooks, but never in church. Back Then, men wore suits and ladies wore gloves, rather than tampons. Children said *ma'am* and *sir* and not *I want to kill you with my dad's gun.*

"That sermon just hit me right in my heart!" congregants said as we filed out of the sanctuary, Sunday after Sunday.

"That sermon will give us something to talk about!" they said.

"What a pastor. So wise!"

I felt crazy. Was I crazy?

"Everybody worships this guy," I often said to Lauren on the way home. "I don't get it."

"I liked the sermon," she'd say.

But now I think I got it. He seemed so fatherly up there in the pulpit, grumpy and disappointed and warning us all about the world's horrors. The horrors had always seemed so far away, out there, but now they were in my home, and I very much needed a wise father. Mine had been dead for three years.

Hairshirt opened the door and stepped inside his study, where I sat on the couch, waiting. As soon as he saw me, you could tell he could tell something big was up. He sat down.

"My secretary said you said this was urgent." He did not look bothered. He looked concerned, which is exactly how you want someone to look in this moment. I told him everything. I just laid it on him, the whole story, or as much of it as I knew.

"Another man?" he said, duly horrified.

"A friend."

"My goodness. You just never know, do you?"

"You don't, until you do." I was crying now.

Hairshirt offered to pray for my marriage. It was a good prayer. In private, here, with me, he could speak freely about real human pain. I was shocked by the particularity of his words, where he said my children's names and prayed for me to have the boldness to throw myself between the world and my family and for my marriage to be restored. Gone were the subordinate clauses and the King James word bank. He used words like *divorce*, *madness*, *vengeance*. He wanted me to know vengeance belongs to God, not me.

As he prayed, my eyes opened. I finally understood why I loved and hated this church. My highest virtue has always been radical transparency, to a fault: The book you're holding is proof of that. This, I believe, is how you heal. Banish sorrow by shining light on it. This is why the prayers and sermons and discourse of this church always felt so bogus. They weren't lying, covering up, pretending we were all perfect. They were just intensely private people. They came from a different century. It was just not my century.

After his prayer, I entreated him for advice. "What do you think I should do?"

"We could discipline her."

"Whoa, daddy" is what I was thinking. But what I said was "I'm not sure that would help."

"We could call her in front of the elders."

It's just, I don't know: Lauren seemed in wholesale revolt

against paternalism in all its forms: our marriage, our religion, and this church, too, which she clearly now seemed all too eager to leave. I couldn't see her ever setting foot in this place again.

"I don't think she thinks what she's doing is wrong," I said.

"We could give it a try."

"And what if she doesn't, you know, stop the affair?"

"Excommunication," he said grimly.

Excommunication: one of those ancient church traditions, formally calling a member to repentance, and if the member won't recant, expelling the person from membership. But how do you boot a woman from a church she clearly had no problem deserting? Excommunication felt like the placement of medieval leeches upon mortal wounds.

Sitting in Hairshirt's office, contemplating how this church might help save my marriage through the potent magic of forgiveness, I felt only the same distance, the same vague, bewildered judgment I've always felt from so many in the pulpit. This man was no monster. He loved babies and had four sweet children and a wife as funny and pretty as mine. He's a good man, but he seemed to feel no goodness for Lauren, not then. After he prayed for my family, I took a Kleenex, thanked him for his compassionate offer to have my wife banished like a witch, and left.

Excommunication hadn't worked for Lauren's family, had it? When her father's affair had been discovered years before and he was unrepentant, he'd been excommunicated and exiled, where he's lived ever since—first in Alabama and now somewhere in the suburban wastes of Florida. He may be happy now, he may not be, we don't know. But we know the threat of exile had not sent him running back to his wife, Lauren's mother. Judgment had only hardened the man's heart. Thirty years later, he remains estranged from his children, doesn't even know his grandchildren. Excommunication might have worked a thousand years ago, when banishment from the village church might actually mean you got eaten by wolves in the enchanted forest, which has a way of making you contrite. But these days, was exile really the answer?

I walked to my bike, locked to a trolley sign, and sucked in a great breath of October air. Where was Lauren? Maybe she was with Chad, another hidden rendezvous, working out their new life together. Had any of her church friends known of the affair? Surely someone had. I knew in my heart that someone had to have known. Later, this would be confirmed by Lauren, who confessed that one of her friends had known. It would be many years before I discovered that this woman had said nothing because she was soon to have her own affair. What a church!

In that moment, I saw that our congregation was an exquisitely handsome farce, a Saturday-morning cartoon about a happy land where woodland creatures fart cotton candy and rainbows taste like gumdrops and nothing bad ever happens because nothing bad can ever be allowed to happen because the bad place is somewhere else, out there. These churches are Disney parks of make-believe. When Tinker Bell has diarrhea, you have to clean it up quickly and quietly so as not to ruin the experience for the guests. Brokenness must be banished. The fairy tale must go on.

I pedaled my bike down Bull Street and wondered if I should leave this church the way Lauren was leaving me. I knew Hairshirt was only trying to love us in his paternal and protective and medieval way. I don't think Hairshirt truly wanted to see Lauren exiled. But when all you have is the hammer of God's loving judgment, everything looks like it wants to be pounded into the floor of hell. I was grateful for the man's prayers, but knew I had to leave this church, for the same reason you sometimes have to find a new doctor. Despite its glorious architecture and many beautiful traditions and the good people who tried to be my friend, this place was not a safe place for my family. We didn't need beatific and pious masquerades. We needed the masks ripped right off.

Chapter 14

BANNERMEN OF LOVE

2017

After class that morning, during which I delivered a lecture on the wonders of literary humor and managed not to have an emo stroke in front of my students, I called some folks. We had a few good friends outside the church, and these people did not offer to stand around my home with pitchforks until Lauren recanted. They said what you want good friends to say when you give them bad news.

They said, "Oh, shit."

They said, "I don't know what to say."

Nobody knew what to say. Although one of them did say something that changed everything. Her name is Angie, a family friend and one of my wife's colleagues, a woman of Anglican faith who'd been around enough blocks to know a shit show when she saw one.

Angie said, "You're going to fight for her, right?"

"I love her." Then I said, "I hate her."

"Fight for her."

People had and would say many things to me in the coming days and weeks—*I'm so sorry; Let's go beat this dipshit's ass; I know a guy; Call my lawyer; Praying for you*—but only Angie said, "Fight for her." I held the phone to my face and looked upward into a sky so painfully blue you almost wanted to cry for the beauty, and I thought, "You know, that's not the worst idea."

Love is never a bad call. It might seem impossible. It might even seem silly when every atom in your body screams for blood. But how else, other than with love, can a broken thing be made whole again? The book of Ezekiel says God likes to work on broken things, to build up the ruined places and plant the desolate land. Our church leaders seemed to have little interest in building up the ruined earth of my marriage. It was Angie and others, newer friends such as Jimbo and Jason, who suggested mercy might be the better way. It was they who encouraged me to stop imagining how judgment would work and start trying to imagine how love might.

I soon turned to these other friends, outside the storied fortress walls of Independent, for help. I'd only known Jimbo and Jason for a couple of years. Our kids went to the same school. Jimbo is a marriage and family therapist, and unlike so many Southern men who strut about in the pallor of their virile achievements, he had no problem weeping in front of his friends. His heart was big as an ocean, and that's what I needed. Jason, a former missionary who'd coached basketball in Uganda and now taught high school English, is a writer who seemed, from the very first, incapable of bullshit. I needed these men in my life. I needed people who would show compassion and speak the opposite of fantasy and vengeance. There would be others like them in the days and years ahead, an army of goodness who would stand behind me like bannermen.

·   ·   ·

In the aftermath of her revelation, I'm pretty sure Lauren believed I would be so overwhelmed by her passion for Chad that I would banish myself from my own home, at which time Chad could move all his cargo shorts into the house, but I was going nowhere. I didn't quite know what *fight for her* meant, but I figured it did not mean leaving.

The next afternoon, before the girls got home from school, we stood there in the kitchen.

"I'm not leaving," I said. "I don't know what you thought would happen."

"You can't kick me out."

"So then we'll live here together. Fun!"

Every human on the planet, I tried to explain, would agree that she should be the one to leave. I wanted to love her, to fight for her, but like an old pickup out of alignment, I kept listing to the judgmental side of the road, where she might be punished. They say to follow your heart, but my heart wanted to hurt her, and I think that's precisely what she wanted me to do, too. If she was lucky, I might work up a decent lather and spew and rage and speak unspeakably hurtful things that could never be forgiven and get so fired up I punched one of those toxic masculinity holes in the drywall, which would allow her to call the police and demand my immediate extraction from the home. It would make things so much easier for her if I would just leave, pleasantly or violently, whatever it took.

"I want to drive you somewhere," I said.

I think she hoped I would drive us both into one of our city's many deep waterways, but instead I drove her to a hotel and walked her up to a door on the third floor. Was I about to smother her with a pillow and leave her for dead? It seemed like that's what she wanted.

I knocked and her sister, Shelby, who had driven all day from Alabama, opened the door. I left them alone to do what sisters do.

I hoped her big sister might knock some sense into her or at least get Lauren drunk enough to talk. What would they speak about? Would there be unearthing of family traumas? Recriminations? Of the three siblings, Shelby, the oldest, a mother of three and the wife of an interventional cardiologist, is the most likely to have been a prosecuting attorney disbarred for making witnesses cry with passive-aggressive statements about their bangs. She can be brutal. I once attempted to flirt with her our freshman year of college, complimenting her sandals before class. She didn't respond, just glared at me with a scowl that would've liquefied helium, for which I repaid her many years later by marrying into her family and sitting next to her every Thanksgiving.

I loved Shelby's dogged love of law and order, her refusal to coddle. She would not urge Lauren to seek her bliss with Chad, I knew that much. She would, I hoped, perform an emotional Heimlich to dislodge this man from my wife's heart in a way that only a big sister can.

It had been mere hours before when I called Shelby to tell her what had happened, and this woman, who had so often found me foolish and tiresome, said, "Do you need me to come?"

"Yes."

I wept on the phone, and Shelby, a good six hours from us, said she was on her way.

Now they sat in a hotel room together, saying God knows what.

Later that night, Shelby texted, "We're eating Mexican. We're drinking. I think things will be okay."

Okayness seemed impossible. The next morning, I got the girls ready for school as Shelby drove Lauren for an emergency therapy session with a counselor recommended by a friend. I received a text after lunch from Lauren:

"I'm coming home this afternoon."

"Okay," I said.

Would she demand a separation? Offer me joint custody if I would agree to leave? I arranged for the girls to be elsewhere after school and left work early and waited for Lauren to come home. I waited, and waited, and still she did not come. Three o'clock, four, five, six, nothing. I panicked. Where was she? Shelby did not know. Lauren would not answer.

She was gone. Eloped with Chad. Dead, maybe. Who knew. The gentle rhythms of my life had given way to chaos. How astonishing to believe, with fair certainty, that your wife, who two days ago had been one of the sanest and strongest people you knew, was quite possibly bleeding out in a Honda Pilot in a far corner of a Target parking lot, having made everyone's choices all the easier. Tragic, but clean. This, too, was not the worst idea, though I felt shitty for thinking it.

Then, just before seven, she pulled into the driveway.

She came through the back door, eyes red.

"I ended it," she said. "It's over. I told him it's over."

Her words limped out into the air like a flag of surrender. Here was my victory, though I cannot say my mood was all that victorious. Lauren looked like a woman who'd just come back from putting down the family mule.

The next morning, I found her in our bedroom. She stood in front of a large mirror. Our eyes met in her reflection, and I saw in her so much rage. I tried hard to see every good thing she'd ever done in her life, for me, for our girls. I tried not to see the betrayal. I tried to see through it to the thing underneath.

She said, "This marriage is a prison."

"I'm going to stay in the prison with you. We'll bust out together."

She stormed out past me like an employee hoping to be fired.

"Where are you going?"

"Counseling." She rolled her eyes. "So they can fix me."

"Why are you so angry?"

She slammed the door and shot off down the street to be "fixed," whatever that meant. She clearly had no interest in falling back in love with me, and nothing I said seemed to help.

Darkness was all around, but hope, too. Serious people of faith talk about spiritual warfare, this trippy idea that angels and demons do battle all around us. I encountered many angels and demons in that season. What the demons said, via blogs and TED talks and occasionally at hotel bars while I traveled for work, was "You deserve to be happy."

The demons said, "To hell with her."

The angels said, "Love her."

The demons said, "Let her die."

The angels said, "If anybody dies, let it be you."

If you want your marriage to survive, you need people in your life who believe in the idea of it. My believers were the men and women who listened and wept and moaned with me and brought beers and cigarettes to my driveway and said, "God likes to work on broken things."

For several days, a small group of friends, Angie and others, descended on the house to sit and listen to Lauren. I stayed outside. I mowed the lawn. I cleaned out her car. I wanted to kill her with kindness. Part of me hoped she might die. I even let her have the big bedroom. I slept in the guest room. I liked it this way. More kindness, more killing. That's the thing they don't tell you about love. You can love somebody, really love somebody, while being totally okay with their unfortunate mauling by an escaped Siberian tiger.

. . .

I found the yardwork meditative. I wanted to sever Chad's limbs but settled for the pecan's, lopping its lowest branches above the firepit. With zeal I sliced the top third off every shrub in the yard, imagining each was Chad's unremarkable head. While I worked outside, Lauren stayed in, where she talked it out with a few friends who'd come over to do a little ice fishing in her heart. I imagined these women sitting in the living room, staring at Lauren while she regarded the floor and said nothing. I was later told someone threw an accent pillow at her in frustration, which pleased me. I knew Lauren needed to feel loved, but I didn't want her feeling good. I wanted guilt to break her in two. I am ashamed to say it now, but that is what I wanted.

My wife had done a Very Bad Thing and I wanted her to pay for it, which perhaps made me no better than Hairshirt and his imperium of Puritan righteousness. The greatest punishment imaginable, I secretly knew, would be to force her to stay married to me, a forced excommunication from the Land of Chad. She probably even resented my working in the yard. *You had an affair, and, look, here I am mowing the lawn, the world's most helpful martyr.*

I'd been paying others to mow our yard for a few years and enjoyed this luxury. When you trim your own hedges, you learn a lot about your home, and what you learn is that your property is aggressively and continually doing the opposite of what you would prefer: gutters stop, eaves rot, crabgrass runs riot, feral cats colonize crawl spaces for their fun cat orgies. A mowed lawn on a midsummer's morning is a thing of beauty, but doing it yourself won't let you ignore all that has gone sideways in your little world. Every time I cut my grass, I dream of selling, or perhaps torching, this home. But now I had a home to save.

I could start with the landscaping.

Chapter 15

THE LITTLE LAWN BOY
LEARNS HIS ABCs

2017

E mergencies reduce complexity to flatness.

Save your family.

Bop the shark in the nose, hurry!

Get the baby out of the burning house!

Your wife had an affair and is a very bad lady!

You did not have an affair and thus you are a very good boy!

Did she want to come back to the good side, where we had nice yards, or did she want to stay over there in her weedy tent city of guilt and badness? But then, in great books, no character is truly flat. They're all craggy and curvy with paradox. They vote for the "right" candidates but thieve UPS deliveries. They feed the hungry but steal parking spaces from paralytics.

"In these situations, if the marriage is going to recover," Jimbo said, in his gentle and supportive therapist's tone, "then the betrayed spouse usually has to own their part in it."

Which sounded a lot like *You are not as good as you think and she may not be as bad*.

But then other people said, in equally soothing tones, "This is not about you."

I mean, fine, okay, while my wife had perpetrated the most grievous breach of trust imaginable between two adults, maybe it was also true that I left empty White Claw cans on the back of the toilet. Is that what Jimbo meant?

I mowed and mulled, raked and reflected, considered these two options: banish, or threaten to banish, my wife, as Hairshirt recommended, versus Angie's exhortation, not to fight her, or with her, but for her. So I prayed for wisdom. Of all the lessons taught by Hairshirt, the one I most remember was an acronym he encouraged us to use in prayer: ACTS.

Adoration: Tell God he's awesome, which casts the heart in humility.

Confession: Tell God what you've done wrong, because only the humble heart can.

Thanksgiving: Thank God for everything he's done for you.

Supplication: Ask God to do maybe a little more if possible.

As I prayed, I followed this wisdom as best I could, but skipped almost immediately to supplication, asking God to revive my dead marriage with electrified paddles of divine power. I kept having to back up and spend some time adoring him, which felt weird, but then I became untenably stuck in the morass of confession. Did I really need to dwell on my own shortcomings to save this marriage? It would take all day. I could cut a thousand lawns and not be finished.

"I admit, I am not amazing," I prayed.

And I heard the still, small voice say, "How, exactly?"

And so I figured, "Fine. Let us consider."

I'd been dumped before. In first grade, a doe-eyed beauty named Shauna cut me loose. She never said why, but she did ask to move desks. In sixth grade, I'd been dumped by a sweet little Southern Baptist with gorgeous brown hair. When I asked why, she quoted a series of Janet Jackson lyrics prepared for this purpose.

"What have you done for me lately?" she said, with a snap of her chin, and ran away.

I was blindsided, not by a self-reflection of my flaws, but by the stunning realization that Baptists were allowed to listen to Janet Jackson.

In grad school, I was dumped by a seminary student, who explained that God did not want us to be together.

"Did God tell you this?" I said.

"Yes."

"Does he have a deep voice, like Barry White? I've always wondered."

A year later, I was dumped by a young illustrator who created greeting cards for Hallmark. When I asked why, she said, "You're too self-involved."

"I try not to be, but I'm the most interesting person I know."

"That's your problem."

"You should put this on a greeting card."

I was not perfect. I understood this at a theoretical level. Yet, next to an adulterer, I did look pretty amazing. Yet, others had occasionally suggested I was not amazing. By this point in our story, you should already know that I am a naïve and needy man who helps too little around the house and may or may not have marginal body dysmorphia, due to being a big, fat walrus. What else might be wrong with me?

A

I am an ASSFACE. If compelled by a majority vote of my family to watch *Frozen*, I have been known to ruin the viewing by a DVD-style commentary on the implausibility of Elsa's ice powers, slowly turning my children into militant activists who might one day hate all men.

B

I BRAG, once boasting so proudly to Lauren about the moral superiority of my owning a flip phone that she assaulted me with a Yankee Candle.

C

I am CONTRARY. In our first year of marriage, as we shopped for a new place, I took issue with everything she loved about every apartment, not because I didn't like these apartments, but because I privately resented any opinion that was not mine, which I felt was the right opinion, being mine. On that occasion, idling in a parking lot and fighting about the number of bathrooms necessary to feel happiness, she got so frustrated with my impertinence that she hit me in the chest with such force, I briefly considered the possibility that I was not a good man.

"You hit me," I said, stunned. "Are you fucking crazy?"

"Yes."

D

I was, for most of our marriage to that point, DISTRACTED by my dream to write a book that would prove to everyone, mostly my father, but also perhaps the entire world, that I was amazing. Writing is a jealous god. To ferret out one's creative truth requires a great deal of tunneling down through the hard leathery armor of the ego and the fleshy superego and all the way to the trembling, quivering id to see what life is really about. You ferret into yourself, and sometimes when you're ferreting you catch the whiff of some rank memory that might, if you can drag it back up into the light, provide the truth you've been searching for, and as you devote yourself to the task of taking out the trash of your trauma, you find that you have not taken out the trash of your kitchen, which Lauren very much wanted me to do.

E

I lack EMPATHY. While I do give dollars to vagrants, I find more distant concerns hard to care about. Remember Standing Rock, a few years ago? Everybody was all "I stand with Standing Rock!" You either stood with Standing Rock or you lacked all human decency. I had no idea what was going on. Something with a pipeline. It just seemed another reason to hate whomever you already hated. I envy people who consume all the reporting and commit themselves to nuanced positions of righteous anger. I barely have time to mow my grass. I stand with my lawn mower, and then I push it, after which I hunger and thirst for food and water.

F

Speaking of FOOD, I have this weird thing where I insist on liking it. I was slow to realize that being married often means eating meals you would rather load onto a trebuchet and launch at an invading army. Corn, for example. On the cob, fine. In a soup, call the police.

"I love corn," Lauren often said when I observed rogue kernels in my bowl and lifted them out with the skill of a trauma surgeon removing buckshot from a victim.

G

I am terrible at receiving GIFTS. I cannot hide disappointment. One birthday, Lauren presented me with a new porch swing. I sat down, determined that the angle was all wrong, stood up, and asked her to return it. What the hell is wrong with me?

H

I'm HALF-HEARTED about so much that matters most. Ever since boyhood, when I first faced the reality that God was quite possibly imaginary, a fiction invented by a nomadic people to help solve the puzzle of being, my heart just hasn't been in it. As a result, I've never been good at the nice Waspy button-down religion or even the honeysuckle sweet kind that treats Jesus like a baby kitten who sleeps in a box at the foot of your bed and demands nothing of you.

I'm not good at the arrogant triumphalist right-wing religion where Jesus carries a flamethrower, and I'm pretty terrible at the righteous social justice Christianity that longs to effect lasting political change with protests and placards utilizing clever genital puns. I don't participate in the Women's March or the MLK Day Parade, and when abortion-themed parades head my way—pro or con, doesn't matter—I run the other way. I marched once in a Pirate Parade and instantly regretted it.

I

I INTERRUPT others because I am blessed with a gift for telling more interesting stories than the ones currently being told to me, and which I cannot wait to tell, because I want to communicate to the person that while he or she is interesting, I once met Jim from *The Office*.

J

For much of my marriage, I have often found myself JEALOUS of other husbands whose wives seemed more fun. Why would Lauren not dance with me at weddings? Was it because I danced like a cowhand attempting to break a small bronco in slow motion? Why did she eventually stop coming with me to parties at all? Was it because when she did come with me, I would promptly abandon her, bouncing around the room to flirt with other women, adopting the posture of a mayor who'd saved the town from some vicious, film-worthy disaster?

K

There are many things I don't KNOW and really should, like what medicines my children take, what diseases they may or may not have, what their teachers' names are, and how much school uniforms cost. I delegate this knowledge to their mother because I need to focus on knowing other things, like Jim from *The Office*. Did I ever tell you I interviewed Michael Scott and once saw Dwight at a bar?

L

After birthing three children, I secretly began to resent my wife's strange new body, which was, let's be honest, simply a projection of the hatred of my own body, which had grown grotesque in its own ways, as will happen to those of us who grow fat, which meant that I could be weird about LAUNDRY. Everything I loved shrank, it seemed, which only made me hate my body more. When Lauren had the gall to dry one of my shirts, the tragedy could send me spiraling into a rage beyond all good sense.

"Then do your own fucking laundry," she said.

So that's what I did. She did everybody else's and I did mine, and in this small way, our lives had already begun long ago to feel sorted and separate.

M

I drink MILK from the carton.

N

I sleep NAKED.

O

I OVERSHARE, for example, by telling the world I sleep naked.

P

I PESTER. I pat. I poke. I tickle. She hates it. I do it anyway. She hits me. She digs her fingernails deep in my forearm and demands I stop. Our girls rush to her defense. Coco screams, "Stop!" Pippi, less reserved, has lately begun kicking me in the nuts.

Q

And yet, still I won't QUIT. I push Lauren so far that she hits me with something and I sulk off to lick my wounds. Hitting was how my father often expressed love. Perhaps the hitting is what I was after. Perhaps I was the one who needed therapy.

R

I RESENTED Lauren's fondness for bourgeois symbols: cute houses, private schools, personal hygiene. My office, she explained, smelled like a barnyard. I reused towels and wore shoes without socks and draped soiled workout shorts, redolent of farm life, across furniture. Mostly I resented her gift for parenting. She was a great mother, and I was, at best, a serviceable father. When she left the girls with me to go shopping, they'd cry as if they'd been locked inside a cage with a bear. They'd run to the window as she drove away, touching the glass like wistful orphans, while I stood there trying to remember what they ate for lunch. I'd inevitably prepare the wrong lunch, which only made them cry more, and when I had to change their clothes, due to their having poured the lunch over themselves in protest, I'd invariably dress them in the wrong outfits.

Lauren would come home and make a face.

"Fuck you," I thought. "You get to dress them from now on."

S

"You're SELFISH," Lauren said to me often, as when I tried to stop at Wendy's for a spicy chicken sandwich while she sat in the passenger seat in labor with our third child.

T

Like many men, I am fond of the TOILET, especially when I might be needed elsewhere, as when packing up to go to the beach or the pool.

"You always do this!" Lauren would say through the door, stomping around the house to fill a beach bag with snacks and water bottles and towels. Did I unconsciously seek refuge in the toilet to avoid helping my wife? No, it's not possible, though it suddenly seemed very possible.

U

I am so often UNKIND to my friends, my coworkers, my children, my mother, Lauren. This unkindness almost never feels intentional. I often don't know it's happening until immediately afterward, when the unkind remark (always a remark) feels like a hateful raptor that has swooped into the picnic of this interpersonal moment and stolen the small puppy of our shared good-feeling in discussing whatever it was we are discussing: Taylor Swift, La Croix, people who say *autumn*. Perhaps we disagree about the solipsism of Swift, or the virtues of sparkling water, or precisely how long people who say *autumn* should be imprisoned. The raptor appears with frightening speed into our midst ("That's the dumbest thing I've ever heard." "Don't be an idiot." Et cetera.), and I watch the beast beat its heavy wide wings and airlift the puppy to a grisly death, shocked at what has just happened and astonished that this raptor is me, or a part of me: the worst part of me. A part of me who doesn't seem to love or even communicate with the rest of me, a predator who sits hidden high in the boughs of my heart, waiting for some sweet goodness to devour.

Once, as I sat with my closest friends at a hotel bar near our home, where a wild (and what sounded fun) wedding reception was being held across the lobby in a ballroom, several of my companions suggested we sneak into the party and do a little dancing. We were not dressed appropriately. I wore a T-shirt for Kool cigarettes. One of our party wore a clerical collar. (It was not Halloween.) Plus, I was surly, I suppose, though I wasn't quite aware of my surliness. I had just paid $42 for a single bourbon on ice, which can make any working man surly. Why couldn't we go somewhere cheap? I do not belong to a socioeconomic class that can withstand such grift. A sign read PRIVATE PARTY outside the ballroom.

"Let's do it!" one of my friends said.

A few more joined in, attempting to goad each other into a froth of courage.

"We should!" they said.

"Why?" I said, in retrospect rather aggressively. "It's a jackass thing to do. No."

My friends looked rebuked. They were only being facetious. Probably. As soon as I saw their faces, I knew: the raptor had struck again. They were not trying to crash a reception. They were only being silly. How many times had I mischievously suggested something similarly silly? How many times had they laughed at my suggestion, rather than call me a jackass? The raptor flew away, taking most of the fun with him.

The counterpart to the unkind raptor is the Greater Prairie-

Chicken of comedy, which also lives inside me, and which can also appear suddenly, like sunshine after a storm. People love the chicken. He doesn't eat puppies. The day before the hotel bar incident, I stood in line outside a comedy club, behind a hot weird Goth girl, who turned to me and asked, without introduction or prompt:

"What's your favorite fantasy fiction?"

"*The Firm* by John Grisham," I said.

Everybody laughed, because the chicken makes people laugh. I never know when he's going to show up. Sometimes I think people keep me around just hoping to meet the chicken. Sometimes I think the raptor and the chicken are the same creature—my bifurcated psyche, my angel and my demon, my Soul and my Id—which I, being an artist, permit to run wild, for better, and for worse. Lauren married me for the chicken, I fear, and did not meet the raptor until later.

V

I can be VINDICTIVE. Sometimes I summon the raptor, knowing full well what he will do upon arrival. We're told twice in the Bible, once in the Old Testament and again in the New, that vengeance belongs to God, though I have often behaved as the Lord's vice president for minor reprisal operations. Cut me off on the interstate, I will teach you a lesson and get both of us killed. I have been known to throw rocks at cars that drive past my home at unsafe speeds because I hope to one day be shot by a motorist.

I had often practiced this vile pettiness with my wife. A few days before our wedding, while out for a casual dinner with friends, she asked for a bite of sausage from my red beans and rice. I politely declined, as she had her own food and I was a growing boy with a great fondness for pork and there was little sausage to be had. When

I wasn't looking, she shoved the last delicious fatty coin into her mouth. She laughed, as did my friends, so I poured the entirety of Lauren's uneaten salad in her lap. Who's laughing now? Nobody, it turned out.

W

You already know I WORK too much, or at least I did during the first decade of my marriage, when Lauren was home with three tiny machines programmed to cry, shit, and vomit in alternating sequences while violently sucking the nutrients out of her body. What you don't know is that I was often so frightened by these children, as any reasonable human would be by a colony of vomiting Dracula babies, that I often lied about having to work. I didn't have to work late. Nobody made me. I could've come home. I felt such guilt about these little lies that I convinced myself they were true, like the kid in first grade who insisted his family once drove to Hawaii. When we explained one could not drive to Hawaii, he doubled down on the lie so intensely, describing an elaborate oceanic interstate, that you could tell he had begun to believe it. He seemed insane. I, too, was insane during those early years of parenting, when I failed to parent much at all. What had she said the night she confessed? Chad was "helpful."

Looking back, I knew that our sweet girls were not, and never had been, vomiting Dracula babies. They were perfectly normal and sweet children who vomited and shat with great tenderness. I deeply regret, and will always regret, how fearful I allowed fatherhood to make me.

X

I do not play the XYLOPHONE. Rather, I play the drums, an instrument that has caused more divorces than any other musical instrument in world history, after the banjo.

Y

I have a Y CHROMOSOME, which means I am a man. I felt and feel certain that my masculinity was and is nontoxic, but nearing the end of this list, I am no longer sure.

Z

My only real talent is comedy, not always beloved, and not even always that funny, but I am handy with a ZINGER if I need to hurt someone and want to avoid breaking any laws. Most of my humor is born in heartache of one brand or another, a mechanism for defense against the tragedy of being born into a world with a body I do not love, a family I do not understand, and a heart too proud to love others like it loves itself. How quickly a gift for provoking laughter, the transmutation of pain into truth, elides into bullying. Life had turned me into a lethal comedy hedgehog, with quills I could aim with deadly precision, as when Lauren would clutch her temples, complaining of another migraine.

"I think I'm dying," she'd say.

"Finally," I'd say, fingers crossed.

Having concluded this brief and incomplete catalogue of my faults, naturally I would like to defend myself. I am an assface because I'm direct! I'm contrary because I see from many interesting perspectives! My oddities make me more original! My refusal to quit tickling Lauren, even while being kicked in the crotch by my own offspring, is a sign of fortitude! My workaholism is dedication! My toxic masculinity is just masculinity, which the world is too delicate to appreciate! My cruel comedy is really just delicacy! Tenderness of spirit! I was abused as a child! At least I'm funny!

My flaws could not be blamed for the affair, but they hadn't helped. Take infidelity off the table and I was, from just about every angle, the least likable person in my marriage.

A few days later, after I'd mowed the lawn to within an inch of its life and edged every edge and cleaned out the garage and emptied out my closets and bought fragrant and manly candles to reduce the barnyard quotient of my office, all the while considering how I might have given Lauren a thousand million reasons to hate me over the years, I sent her a text:

"I don't know much. But I know this: I'm an assface."

And the wildest thing happened. She said, "I am, too."

Nobody told me fighting for my marriage would be less a fight than a kneeling in humiliation at the feet of my enemy. In those delicate days in the autumn of 2017, our marriage motionless in the critical care unit of the burn center, this admission of such an obvious truth, that we were both deeply flawed assfaces, was the first thing we'd agreed on in a long, long time.

Chapter 16

THE TREATY OF VERSAILLES

2017–18

The first few battles were won. The war dragged on. Admitting my role in all this helped. In snatches of conversation, tenuous steps toward healing, I confessed many of my aforementioned imperfections to my wife, a few at a time, spreading them out like fertilizer in hopes of a healing harvest.

I found myself less bitter toward Lauren, and she softened, too, in small ways. She no longer stormed off to therapy. I prayed every morning, tried to be less contrary, more empathic, drank milk from glasses. Baby steps. We still didn't share a bed. The ghost of Chad haunted our home. Lauren handed me a set of keys to Chad and Lane's house, given to her by Lane months before, for emergencies. The breaches of trust were vast and deep.

"I'll take care of it," I said.

I put the keys in an envelope and drove to Chad's office. I saw his truck in the lot, entered the lobby, approached the receptionist. I gave his name and waited. The receptionist rang him. I waited, my skin tingling now. I channeled my inner redneck, summoned the bellicose spirit of my ancestors, who would've whipped Chad with his own belt like a child and then thrown him out a window. I could feel the spirit of a thousand righteous hillbillies swarming inside me. The lobby featured many potential murder weapons: lamps, chairs, vases of cut glass.

Chad never showed. I left the keys with the receptionist and sauntered out like a disappointed Wyatt Earp. Probably for the best. Hospitalizing Chad might have sent Lauren running to the ER while I stewed in county lockup. No need for all that. I drove home.

Days, weeks, her sleeping in one room, me in another. She went to counseling, I went to counseling. She insisted Chad was out of the picture. Lane texted me often with damning facts about my wife, further recriminations. I expressed my sorrow to Lane and explained we were moving on. The angry texts persisted. She wanted to talk with me, wanted to grieve together. I had to block her number, though I wanted to talk to her, desperately, hungry for the thrilling details of how the lovebirds had lied to both of us.

Lauren wept every day. She maintained that Chad no longer texted. She spoke of him with anger now, a girl jilted by a prom date. I tried to understand. Here was a man who promised to rescue her into a new life, and here she was, stuck with the old. She said he was chickenshit. Said he hadn't fought for her. She cried so much while saying all this, and I knew she wasn't crying for me. It's a sad thing to see your wife weep because she has to stay married.

One month, three, six. How do you know when you're okay? Would there be a surging, tearful moment of reconciliation as we leaped into each other's arms in an airport terminal? Would it be quieter, a soft and loving gesture, a hand, held, squeezed, which signaled rebirth and resolution? Or would it be a passionate rejuvenation, naked, where we rolled around on a bed in the dark and, you know? You know?

Best friends remain best friends because you can take breaks, but a marriage is the sleepover that never ends. Long ago, my wife had been my best friend, but somewhere, we'd gone from making out on city streets to playing the dozens. I got so distracted by our comedy that I failed to notice she had planned to run off with a man whose only real virtue was not having been married to my wife long enough to make her hate him.

A lifetime of the mildest insults had deposited a grand pile of hurt on both our hearts. You can email a list of your many flaws to your wife, which makes her hate you a little less, but it won't necessarily make her love you again. We'd forgotten how to hear each other. It had been easy for her to talk to Chad. They hadn't spent a decade and a half making meal plans and fighting on the way to parties about the height of Ryan Seacrest. My wife had wanted a husband but needed a friend, and Chad let me do the heavy lifting of being the husband while he played the friend. I had failed in so many ways.

Feelings had made us funny and feelings had been hurt and feelings had been lost and new feelings had been sought. But Lauren and I had something more final than feelings. We had three children, and we had facts, too. New facts. We knew things about each other that we had not known before. I knew that she had wanted to leave, and she knew that I would fight for her like no man ever had—her father, or even Chad, who'd pledged his undying love and walked away. Lauren had been left by every man who'd ever loved her, but I would not leave. I owed this much to my daughters. I knew that the only way this could work was for me to own my part in whatever wicked thing had happened and then to do the harder thing: to use this information to become a less shitty person.

"I want to be friends again," I said to her one night.

"That would be nice."

We retired worn routines and wrote new material for our act.

"You have to ask about my writing," I said. "You have to ask and you have to care."

"But I don't."

"You have to act like you do."

"You have to take out the garbage without being asked."

"Fine."

I checked my belligerence and worked hard to be less distracted at home. If we ever again went to a party together, I determined not to wander off. I did keep doing my own laundry. This, I think, she liked.

I soon took over the bill paying, which had been her thing. She tried talking about her feelings, which had been mine. She texted me for no reason in the middle of the day to tell me about her recently discovered fingernail cancer, and I did not make jokes. When one of her friends had a girls' night and didn't invite her, I offered to burn the woman's house down. I was in her corner from now on.

Healing would take time, we knew that. I knew the renewal of conjugal visits might be months, maybe even a year, away. I made a sexy playlist with songs I felt might imperceptibly communicate the thirst of my loins, tracks by D'Angelo, Sade, Nina Simone.

"What is this music?" Lauren said in the car when I first played the playlist on one of our first real date nights in this delicate season of our marriage.

"It's just a playlist."

Nina sang about wanting a man to work on her lawn, which sounded like a fine idea.

Within months of the affair ending, we even discussed the very real possibility of having another baby, or maybe adopting. Newness was all around. We even started sitting next to each other on the couch again, which triggered a federal investigation by the children.

"Why are you sitting next to Mommy?" they asked. "What's going on here?"

A veil had been rent. We cooked together, danced in the kitchen. I learned to see the world through her eyes and not my own. I cleaned out her car with no provocation and put away everyone's laundry. I brought her coffee in the morning and Cokes in the afternoon, and she brought us tequila shots at night and we stood outside and looked at the moon. It seemed like the war might be over.

So much comedy is a kind of redeemed mourning, turning the dross of pain into gold, just as visiting Disney World in matching HIS BEAUTY and HER BEAST tank tops is a kind of psychosis. I stopped mocking those lucky people who pretend to be married to their best friends, even though I worried they were pretending marriage isn't an impossible riddle only solved by breaking both of you in half. I thank those weirdos for reminding me that a good marriage often looks like a joke to those outside it.

I vowed to fight for my wife and would have to again in ways I could not even begin to fathom. Some new Chad could come roaring into our lives with a leaf blower at any moment. But this: this was not about Chad, I finally saw. He may have conspired with my wife to put my marriage out of its misery, but I, as much as Lauren, had starved and weakened and hobbled this marriage to the point where its death felt—for my wife, at least—the only option. Chad had been no knight-errant. He was, as I had been so long before, just another rebound, and now he'd vanished into the reeds as swiftly as a frightened snake. Our greatest enemy was us: we were the people who had killed our marriage, and we, with the help of beings both divine and mortal, would have to be the people to make it live again.

Our few friends had done their best to help, but there's nothing like infidelity to show you just how small your community really is. Somehow, we'd made it through this season. We got a little better every day. After more than a year of work and learning and unlearning, after the sexy playlists and tequila shots and kitchen dancing, there I stood with my wife next to the Savannah River one night, and right there in public, like a total weirdo, I pulled her close and kissed her the way I'd forgotten how, and she kissed me back, and I won't lie: I felt baptized by love.

"I feel a strong desire to mow your lawn right now," I said.

"Gross," she said, and we kissed again and went home and, you know.

Chapter 17

THE CHURCH OF
BROKEN WINDOWS

2018

Life had been hell for our family, then so much better it seemed impossibly miraculous. We never spoke a word of this hell to our girls or my mother. The circle of trust comprised a few close friends and Shelby. Motivated as much by fear as prudence, we hoped to contain the fallout while confronting our demons, a decision that would, in time, prove as naïve as Lauren's dreams of a life with Chad.

For months, every night, my head on the pillow, Lauren on the other side of our bed, I closed my eyes and relived her confession. I remembered each line of dialogue, the coolness of her tone, the deadness in her eyes. The show played every night before I could sleep. The moment could, I believed, be drained of its power by this ritual.

Where was Chad? I wondered. How was his marriage to poor Lane working out? Lane, a nurse with all the latent rage of anyone condemned to working at a hospital, seemed capable of blood vengeance. I liked to imagine reading in the *Savannah Morning*

News of a sweet pediatric nurse who ran over her husband in the driveway, repeatedly, which helped me sleep. I knew we might bump into them anywhere—a basketball game, a soccer field—and ran through scenarios in my head. The girls often asked why we didn't see Chad or his wife or son anymore.

"Sometimes you just stop being friends," I'd say.

Did Lauren think of him? I had to assume yes. Jesus says you don't forgive once. You forgive so many times it almost seems silly. "Lord, how oft shall my brother sin against me, and I forgive him? Seven times?" asks Peter in the book of Matthew.

Jesus says, "No, not seven times. Seventy times seven times."

I've always found this passage a little ridiculous, just more evidence that Jesus, had he been born in my century, would've told jokes for a living. I had to forgive every imagined text message, every furtive phone call when I was at work, every time she opened the door to let him into our home. I had to let it all go and forgive all over again, every time I remembered.

Things got better. Date nights. Romantic dinners. Contemplative walks. Vacations. She started going back out with me on tour, where we enjoyed stolen weekends away to roll around in hotel rooms and waited six hours for a room service burger. Once we had makeup sex for two months straight, at all times of the day and night and on most of the furniture and several of the rugs. It felt like we were preparing for a paired event at the U.S. Olympic Trials. In the year following the affair, the year she turned forty, we made out at least seventy times seven times.

Our sexual ardor was, for me at least, an expression of the wonder we'd found in forgiveness, the giddiness at the miracle of how our marriage and our family had been saved, but our healing was incomplete.

. . . .

What we needed was full-hearted joy. Christians talk a lot of joy, but I'd so rarely seen it manifest in Christian communities—the joy of play, a carnival embrace of healthy chaos. From the pulpit, Hairshirt had often spoken in despising tones of the St. Patrick's Day Parade, our city's biggest party, one of the largest in North America. For several years now, our family had been celebrating this parade with a motley crew of friends from around the city, Jimbo, Jason, Chip, Soren, others. We camped out along the parade route two or three days before every parade, to guarantee our families a front-row seat at the carnival mayhem.

You learn a lot about men you've heard vomit in a portable toilet at two in the morning, and what you learn is that you can, from then to the end of your days, tell those men anything. These guys and their families listened to our pain and invited us out on couples' dates, beach dates, boat dates. Rather than sit in pews and listen about how disappointing all of us were to God, I sat on porches with these men, laughing, occasionally crying. Most Savannah men I knew only cried when talking about their boats, or Georgia football coach Vince Dooley. We were all romantics deep down, dreamers. The abiding mood of our gatherings was a pining hope, like enthusiastic fans at a game you know you're probably going to lose. We laughed about our disappointments and dreamed of becoming better men, better husbands, better fathers.

Our St. Patrick's Day parties had grown into wild and raucous and holy moments of celebration. One March morning the year after my marriage imploded, as we sat out on Lafayette Square amid one hundred thousand neighbors, Soren—a local college minister—perhaps feeling the effects of his morning whiskey, got poetic on us. This experience was too beautiful to save for just one day a year, he said: the joy, the feasting, the dancing, the turning of strangers into friends.

"What we need is a church like this," he said.

He envisioned a place that would be animated by joy and hospitality, a church where you could drink a beer or try to leave your husband and not be shunned.

Soon enough, Soren made good on his threat. Jimbo and his family joined in the madness and so did a few other families, and they had the audacity to ask me if I would bang on a drum for the Lord. I never saw myself as a church drummer, but God has a way of not caring what you see yourself as.

We first met in Soren's tiny living room and then an empty art gallery, and eventually we moved on to a modest little sanctuary just like the churches of my youth, except with guitar amps and a small four-piece kit I played so loud that drunks wandered in for the free show. I showed up to services an hour early every Sunday for rehearsal, and most days the girls would come with me to fold bulletins and draw. It was three blocks from our house, close enough to walk. The church was called Christ the King.

"The name is a little much," Lauren suggested at first, but we went anyway and loved it. This was no historic downtown church and neither was it a gleaming new megachurch with Broadway lighting systems and handsome restrooms smelling of fresh-baked bread and evergreen forests. The building had one toilet and shattered windows. We shared the property with a homeless shelter.

Here was a church that didn't hide brokenness, because brokenness was everywhere, including many of the lights. You might see people in shorts and neckties and jeans and ponchos, sometimes all on the same person. For a while, I wore swim trunks just to see if anyone cared. One Sunday after a rainstorm, I took off my waterlogged Vans and played the drums barefoot and nobody said a word.

Soren was a fine preacher who never seemed preachy. He didn't

give pep talks or opine about the depravity of coastal elites: a welcome relief. What he did was come off like one of those high school
English teachers who know you didn't read the assignment and
aren't going to get their feelings hurt about it. His preoccupation—
every preacher and professor has one—was how to stop being an
asshole and how to throw a party and invite neighbors. He cited
films often during his sermons and ruined every decent M. Night
Shyamalan film that first year, but I grew to love the spoilers, for he
had a way of exposing his heart in all its confusion and anguish and
wisdom and delight, and something about that vulnerability compelled me to stop making to-do lists or outlining new TV pitches
during sermons.

Lauren couldn't decide what she thought of it all. I know it
must have been strange for her to see me up there pounding on the
skins like a fruitcake, barefoot in a swimsuit. But I think she could
tell that for the first time in almost forever, I felt at home in church.

Soren wore a clerical collar and wrinkled pants and cheap sneakers, just what we needed after a decade at the Church of the Sock
Hop. Services presented a broad mix of high-church formality and
frontier wildness, recitations and confessions and creeds coupled
with cacophonous foot-stomping hymns that made worship feel
like a book-of-Revelation hootenanny, when all those Guillermo
del Toro–looking creatures clap and shout around the enthroned
Jesus. We had those people who sing with their eyes closed and
arms spread wide, like children catching snowflakes, right next to
conservative Presbyterians and lapsed Baptists who let their hands
fall to their sides, where hands belong.

The whole thing felt funny and floppy and fullhearted, always
at the edge of chaos. You never knew who might show up: old Black
men with walkers and U.S. Army pilots and tattooed vegans and addicts looking for a few dollars and women in heels and grizzled old

artists, drunken and ready to fight with God, Jimbo emoting into the microphone like a man at a tent revival and a Calvinist pastor in a Catholic collar guiding us into the abysses of his own existential anguish while spoiling every good HBO series.

Soren's preaching and the music and the mise-en-scène of it all—the old pews, the odd cockroach corpse, the happy children, the random musical instruments scattered about, the open bottle of cheap red and the loaves of challah bread on the communion table every Sunday—felt somewhere between *Ted Lasso* and *The Muppet Show*. It was the kind of church where you could show your ugly heart to everybody and they just loved you harder and handed you a beer.

They say God is love. I'd heard this remarkable axiom all my life, and I think I finally understood. Heaven and hell and smitings and virgin births and fishes and loaves, it was all a story to celebrate and make sense of the strangest fact of all: love is what saves you. Love, love enough to confess your failures, love to forgive the failures of others, is always what saves your life, your soul, your family, your marriage. Love lived in the people of our new church, others, like us, in exile, refugees from abuse and scandal and estrangement, people who were far from home or from right up the street. The only thing that needed to be excommunicated from my home was the idol of perfect obedience: hers or mine. Our story was no fairy tale. A church with broken windows is just what we needed: the community that would make us whole again and pull us through what had happened, and what was yet to come.

Chapter 18

RAPTURE

2019

I felt freed from the illusions of the past, our family heading for new territory. When Lauren split on weekends to run errands, I still found myself wanting to know where, exactly, my wife was going, but knew too much asking could push her away. Tailing Lauren with an ankle monitor seemed the opposite of love. We rebuilt trust one breath, one meal, one joke, at a time.

Sundays were happy days now. I'd taken over the cooking almost entirely and bought power tools, repaired toilet seats and doorknobs poorly. I hung new art, illustrations, paintings, photographs, portraits of Grace Kelly, Eudora Welty, Teen Wolf. I festooned six pairs of antlers with glitter and colored yarn and hot glue and mounted them across the walls. I commissioned five cartoonishly perfect portraits of the girls and Lauren and me, painted by Katherine, a friend.

My books were selling okay, and a real Hollywood producer offered to work with me on a screenplay, and the girls were all healthy, and Lauren seemed happy in her work at the school. Coco was a teenager now, and Pippi and Ginsburg edged near the cusp of adolescence with wondrous velocity. Things were so much better that, before long, Lauren got pregnant.

When we saw the test results, we both laughed, like Sarah in the book of Genesis when she got put in the family way at the age of ninety. Lauren was forty-one and I was forty-three, and the thought of having a tiny baby in the house made us dizzy with laughter. We'd have one in diapers and three in tampons. I would be sixty years old at this baby's high school graduation, delivering a wedding toast from an electric wheelchair. The baby brought instant joy into our hearts.

On my bike, pedaling to the office every morning after we got the news, the pregnancy test still on the bathroom counter, I couldn't help but smile at this future God had made possible. The baby was a gift, a consummation of the healing of my marriage, a sign, a wonder. I didn't think of the money or the time that this new human would cost, only the gift of love let loose in my heart. I'd been too young and foolish to feel this way when the other three girls had come along, too fretful about the future to let the tides of love carry me away.

We told the girls.

"I'm having a baby!" Lauren said, eyes wet, smiling.

Coco, the oldest, knew what we had been up to.

Ginsburg, the youngest, had a few questions about the mechanics of it.

Pippi, the middle, lover of babies and cooking, fell to her knees, blubbering in adulation. For weeks, the house shimmered with hope: Would it be a boy? Of course not, a girl, obviously, but, no, how perfect if a boy. I'd always felt like the ideal father of daughters, with my love of dance parties and baking, but welcomed the thought of teaching my son to throw a spiral and then to write a sonnet about how it made him feel. I was so happy. Lauren beamed. This is what our marriage needed. She was more radiant than ever. We sent the girls off to summer camp.

It was merciful that the girls were gone the week we lost the baby. The sight of their mother, pale from blood loss, too weak even to walk, limp as a dishrag, being carried by me out the door to the car to the ER in the middle of the night, would've been too much. She lost so much blood. Our bathroom was a crime scene, fauvist strokes of red across the floor.

The hospital room felt so sad and funereal, hushed whispers and prayer and talk of transfusions and a birth that was no birth. I sat there, stunned, watching my wife fall through stages of grief. The nurses did God's work that day. They let Lauren grieve and formed a wall of protection around her, a wall of words and feelings around her bed. Two days later, resting at home, the girls still gone, Lauren said, "Go get my babies."

I drove to the mountains of North Carolina through the night and got the girls from camp and we were home the next day. We lined them up on the couch.

"We lost the baby," Lauren said.

"What do you mean?"

"The baby died," I said.

Coco got pensive. Ginsburg got worried about Lauren and said, "But you're not hurt?"

Pippi fell to the floor, again, weeping a river of the saddest tears. The new baby, this child of wonder and possibility and rebirth, was gone. We held one another, all five of us, for days. We told the church and the church brought food and flowers and everyone came by the house. I know miscarriages happen all the time but this felt like the death of someone I'd known.

. . .

A week after the miscarriage, in a meeting, when a colleague asked how excited I was about the new baby, my grief knocked me to the conference room floor. I stumbled back to my office and sat on the carpet and wept some more. I finally got what love was, that a baby creates love because babies dismantle vanity and pride, if you love them the way you're supposed to, and God had finally broken me enough to see the love. I'd seen the love in Lauren and in our church and in my children and in myself—and then the baby, the bringer and promise of that love, died.

My boss said, "Go home. Go be with your family."

I could hardly pedal my bike the three miles back to the house. Sadness poured from every window and every faucet, the rooms flooded with pain. I took time off work, took the girls to the pool, took apple juice and plates of food to Lauren in bed. For many nights, Lauren and I fell asleep holding hands. We were closer than ever.

I felt love in the house, but also a wobbly kind of weirdness, the scab of healing pulled back, a wound reopened. Things felt un-settled all over again, uncanny, and then God showed us the true meaning of strange, because a few months later, in March 2020, everything got a lot stranger for everyone. The darkest part of the woods now lay ahead.

Chapter 19

THIS LITTLE
BLIGHT OF MINE

2020

It was a season of world history painted in kaleidoscopically weird scenes when any number of psychic fantasias, from the mildly ridiculous to the geopolitically savage, raged inside every human on the planet. I had pals who'd gone full Bob Wiley and followed the science by wearing latex gloves in the shower, and a whole other set who licked all the doorknobs to demonstrate the power of their immune systems. Conservative friends became riotous lawbreakers, and progressive neighbors locked themselves away in vaults of fundamentalist terror. Everybody seemed to have lost their minds. Lauren and I and our friends at Christ the King carried on quieter but relatively normal lives, sans the moral panic that devoured many during those early days of plague. It had been almost three years since the affair. We'd been through hell. Pandemic? Economic collapse? Civil war? We feared nothing.

Our driveway became a watering hole where my friends gathered every Thursday night to sit on lawn chairs and visit, our conversation roving over the Martian terrain of the year, from alien hoaxes and psilocybin to Jesus and Jordan Peterson. Jimbo and Chip and Martin brought their guitars and Soren his bass. We jammed away in my garage, working through every funk and Americana and pop song we knew, pausing just long enough between numbers to hear one of the neighbors scream "Shut up!" from a backyard. We called ourselves the Love Handles and decided what this pandemic needed was a new cover band.

I was now a dean at the university and spent those gorgeous pandemic days pacing the driveway barefoot on the phone with students and staff to make sure everyone had access to ramen and wellness resources and good Wi-Fi. I took breaks from calls to puzzle through fractions with whichever daughter was weepiest about fractions, all three on Zoom in various rooms of the house while my wife zoomed from the breakfast table. Lauren's gift for operational management was on full display. To keep the children from gorging on Chex Mix and Cheetos for eighteen hours a day, she created a monetary point system—peaches cost two points, Cheetos a dozen. The sink was never not full of dishes, so often did we cook and eat and then cook again.

"I can't do it," Lauren said.

"We have to eat again," I said. "We will likely have to eat every day."

"It's too much eating."

The togetherness was a lot. I felt Lauren might be cracking. She'd been promoted to director of admissions, a tough racket for anyone during a pandemic. Her enrollment targets seemed untethered to reality. But we were in it together, all of us, along with my mother, who visited us weekly, banished to a rocking chair in the corner with a plate in her lap.

"If we die, you die," I said.

"Dying would give us all something to do," Mom said.

April and May proved oddly magical. The virus, for all its

chaos, established in my house a peace that passeth understanding, every event canceled, the booming parade of busyness hushed and halted, and for that I was deeply grateful. The affair seemed a hundred years in the past. We threw the football in the front yard. We reinstituted movie night and board game night and cooked cheap delicious meals together every night of the week and ate dinner on the porch like a family from a salad-dressing commercial.

I said we didn't lose our minds like so many in those days, but that's a lie. Whatever madness flooded the zeitgeist leaked into our home, turning all of us slowly senseless. I lost touch with the governor in my brain. My sense of passing time blurred. Minutes became hours, but so did days. With all my speaking engagements canceled, my best friend, Mark, and I decided to write the screenplay I'd been discussing with the producer, though writing proved as hard as anything else during that odd season. I bought an egg timer and made myself compose without stopping for thirty minutes, and when the jangling bell told me to stop, I stopped and did something else: washed a dish, screamed into a pillow, stared at the sun. My mind, like the world's, devolved into a watery mass. I became highly suggestible.

"Can we ride our bikes to the candy store?" the girls asked.

"Fine."

"Can we make a cake instead of doing our math?"

"Okay."

"Can we get a dog?"

"Sure."

I knew I was unstable when I agreed to the dog. The girls had been asking for years and I always said no, because I grew up among guns and blood and meat and death and would've been pleased never to see another animal again.

"Please, Daddy," the girls said.

"A little puppy, sweet little puppy," Lauren said.

They sent me screenshots of puppies day and night, trolling my phone with this hateful dog spam. The thought of voluntarily bringing anything larger than a cat into my home was blasphemy, but suddenly a dog seemed exactly what we needed.

Lauren and I drove alone to pick him up in a Lowe's parking lot on the morning of Coco's fourteenth birthday. At home, we sat the girls down in the living room and made everybody close their eyes and set the wriggling chocolate beast down on Coco's lap and you've never seen so much crying. Pippi knelt as before the Baby Jesus. Ginsburg sobbed.

"Gary," Coco said, bawling. "We will call him Gary."

That first night and for many nights after, Gary slept in an enormous crate in the living room on a bed of old blankets. When he whined in the night, like all babies do, Lauren got up to sleep with him on the couch, and I was reminded every morning how good a mother she was and what a good sleeper I have always been.

"Poor buddy was lonely," she said, sleepy.

His little tail wagged.

"I'll start getting up with him, too," I said.

I woke in the mornings and carried him down the steps into the yard to empty his tiny colon, which would soon grow big, and my heart grew bigger, too, the way hearts always do in dog movies. I sat with him on the couch at one and three and five in the morning and fell back asleep and woke again and wondered if my wife would ever have wanted to divorce me if I had done this with my own children, when they were tiny. I had plenty of regrets. Using a house payment to acquire Gary the chocolate Lab was not one. He became the son we almost had.

·　·　·

By June, the virus was no longer a terrifying mystery from the deep, less the phantasmagoric beast who might devour everybody you ever loved than an invisible houseguest who wouldn't leave. All the markers of season and ritual had been deleted from the document of experience. The school year ended with the ceremonial closing of a laptop. No convocations, no parties, no recitals: anti-pomp, non-circumstance. These customs shape time and set your feet in history, but all that was gone and the effect was dizzying and dark. The workday never started nor ended. Wednesdays felt like Fridays and Fridays felt like Mondays. All those distinctions of Genesis 1—God defining heaven and earth, day and night, land and sea, sun and moon—got scrambled. Consciousness was formless and void. The only marker of a week's passing was church.

A few months into the pandemic, we were all back in pews and masks. I was always there an hour early for music rehearsal.

"You coming?" I'd ask Lauren, still in bed.

"I guess," she'd say, putting her phone down.

She and the girls would eventually arrive, and Lauren sat there in the pew while I looked out from behind the drums and wondered what was up, all the faces and mouths cloaked in N95s and secrecy. She seemed discomfited, not all there. It was all in the eyes. Lauren worked from home half the time, but was out and about, too, hustling, touring families, interviewing parents, enrolling a queue of public-school refugees whose parents had finally admitted to themselves that a government does little well but make war and debt. She was busy, and I had my summer assignments at the college. All was well, except for a creaking in the floorboards at night, hairline fractures in the air.

"It's been a weird year," I started saying when people asked how I was, a polite swatting at the horsefly of existential dread.

· · · · ·

"Everything is a clue," Soren said once, in a sermon. He was trying to get us to open our eyes to the unfurling mystery of being, I guess. Everything became a clue that year, the year that had been either stolen away from us or given as a gift, a time out of time. Reality had begun to seem like a simulation, poorly rendered. Everywhere I looked, I saw incompleteness.

What was odd, exactly? Hard to say. The world. The neighbors. Everybody getting weird at the grocery store. The grass started dying, due to Gary's prodigious bladder. The trees started dying, too. That spring I planted three gloriously mature Leyland cypresses in the backyard, a green screen to keep the neighbors from being forced to see me standing naked in my office while reading drafts. I watered the trees daily, but as soon as I got them in the ground, this expensive foliage turned sad and brown. Out front, the limes on the lime tree, always so fragrant and perfect, came out withered. The lemon tree refused even that much.

"Where are the lemons?" Ginsburg, nine, asked, tugging at a branch.

"In lockdown," I said.

No fruit in the streets, no fruit in the sheets. The Tokyo Summer Games had been postponed and so had our own sexual Olympics. I've never been a Sex on Demand husband, as far as I can tell. Weekly lovemaking was plenty. It only seemed fair after seventeen years and five pregnancies. A man whose wife was great with child for the better part of a decade can transform himself into a conjugal dromedary, when necessary. Monks and nuns do it all the time. Weekly relations were fine, especially with Lauren's zonked-out body chemistry, the migraines and MRIs and mammograms and menstruation deluge that followed a lunar cycle from some undiscovered planet with two or more moons. Her periods lasted for years, it seemed. Who was I to question it? A woman's insides are a chaos of Gaia energy that frightens mortals. My wife was a Leyland cypress, watered but withered. This, too, was a clue. I pinned these thoughts to the bulletin board of my heart like a police detective in a TV show but couldn't find the pattern.

Just before midsummer, we took a weeklong vacation up to the mountains. How could things be bad if we could afford a holiday during a world-historical crisis? We'd saved so much money during quarantine—no restaurants, no bars, no new soccer cleats. A road trip might loosen the desiccated earth and get water where it needed to be. But at night in the little cabin with the decent view, all I saw of my wife was her back, as she turned toward the wall. A week in the mountains and we hardly touched.

I observed. We talked. I listened. I asked questions. About work. Colleagues. Migraines. Maybe it was pills. Maybe my wife did pills. Hell, the woman could be shooting up under an overpass, but you can't go asking your wife if she's shooting up under an overpass without ruining movie night.

"Let's go sit in the driveway" is not a thing I said. I should have.

"Why?" is what she would have said.

"To talk."

"About what?"

"Alien hoaxes. Gary. Why we never have sex anymore."

Who knows what she saw or felt? I didn't know how to ask without making every conversation feel like an interrogation. I thought a lot about the miscarriage. If the baby was a sign of a new covenant of love, then perhaps Lauren saw the miscarriage as a sign of its breaking.

"Let's go for a walk," I sometimes asked.

"It's too hot," she always said.

I took Gary instead. I devoted myself to the dog and watering our tomato and pepper and cucumber plants and riding bikes with the girls and trying to carry on the work of co-running a household. Something about the inside of the house had turned stale. Beautification had ceased. The art I'd hung on the walls suddenly seemed old. Gary discovered a talent for eating everything we loved: furniture, jewelry, the cat. More clues.

Clues to what, exactly? The riddle concerned all of us, would touch everyone in the house, somehow, would transform the simulation into a whole new reality. And I want to make this clear: I'm not saying she was keeping a secret. It didn't seem like a secret. It seemed like a hidden thing, a plague of unknown origin, like in *Oedipus Rex* when Thebes is suffering and King Oedipus is doing his best to find out why the city is suffering. The priest explains:

> A blight is on our harvest in the ear,
> A blight upon the grazing flocks and herds,
> A blight on wives in travail; and withal
> Armed with his blazing torch the God of Plague
> Hath swooped upon our city emptying
> The house of Cadmus, and the murky realm
> Of Pluto is full fed with groans and tears.

What Oedipus discovers, by the end of the play, is that the thing that's wrong with the city, which has turned it full red with groans and tears, is him. Maybe I was the cause of the plague on my house. It was possible. Anything was possible. Had I missed something three years before, when she'd confessed? Had I papered over the wounds of the infidelity too quickly? I suddenly felt as if I'd overlooked important clues to the truth of this woman and our marriage. "For nothing is secret that shall not be made manifest,"

Jesus says in the book of Luke. "Neither is anything hid that shall not be known."

I tried asking her questions. Was she okay? How was she feeling? How was her day? But I got nothing. I began devouring books and plays about infidelity: Tolstoy's *Anna Karenina*, Jamie Quatro's *Fire Sermon*, Elena Ferrante's *The Days of Abandonment*, Jenny Offill's *Dept. of Speculation*, Nick Tosches's *Hellfire: The Jerry Lee Lewis Story*, Harold Pinter's *Betrayal*. I watched all seven seasons of *Mad Men* so many times I dreamed in spec scripts. Was Lauren terminally unhappy, like Anna? Was I still blind, like Ferrante's mad heroine? Was Lauren a serial cheater, a heartbreaker with a broken heart, like Don Draper?

I watched *Marriage Story* and *Eyes Wide Shut* and *The Bridges of Madison County* alone, in fragments over lunch at the office, trying to divine the mythos of infidelity from these stories. What of these stories was in ours? Had the couples made it through? If so, how? The internet told me to follow the science, but my heart told me to follow the literature.

"You're obsessed," Lauren said to me. "Let it go."

"I'm just trying to understand our story."

Truth was, I'd never felt capable of infidelity—most of my lusts involve being adored by auditoriums of strangers, rather than a neighbor—but the affair had torn a hole in my willpower. Suddenly, an affair seemed not only possible but perhaps even exciting. Most of the books I read made affairs seem less like hell and more like undercover adventures to exotic, faraway lands. I could not let myself believe these tales. I wanted a book that painted pictures of the hell I'd lived, and so one day I put away the shows and books and pulled out the biggest, weirdest book of all, looking for answers.

Chapter 20

EASTER EGGS

2020

Islogged through the Old Testament that first summer of the plague, a year after the miscarriage. The answer to the riddle of my life was somewhere in this book. I can't say how I knew, but I knew.

Genesis never disappoints, crammed as it is with nudity, murder, and many delicious set pieces involving nudity and murder, in addition to DIY boatbuilding instructions. This opening book rocks you with its audacity, the greatest opening montage in world literature. There's a big bang and epic scenes of world formation and a man and a woman having the best of times and effing it up anyway, in a garden whose fruity trees turn sour. Suddenly, this cryptic book felt radically personal. I devoured it. I read whole chapters in a breath, whole testaments in a month.

You can't help but laugh at these people, who behave exactly like people. When Adam and Eve break the rules and eat the fruit and their eyes are opened and human history begins and God shows up and asks if they did the One Thing He Asked Them Not to Do, Adam, the first man, paterfamilias of all humankind, the archetype for every loving husband in human history, rats out his wife and disappears into the shrubbery.

Exodus read like *Star Wars: Episode IV—A New Hope* and the book of Joshua now felt more like *Return of the Jedi*, with the addition of extensive real estate transactions. The book of Judges is the bloodiest and wildest and most absurd book of the whole bunch, somewhere between *Groundhog Day* and *Game of Thrones*, all bloodshed and burlesque. Every page was pure tragicomic farce, which is how my life had begun to feel. As a young man, the book of Leviticus was easy to mock, all the evidence you needed of God's pettiness, but after reading CDC recommendations for the reopening of schools, Leviticus now felt familiar, whole chapters devoted to reminding people to wash their hands.

As I got deeper into the Old Testament, I saw grand metaphysical comedy everywhere, where the good guys go whoring and murdering and are chastened and humbled, where the high are brought so low so often that the book induces moral vertigo—and yet these fools are loved by God anyway. Comedy and absurdity brightened every page, as in Deuteronomy 25:11, where women are encouraged not to grab men by the genitals, or 1 Samuel 6, where God avenges the theft of company property by giving everyone hemorrhoids. I'm sure these passages weren't funny to the average ancient Israelite—but, no, actually I'm not sure at all. I'm definitely sure that in 1 Kings 18:27, when the prophet Elijah taunts the priests of a sex cult, he knew he was being hilarious. The whole book of Ezekiel, one of my favorites, comes off less like prophecy and more like a close friend relating his weird NyQuil dream that somehow gives you hope, especially the part where God animates a great pit of bones and makes them dance again.

•   •   •

By September, my home and my yard were still a desiccated depression of skeleton shards. I dug up the cypresses and carried them to the dump and pruned the citrus trees and weeded every tomato in the yard, but inside the house, weeds of circumspection grew tall. Lauren stopped using our pet name for each other: Presh.

"Harrison?" she said one day. "I think Gary's eating the cat litter. Can you go check?"

Harrison? When did I become Harrison? I filed it away.

We often talked during the day, around lunch, maybe midafternoon, a friendly check-in, but all that had now ceased. I sent her flowers on the first day of school that fall, for how hard she'd worked all summer to fill the classrooms with new students and hoping to woo her to help me fill our marriage bed with some new affection, but the flowers earned me little more than a text and one solitary emoji. Heart eyes? I'd felt more warmth from the auto warranty spammers. Good might win in the end but our story dragged on, just like the Bible.

Halfway through the Old Testament, the grand comic fugue of Scripture devolves into an excruciatingly slow-action movie that made me want to eat a bag of glass. The book of 1 Chronicles felt like a history textbook written by somebody who kept blacking out. Reading the minor prophets—Hosea, Joel, Amos—felt like reading YouTube comments written by people who hate a video of Israel. Lamentations is quite obviously a sad book and so is Jeremiah. The gloriously poetic book of Isaiah reads as if a clinically depressed Middle Earth elf king wrote it, and Ecclesiastes now sounded not unlike an elegantly dismal Edward Albee monologue delivered on a park bench by a wealth manager pondering suicide, and the Psalms read like a high school friend's Facebook posts about all the cryptic drama in her life that she won't fully explain, but you know it's not good and also that she might be high. I didn't feel high. I felt lost.

Our marriage had given birth to many rituals, though most hadn't lasted. The one custom that persisted longest was our Sunday nap, the unspoken sacrament of Christians across history, but somewhere that year, Lauren stopped napping. Most Sundays after lunch, I found myself in the bed alone.

"I'm going to get my nails done," she'd say, closing the door. Sometimes it was groceries or coffee with a friend or long, luxurious excursions to find new clothes for the cooler weather we all prayed would come. Whatever it was, it took her away from me. I'd lie in the dark with slivers of sun knifing through the blinds and crack open the Bible. After three months in the Old Testament, the best part about reading had been falling sleep. But some ideas had become clearer to me: suffering spares no human, neither good nor bad, because even when we're good, we're also idiots who eff up the little good we've done.

"I am a brother to dragons and a companion to owls," says Job, whose life had not turned out the way he hoped, and though his troubles were a sight worse than mine, we were the same man: sad little creatures in sad little caves, alone in the dark, owls hooting into an empty wood.

The good news of the Old Testament, as far as I could tell, was in the frailty of its heroes. You've got to appreciate a world religion that does not attempt to make the good guys look too good. Name some grotesque character trait of Barack Obama or Dolly Parton. You can't. You know they're probably jackasses in specific ways—we all are—but the official narrative won't allow for it. Too much is at stake. Maybe Eleanor Roosevelt was secretly cruel to family pets. Albert Einstein probably had some weird mustard fetish. Tell me, where do we openly declare that even the greatest among us are flawed and broken, other than on the stages of comedy clubs and in the Holy Bible, with its gallery of liars and rogues stripped of everything, at which point they throw themselves across the altar of their defeat and find, in their weakness, grace? There is Jacob, as phony and desperate as George Costanza. There's Solomon, the sex addict who awakens to the vacuity of his desire. There's David, an adulterer and murderer after God's own heart. David's story of adultery, for those who don't know, shocks with its audacity. Go read 2 Samuel 11, it's all there: "And it came to pass in an eventide, that David arose from off his bed, and walked upon the roof of the king's house: and from the roof he saw a woman washing herself; and the woman was very beautiful to look upon." David, the man after God's own heart, we're told, was also a creep, and he fetches this hot naked woman to his bedchamber, as kings do, and she goes, because he's a king, and he lords his power over her so many times she gets pregnant. He then conspires to murder her husband, Uriah, one of David's top soldiers, via a *Game of Thrones*-worthy stratagem. "And when the wife of Uriah heard that Uriah her husband was dead, she mourned for her husband," we're told. "And when the mourning was past, David sent and fetched her to his house, and she became his wife, and bare him a son."

What to make of this nonsense? Never mind we're told that "the thing that David had done displeased the Lord." Of course it had. But what to make of how in a very real way the adulterers lived happily ever after, giving birth to a son who would go on to write the selfsame Song of Solomon that drove me mad with lust as a boy? Solomon's gift for lust suddenly made all kinds of sense. He came by it honest. And it would be through his bloodline that the very savior of humankind came into the world.

The Bible gave no easy answers about adultery. It was wrong, sure, but those who committed it could still be loved, and the fruit of their crimes could create much goodness in the world. How stunning that David, the hero of the Old Testament if ever there was one, was also one of its most cunning villains. David, Solomon, Jacob, Noah, these men were no better than Oedipus and actually far worse—they failed and caused the failing in total consciousness of the failure. Maybe I'd been right. Maybe I was the problem here. That time she tried to leave, maybe I should've done like Uriah and let myself be written out of the story to make room for her and Chad's love.

It's just, I didn't feel like the problem. Uriah's only crime was, so far as we know, having a wife who bathed on the roof. But I'd committed many crimes and done penance. I'd come a long way in seventeen years of marriage. I was now a doer of dishes and a cooker of dinners and a highly engaged father of daughters, taking them on epic bike rides to give my wife time to wander the city alone, a thrower of footballs and a server of volleyballs, and a signer of homework, but I remained a quiet pouter, a loud laugher, a downer, a one-upper, an overthinker, an underempathizer, wordy, able to process nothing without talking so much that my wife wanted to hurl herself in front of a city bus. How could anyone stand me? Had the admission of my many flaws been an empty gesture? Was I still the assface I'd always been? Did she still hate me? One Sunday after church, I decided to ask. Lunch was over and everybody had left the table.

She had nowhere to be. It was Sunday. Maybe we could nap like old times.

"Something's wrong," I said. "Don't you feel like something's off? With us?"

"Yeah, I guess." She stared off toward the door.

I let the words fly around the room and worked hard to keep my mouth shut. This was her turn to talk, but she said nothing.

The most precious commodities in any life, the Bible seems to say, are disconcertingly paradoxical: wisdom, but also childlike wonder; courage to venture into alien lands and fight monstrous beasts, but also prudence to remember the dragon in you is the scariest of all. The Old Testament wants you to know that existence is rough, rough as they come, but good, too. When you eff it up, a life can still be made beautiful. Hearts of stone can be made into hearts of flesh. Dead things can dance again.

The weirdest part is that as much as my wife's heart had quietly turned to stone against me, she did look very much alive. She'd gone mostly vegan and was thinner than she'd been since forever. She seemed alive everywhere but in church and with everyone but me, as if my presence cast a darkness over whatever secret joy lit her up from the inside. The housing market was wild then, everybody making moves, the virus severing the shackles that chained people to desks in overcrowded urban kingdoms.

"I think I'd be good in real estate," she said one day that fall.

"Like, an agent?" I said.

"Yeah, maybe."

Odd. Lauren loved her job at the school, always had.

"You'd be great at real estate," I said. "You'd be perfect."

She possessed the qualities of all the best agents: beauty, charm, a sense of humor, straight teeth, a willingness to judge home furnishings and to cut those who cross her. But I know now she had other reasons for wanting a new career.

"I need a vacation," Lauren texted one day that fall. Work was killing her. She wanted a day or two away.

"Go for it," I said, the good and supportive husband.

I was trying to be kind while also being circumspect and observant and wily as a bobcat. I suggested she get a hotel room downtown for a Friday night sometime, just lie around and do nothing for a day but enjoy the exquisite pleasure of room service fries and Netflix and nobody else around.

"I'll use my money," she said. Another clue: this talk of *her money* and *my money*.

A couple of weeks later, she spent a Friday night alone in Hilton Head, in a room with a balcony where she said you could almost see the beach. The girls and I spent the night wandering downtown Savannah. While walking out of a candy store on River Street, I looked across the river at the darkness of the South Carolina marsh and knew she was over there, somewhere in the dark. I hoped she was getting a little rest, untangling whatever seemed so tangled.

She came back the next afternoon looking like a new woman.

"Thank you," she said. "I needed that."

I pressed on, into the last big chunk of Bible. The first thing you notice about the New Testament is how intensely contemporary it feels. The Old Testament is mythic and teeming with monsters and death, like hearing your great-grandfather describe what it was like to ride woolly mammoths. Then, after a thousand pages of *The Silmarillion*, you stumble into pages that read almost like a real novel, stories of tenderness and hope and dialogue and real people walking around real cities that still exist. It's a shock, after all the war and blood feuds and burning bushes and armies and leviathans and foreskins and bellies sliced open with blades and wooden pegs driven through foreheads, to turn to the New Testament and there it is: a little baby.

Our little baby had been dead more than a year, and now Lauren planned for herself a hysterectomy. She mentioned it casually, offhand, while preparing dinner one night. So many years of pregnancies had done their damage and the doctor suggested this surgery to quell the biochemical madness and perhaps to keep her bladder from falling out of her body.

"If you think it's best," I said. "This is your decision."

"This will help my migraines."

"No more headaches. That's huge."

"No more babies, either."

The thing I'd been thinking but hadn't wanted to think is that maybe she'd never ended things with Chad. The thought of this man lurking at the edges of our marriage like a snake had dissipated over time, but still I woke at night fantasizing about driving to his house, to be sure the thing was dead.

My curiosity and self-reflection soon gave way to a quiet rage, as I knew I could never bring all this up with Lauren without going backward in our marriage. She'd get angry, defensive, hurt, would pull further away into whatever hole she kept crawling to. Maybe I needed to be more of an asshole about the matter. It's possible I'd been too kind, inventing excuses for her distance when what I needed to do was be more like Jesus. Because the thing about Jesus is, when you get to the part where he's fully grown, when you shelve all the platitudes and chestnuts about him that you absorb in a lifetime of Sunday school lessons and sermons, when you step back, what you find is that Jesus can seem like a real asshole.

In Mark 11, he instructs his disciples to go steal a baby horse in another town, and right after that, he kills a tree that didn't do a thing to him. In Matthew 8, he ruins a perfectly good herd of pigs by filling them with demons and sending them plummeting over a cliff. In Matthew 25, he at first ignores a woman whose daughter's vexed by the Devil because she's carrying the wrong passport. He tells confusing stories. He causes legitimately awkward moments. He is not cool, his only weapons being the ability to perform mostly food-based miracles and to tell a great story in such a way as to amaze his hearers while also insulting them. He's slippery.

He says, "Love your neighbor."

Then he's all "You may have to slay your neighbor."

When it's time to get angry, Jesus gets angry. When it's time to weep, he weeps. He's fully human and extraordinarily weird, the baby, the boy, the man, the God who refuses to be what you want him to be and instead is and remains the most cryptic and magnetic and heroic figure of world literature, unjustly executed by the state, slaughtered by his community, abandoned by those who claimed to love him. You can understand the anger.

I had begun to feel some anger in me, too, and very little happiness. The Bible seems to think the happiness question is moot. Saying you deserve happiness is like saying you deserve fresh, minty breath. Nice to have, enjoy it while it lasts. There are more things in heaven and earth to want than happiness. Purpose. Community. Duty. Joy. Goodness.

I finally understood the point of the Bible, this book of operating instructions crowdsourced over thousands of years, a sort of vast cosmic Wikipedia of wisdom about the human comedy, each story a case study in the long war between darkness and light, proud and meek. Present urges and passions can drag you and your loved ones to hell. Think of the future. Think not just a year or five into the future. Cast your vision a generation ahead, twenty generations even. What you do now echoes across future history. David and Bathsheba had that baby, and the baby grew strong, but the kingdom David ruled is no more.

By Halloween, I finished the Bible and had to admit, there was real hope in it. The story has a wondrous climax, a comic finale for humankind, a miraculous consummation too wild to be believed, where all tears are wiped away and all riddles solved. Our own finale was nearing its moment.

Chapter 21

SECOND REVELATION

2020

"I think I'm going to get my nails done," Lauren said one Sunday afternoon, a couple of weeks before Thanksgiving. "Might look at furniture."

We needed something new for the living room, as Gary had eaten much of the love seat and attempted to mate with several of the cushions. A sectional had been discussed. She left, and I lay down for a nap. When I woke midafternoon, I took Gary for a long walk.

"What's Mom's password?" the girls asked, when I returned an hour later. They brought Lauren's laptop into the kitchen. They wanted to watch a movie. Lauren's computer, like mine, was a kid-free zone, dedicated for work and little else, but the girls had played outside for two hours and earned themselves some screen time. I knew Lauren's password—I had set it up for her two years before—and input the keystrokes, to little effect.

"What's your password?" I texted Lauren. "The girls want to watch something."

"I don't have a password," she replied.

"Your computer thinks you do."

Lauren was gone until dinner, just about: long enough to have cased every furniture store in Savannah and gotten nails done for more hands and feet than she possessed. When she walked in the door, she looked, well, I'll tell you exactly what she looked like. *Glowing* is the word I hate to use here but have to, for she glowed. She looked gorgeous, in her white cable sweater and jeans and new nails and fresh makeup. She moved with lightness and energy, smiling at the girls, caressing their hair, asking about their afternoon. Did Pottery Barn now offer makeovers?

Later that night, Lauren cracked open her laptop. "The password was missing an exclamation point. I always forget!"

I would not confront Lauren about why it had taken six hours to look at sofas or cross-examine her on the silliness of her misremembering a password or that she had one at all. An accusation would only deepen the lie and heighten the fortress around her heart. What would Jesus do? Jesus was Superman. Jesus would look straight through the laptop screen and see the truth. But I could not go full Jesus and overturn the money changers just yet.

I got the opportunity a couple of days later when she got her hair done. Afterward, she sent me a photo, as she always did, of her new color.

"Cute" is what I'd normally say, but I texted back "Hot."

Then I said, "Might have to get naked later tonight."

This was not my usual way. I do not sext. I was born in a generation where lewd messages, should you long to send them, should be communicated via bridge overpass. Whenever I've asked to see a woman naked, I've always had the decency to do this in person. The only photos of my genitals, as far as I know, have been taken by X-ray technicians. But I was determined to make love to my wife this very night. I would flirt all day if that's what it took. I would do the dishes extra-good. I would sweep the floor and fold the laundry and floss. We'd had sex maybe three times in six months, a historic drought. Her response to my gently flirtatious G-rated sext was the emoji face with the monocle. No bites.

That night, I made dinner and did the dishes and moved a load to the dryer and was sweet without going overboard. Sex on a Thursday night. This would be wild.

When it was bedtime, I brushed my teeth and climbed in and cracked open *Lonesome Dove* while she checked her phone one last time. She put the phone down and I closed the book and turned off the light and moved across the expanse of bedding with the quickness of a cattle stampede. I put my hands on her with as much sweetness as I had in me.

"Hey there," I said, with my minty breath.

"Don't come over here unless you want your feelings hurt," she said, not even turning to face me in the dark.

She'd been snubbing me for months. So I was ready to snap, and snap I did.

"What the fuck," I said, into the dark. "Something's going on."

I'd been as sweet as a toothache for six months. What the hell? I lay there in the dark. I'd reached into the blackness and felt the scales of something, unmistakably.

The next morning, she came into my office, sheepish, softer, apologetic. This never happened. The words *I'm sorry* have no home in Lauren's brain. You'd sooner get Vladimir Putin to ride a unicycle in the Pride Parade than hear my wife apologize. She'd back over me with a cement mixer and tell me it was my fault for being so close to a cement mixer. But that morning, she seemed genuinely sorry for rebuffing my fervent nudity the night before.

"What the hell is going on?" I said, like a movie character when the plot needs a push.

"I don't know."

But she knew. She knew more than I did.

"I love you," I said. "But I cannot be married to you for another forty years if this is what it's going to be like. We've been here before. I thought we got better."

"I have to get ready for work."

I stopped her on the way out the door, an hour later. "Do you believe in our marriage?"

"Sometimes." She left.

Later that day, she sent a nice text: another gently sweet apology, an admission: yes, the last few months had been difficult. Two apologies in one day. Wonder of wonders. Reality had begun to tilt with all this gentleness from Lauren. Something was in the air, a vibration, puzzling new pastels. It's like something inside her had warmed, almost against her will. I had to press this advantage. I suggested we go to breakfast the next morning, a Saturday.

"I'd like to ask you some questions," I texted.

"About what?"

"Life."

The next morning before dawn, I opened to the book of Psalms. I looked for any last wisdom before asking the unaskable question. I got down on my office floor, on hands and knees, and touched my head to the earth and prayed like a monk, rocking, reciting, "Deliver me out of the mire, and let me not sink. Let not the water flood overflow me, neither let the deep swallow me up, and let not the pit shut her mouth upon me."

The Word of God calls itself many things: a sword, a hammer, a lamp. In places, the Word is called fire. In others, food. The book of

John says that the Word isn't just with God or from God—it *is* God. I don't even pretend to know what this means. Over the years, the Bible has cleaved me in two like a sword and broken my brain like a hammer and cut through fog like a lamp. It has filled me and burned me, but mostly it has given me hope: that I am not as alone as my dolor might make me feel, that my travails are mine but they are not new in the world, that humans have cried out to the heavens in astonishment and want for as long as we have had lungs to cry. If our species can feel such anguish and write it down and pass it up the branches of the family tree, then that gives me hope. I stood far out on a branch now and had little else to comfort me but this old and weird book. I finally felt equipped to do what I hadn't possessed the wisdom and strength to do ever before in my life: I felt as courageous as Saint George before the monster of being itself, fearful, yes, but armored, wilier, wiser, possessing a hope and faith that felt stronger than any dragon.

I wrote out a few questions I wanted to ask. A fortress lived inside that woman, an underwater kingdom that she protected with the ferocity of an army of orcas, but something was different now. The orcas had been called off. I could feel it.

We drove to a bagel shop and got our bagels and coffee and sat at a picnic table. It was cool and clear, a perfect fall day, that Saturday before Thanksgiving. We sat at a table farthest from the others, where we could talk.

"So, I wrote some questions on my phone, I hope that's not weird," I said.

"That's fine."

Normally, this would've been her cue to shut down and summon additional orcas to devour me, but she seemed too weak to fight any longer.

"Are there things about you I don't know?" I said.

"There's things about everybody that other people don't know."

"I'm pretty sure you know everything about me."

"Because you tell everyone everything. Most people don't."

"Fair enough."

I looked at my list. Six questions. One down.

"Were you abused? Molested? As a child?"

"No."

I felt woefully unequipped to go further into this disturbing interrogation with a woman I'd known and not known for almost half my life, a woman I'd carried into hospitals and whose hand I'd held through the births of three miraculous daughters now eating Pop-Tarts a few blocks away. How could I ever know her?

And that's when a question came to me. I had not planned to ask it. I had not felt capable of asking it without splintering into a trillion billion atoms. This question was not written into my notes. The words blazed across the sky of my mind as if painted on a banner behind a small plane piloted by the Holy Spirit. I knew that when I asked it, everything would change, forever.

"When you were shopping for furniture last Sunday, were you really shopping for furniture?"

"No."

"Where were you?"

She looked around at the others nearby, eating their bagels. "I can't say it here."

Two minutes later, our uneaten bagels thrown away, we were in the car.

"Where were you?"

And she said it.

Good God. I promise you, this story was not supposed to end this way. I had wanted it to have a happy ending. I had been so naïve.

Chapter 22

BACK AND THERE AGAIN

2020

The fog of that mad season burned away with the hiss of his dumb name. The Great and Powerful Chad! I felt insane. I laughed with genuine shock. I said, "Oh my God."

Three years earlier, I had wanted to fillet this man's face with a lawn-mower blade, until prayer and reflection revealed that Chad was not so much the problem here as the symptom. But dammit all to hell, this little cockroach was starting to seem like part of the problem. Hit him with a shoe a dozen times and he just looks up at you, like, "Nice place you got here."

But, no, I was not doing battle with a cockroach. This was battle with something far more malevolent. This was a monster, vile and immense. A beast of cosmic wickedness with no face, no name. I suddenly felt like a man who'd been tiptoeing through a Cretan labyrinth and finally stood before the Minotaur. It focuses the mind.

"Three years ago, you lied. You slept with him."

"Yes."

"That night you spent in a hotel in Hilton Head, you were with him."

"Yes."

"Was it his baby?" I asked, of the baby we'd lost.

"No."

They didn't start talking again until a few months before, she confessed. For three years, she'd tried to be good, she said, but their swift and sudden breakup made it all seem to her like a movie. The unrequitedness of it all. The idea of him lived inside her like a virus, quiet, silent, working its evil undetected. The germ of Chad, and the miscarried life they almost had, became a parallel universe inside her.

"I guess you want to marry him."

"Yes," she said, though she didn't sound happy about it.

What white-hot pain lived inside Lauren's heart that would cause her to inflict such cruel hurt on those she'd promised and professed most to love? I'd have better luck prying open a petrified clam with a biodegradable straw.

"Why him? Good God."

"I can't explain it."

"Try."

Silence. And then: "You don't want to hear."

They'd been back together for four months, since summer. He'd been hassling her all year, intermittently sending texts, emails. He wanted closure, and she wanted something, too. Release? Freedom? More suffering in the world?

When she'd broken it off before, he went dark for a while, she said, but crawled back the way he always had. She insisted that she'd stiff-armed his pleas, but eventually caved in the hot, lonely pandemic month of July. The virus weakened more than lungs.

"Where did all this happen?" I asked.

"Do you really want to know?"

She explained: They'd met for closure in some piney thicket off in the woods a few miles from our house, where she told him about the new church, the miscarriage, her loneliness, and he shared his own tales of woe. In the three years since their affair, things had gotten bad for Chad. There had been some trouble with the law, though the details were unclear. What was clear is that he'd lost his IT career due to a series of self-destructive choices that sounded like the world's most boring Merle Haggard song. He was now working odd jobs, she said, assembling trampolines, installing Christmas lights. He was a lost kitten, his own marriage all but finished. I don't know: maybe Lauren's nurturing instinct, laid low by miscarriage, found in Chad something new to care for.

"I hope you find what you're looking for," I said, as I cranked the car to head back home. "Although I cannot imagine this poor man is what anybody is looking for, unless you have a trampoline to assemble." Chad needed help, and Lauren needed Chad, and I needed a beer. I had my own country song to write.

I knew she loved him. But maybe it wasn't love. Maybe it was a pain so deep, so inconceivably vast, that it only felt like love. Chad's own wife, Lane, had discovered the rekindled affair months ago—she saw a text—and she and their son were now living elsewhere. I suddenly regretted blocking Lane's number three years before. Maybe she'd have tried to tell me. Their divorce proceedings had already begun. He'd be homeless within the month, nowhere to go, nobody to turn to but my wife, who might be homeless within the month, too, maybe within the hour. I drove us both away from the café.

The day was gorgeous, clear as a picture, Thanksgiving just days away. We were supposed to be packing for a trip to Indian Springs, to roast a turkey and frolic in the Alabama woods at her sister's.

"I need time," she said. She seemed like a woman who'd booked a skydiving excursion and now refused to jump through the open door. "I need to figure stuff out." She scratched at her neck, chewed her lip. She seemed covered in ants, panicky.

When I looked at her, I felt sorrow. I would be fine, in time. I had a genuine community of friends and family who would carry me through this. The girls would be cared for and loved by our community, too, but their grief and pain would unfold over years, marathon sessions with counselors at best, foolish and angry choices at worst. I felt sorrow, deep and bottomless, for my daughters. Lauren must have believed, in some twisted way, that they would benefit from this madness, somehow, convinced herself that living "her truth" would free them to live their own. But truth does not make you look like she looked in the passenger seat of the truck. She looked like those characters in horror films who've seen demons.

When we pulled into our driveway, I opened the door and got out.

"Where are you going?" she said, almost frantic.

She must have worried I was about to go shred all her dresses in the yard with the machete I kept on hand for such occasions or do something equally dramatic or far worse, the sort of stuff you read about online:

"Jilted Husband Jailed for Two Years for Breaking Legs of Wife's Lover"

"Defendant Takes Plea Deal in Love Triangle Shooting"

"Man Admits to Dismembering Wife"

Men do a lot of violence when betrayed. Women do, too. You can find ample stories of vandalized trucks, torched bass boats, poetic castrations. I had no plans for a love-triangle shooting or the dismemberment of anyone. If the theology of the Reformation taught me anything, it was, as the book of Jeremiah says, "The heart is deceitful above all things, and desperately wicked: Who can know it?" This included my heart, too.

"What are you doing?" She followed me into the garage.

"Yardwork."

It confused the hell out of her. That was a good start.

Chapter 23

THE HARDEST THING

2020

An hour later, Lauren found me on my hands and knees, prying fallen pecans from grass. I thought of making a pie.

"I'm sorry," she said. Three apologies in as many days.

"For what?" I dropped another woody nut in the bucket.

"For everything." She seemed genuine, but then, people who are great at lying always do.

"Cool. Tell me why I shouldn't break his legs."

"He knows everything about me. He knows my secrets."

"What secrets?"

"Him. He's the secret."

"Well, now I know, too."

That afternoon, I showered and left for a long drive down the coast, through saw grass and marsh under a temple dome of sky so bright and clear that I hoped to get God's attention. I played spacey music to clear my mind, mostly Beach House: the sort of music you

can imagine hearing as I drive my truck quietly off a pier. I prayed.
I smoked. I drove to the beach, got a beer.

Where would I go now? You don't have many moments in your
life when you feel like your choices on that very day will shape the
rest of your existence on earth. What do I love? Who am I? I am a
family man. What I most love is coming home, to Lauren and Coco
and Pippi and Ginsburg and Gary and Rivers the Cat and Bootsie
the Tortoise. I love cooking dinner and laughing with my family at
the dinner table and cleaning the kitchen and hearing Pippi sing
in the shower and trying to hug Coco, who is allergic to human
touch, like her mother. I love giggling with Ginsburg, who is never
not giggling, except when she's scowling, just like her father. I turn
down many invitations so that I can be at home with these people.

I come from a long line of men who love to be out in the
world—hunting, fishing, killing, running, hitting, scoring, farming,
plowing, milking—and who love being at home with their people
even more, telling stories, eating meals, sitting on porches. I have
inherited that love of domestic life. It is not something I merely
love. It defines my very existence. And now I stood to lose it all. I
was terrified. The girls would live with me, with her, it didn't matter.
They wouldn't be living with us. People ask why I didn't feel more
rage toward Chad. I felt plenty of rage, but mostly I felt terror.

As I drove along, I thought of the men who'd shaped my understanding of what it means to be a father and a husband, the coaches
and preachers and teachers and professors and elders and deacons
and all the waddle-necked cranks at the deer camp. I didn't hear
much ugly talk of women or the glorification of extramarital fondling. A little coarse jesting, not much else. Divorce was not a thing
to be celebrated, though perhaps necessary in grim conditions. As a

boy, I had known good men. Did I have their strength to do whatever it was that needed doing?

I thought of my father, who got left twice by two different wives, but who never spoke bitterly of either one. He appeared to have done some healthy self-reflection before marrying a third time—the woman who would become my mother—and it must have worked. That third marriage lasted forty years, when at death they did part.

His father—my grandfather, Monk—was married to my grandmother for seventy years, and for much of that time she was wearing a hairnet. Did he leave her? Bark about her degraded countenance? Run off for a younger, sprier woman? He drove her to the beauty parlor every Saturday to get her hair set for church. Seven decades of hairnets. That's a man.

Was I so strong as my father, my grandfather, to refuse bitterness? It's true that, as far as I know, my grandmother never did try to run off with a handyman, as my own wife had attempted once and was presently reattempting, but life threw plenty at Monk. He lived through the Great Depression and droughts and heat waves that killed his cattle. Did Monk rail at God about the drought? And when automation finally decimated his dairy operation, he ran traps for fox and beaver, and when fur bottomed out, he got a factory job, and when American manufacturing faltered, he started catching and selling turtles for pets and soups. Did he rail about how fate had sentenced him to spending his twilight years not in a manicured retirement community of gleaming surfaces but in duck waders in a swamp thick with reptilian violence trying to net a few spiny softshells for supper?

He always did the hard thing and the right thing and did it with such quiet diligence that you hardly noticed his life was one long string of reasons to hate God if hating God is what he might've preferred. I don't think I ever even saw him get angry. He might jaw with you all day about farm subsidies or nuclear disarmament, and if you snapped in hostile disagreement, he would simply ignore you and ask if you wanted another biscuit, which, of course, you did. Who doesn't want another biscuit?

Despite heaps of tragedy and suffering, my father and grandfather had not turned cold toward life. I am sure anger and vengeance would have felt so good to them—rage at God, rage at the people who deceived and hurt them—but I never saw it. I saw this goodness in my big brother, too. Bird's biological father was killed when he was only two years old. Bird was raised, for the most part, by people who were not his people. Bird could've turned nasty and hard, but he didn't. He has always found much to love in life: hunting, Cormac McCarthy novels, Van Halen, weed, his sweet wife. I saw this same goodness in our mother. Her first husband, Bird's father, had, before he died in a car accident, just one day up and walked out and never came back, leaving her with a baby and a broken heart, but I never sensed any resentment in Mom, no ill will. All around me, Pop and Mom and Monk and Bird and cousins and aunts and uncles, all those who stood to my left and right in the Great Unbroken Circle, had been betrayed and abandoned by fate and sickness and lovers and liars, but still they held on to and seemed to believe in the goodness of life, the promise of abundance.

I felt God was calling me to love, somehow, too: impossibly. What does love look like in this moment? Does it mean loving my wife the way they say God loves me? If so, what does that mean, specifically? The book of Micah says, "He hath shewed thee, O man, what *is* good." And what is good? According to Micah, it is "to do justly, and to love mercy, and to walk humbly with thy God."

But what is justice?

How to evince mercy?

And to whom?

My wife, or my children? Chad?

Did Chad deserve mercy? Is it possible to express mercy with a pitching wedge to the skull? How does one walk humbly while dragging a dead body into a gully? I don't care what you think about divorce or how much you feel that my wife was clearly just in pursuit of an imagined happiness and ought to have been free to seek it the way the Founding Fathers of materialism deemed was her right. Goddammit, she was hurting a lot of good people to seek her godforsaken happiness. She deserved every horrid thing that might come to pass with the dissolution of our marriage. She was begging for it. And I knew justice would cast my wife to the wolves, send her into the outer rim of being. Everything she loved about her life would be taken from her, even her children. Her happiness was our hell—and her hell, too, it turned out.

Chapter 24

LYING IN BED

2020

When I got home from my long drive, I no longer felt terror or shock or even the delightful masculine compulsion to assault the problem with the brute force of reason. Instead, what I felt was peace. Man, it was weird. It was not a spacey, THC-laced tranquility, but more like the peace you feel when you've ordered a cheese pizza and they bring you one pocked with hateful black olives and you eat the disgusting pizza anyway, it's not so bad, it's still pizza, fuck it. It was the peace of allowing asshole drivers to pass you freely on the interstate, though they deserve slow and painful deaths, the peace of accepting that this ballet recital is going to last three hours and you can do nothing short of calling in a bomb threat. Chill, brother, nobody here is having fun, not even the children. Let it go.

It was the peace of surrender.

I no longer felt an obligation to "win." To win my wife back, to defeat Chad in a lawn-mowing tournament, to prove my worth, to preen my achievements for her review, fuck it. I couldn't fix this. I didn't hardly know what "this" even meant anymore. This is about the weirdest and most terrible feeling a man can have, I think. Conquest of one kind or another—of the self, of others, of danger, of threats, of chaos—this is the spirit that animates our every thought and deed, and when rightly guided, it is this spirit that builds cities and civilizations and strong, beautiful theaters for three-hour ballet recitals. But this bellicose spirit could do no good here. None of the tools and weapons at my disposal worked anymore. So I tendered my resignation from Manly Problem Solvers, Inc., and walked into the house and put away my sword. The meek shall inherit the earth? Cool. Let's give it a shot.

It was night now. I walked inside and lay down on the couch in my office and stared at the ceiling. I showered again for no reason. I put on jeans and a T-shirt featuring two howling wolves underneath the words I'D RATHER BE CRYING TO ENYA.

Lauren came in, crying.

"I'll leave if you want me to," she said.

She was crying because she did not want to leave the girls, but she knew that the leaving would have to be hers to do. Did I want her to leave and suffer and be sad and take a dozen Ambien and slip quietly into eternity? Maybe. But she was too chicken to do us all the favor and would instead run straight to Chad, sending all of us deeper into this hell.

I got up off the couch and stood. In that moment, I felt, not strong: *strong* is not the word. Neither is *weak*. If I wanted Lauren to suffer, all I had to do was put into motion the machinations of judgment within reach: a call to an attorney, a simple disentanglement of banking, and she'd be lost in the frigid chaos with nothing and nobody to aid her.

"Leave if you want. But this is the safest place for you right now."

"Okay."

Looking back, knowing what was to come, maybe I should've kicked her out on that day of that hateful second revelation, though it would have traumatized the girls and cleaved the marriage with finality. She would lose everything. Maybe that's what she needed most, in that moment: to feel what it is to dangle and drop into this dark and hateful crevasse. That might have been merciful. One thing I learned in all this is that sometimes justice is indistinguishable from mercy. But I did not kick her out. I did not take a hammer to her laptop. I meant what I said: she could stay. It's what Monk would've done.

Our house was less a home now than a refugee settlement for a woman who had nowhere else to go. Every path away from our door led to isolation and destruction. I knew it in my bones. I think she knew it, too. If she had a close family member somewhere in town, I'd have told her to get the hell out, but she didn't even have a single good friend who knew what was going on. She'd cut off everyone who could've talked sense to her, the way addicts do.

I set some rules and could hardly believe the words came out of my mouth. I could not keep her from seeing him. She was no prisoner. She had plenty of opportunities every week to slink off to one of Savannah's plenteous marinas to fondle Chad and talk of their future together.

"I know you will talk to him," I said, "but if I find him in my house or on my property, I will do my best to make sure he pees blood, and I do not want to have to do that."

My broadsword was no longer in my hand, but it was on the wall. I might need it again one day, I had no doubt of this.

She looked at the floor.

It's said that when a man steals your wife, there's no better revenge than to let him keep her. Yet, while Chad seemed all too eager to drive the getaway car, it was not this poor man doing the stealing here. Lauren was the agent of this action. It was Lauren who had confessed her love to him via email so long ago on the cul-de-sac. That was around 2012, she said. By her own account, he had resisted, even moved his family away for a time, perhaps because he'd foreseen the hell to come. In 2017, sure, okay, it was Chad who moved back, made the call, invited himself over, finally confessed his love, but it was Lauren who'd left the back door unlocked. It was Lauren who'd ended things then. Now, in 2020, yet again, when he came slinking back and reignited this fire, it was Lauren who'd agreed to meet for closure. She'd held the cards through this whole nightmare. She did the dealing. She decided when the game would be played, and ended, and played again. But I was done with lover's poker. I backed away from the table.

Go, if you want. But this is where your family lives.

If Lauren moved in with Chad, I felt sure she would destroy him the same way she'd laid waste to us. Pain like hers longs only to create more pain. She'd fleece his affections, dominate him, rule him, until she saw that he, too, was not her father, and she would abandon him to a roadside grave, right next to me, another desiccated husk of a man. She was a missile of pain hiding nuclear warheads of suffering. Nobody was safe. I would have to take one for my gender and let her sleep here. I was already dead. She couldn't hurt me anymore.

So, she stayed. I know many reading this book will scoff and wonder why I didn't just drive to Chad's house and whip him with a rubber hose. But this miracle would require more magic than rage offers.

Over the next few days, our home became the setting for an absurdist drama straight out of Harold Pinter, where we carried on a perfectly normal outward life while holding on to this secret knowledge. I knew what she was, and she knew I knew, yet there we were, making school lunches and planning meals and doing our best to laugh with the girls about some funny thing that had happened at school and asking what they wanted for Christmas. The girls never asked about why I slept on my office couch. I was up before everybody and folded the old quilts every morning, hoping they didn't see.

I did not call in the cavalry this time, not like three years before, to come stampeding over the hilltops and surround our home with tough love and straight talk. This had only shamed my wife into behaving, and I didn't want a marriage soaked in shame. That's what Lauren had meant back then about our marriage being a "prison." She felt caged, shamed all her life, forced to conform, to smile. So, okay. No shame. No people. I told nobody. It was just her and me and the thing we call God.

The next two weeks presented a nightmare of turkey and dressing. I lashed myself together with duct tape and kite string and got us to Alabama for the holiday, where Lauren and I spent a week trapped in the same guest bedroom. Whatever softness had once lived in her had been lobotomized. I wept, reminded her of our old affections, the happy times, all those better days we'd shared for so many years, in a whole other life.

"Those people are dead," she said. Ice.

We kept up appearances. I spent most of the holiday reading or walking the roads and hills and woods followed by two small goats and Norman, a colossal Great Pyrenees who seemed to understand my pain. Lauren spent much of her time in the bedroom. I've had plenty of awkward Thanksgivings, and the one where I shared a small bed with my wife while she texted her boyfriend was one of them.

We got home on a Saturday. This situation was untenable.

Something had to be done. But then I remembered about the hysterectomy.

The procedure, planned months ago, was two weeks away. She'd be unable to walk or do much else for many days, all the way till Christmas. You can't exactly boot the lying, cheating mother of your children onto the street when she's nursing abdomen sutures. All's fair in love and war, but what about laparoscopic wounds?

I presented her an option. She could stay until the surgery and would then have to choose where to recover and begin her new life: his home or ours.

"When you leave the hospital, you go there or you come here."

"It's Christmas."

"It's very Hallmark."

"After surgery, I'm coming home," she said, a little pissed.

"Is this still your home?"

My sword was sheathed for now but there was plenty to do. I girded my loins for the storms to come, opened a new bank account, moved most of the money there, refinanced the mortgage, freed up cash, and bought a new pickup truck with the last of my most recent book advance, squirreled away for an emergency. I never did feel like much of a truck guy, but I suddenly liked the idea of hauling shit. Trucks are useful. I might have to haul Lauren's shit to the dump or tote Chad's lifeless body to the marsh. I won't lie, it felt great to walk into a Toyota dealership with a sack of money. I take affection where I can get it.

"Dad bought a new truck!" the girls said that afternoon.

"Wow," Lauren said, dazed. She was more hologram than human now.

God knows, if I'd have left the money in the bank, at least half of it stood to be seized by some avaricious divorce attorney. The

Toyota had deeply tinted windows all around, which looked pretty freaking cool and made it easier to absentmindedly mow over pedestrians and small animals while backing up. To hell with it. I no longer cared about what was behind me, neither the happy marriage that had been a lie, nor the rollerbladers that now plagued Savannah's residential streets. Sorry, guys! I was on a new road.

The Toyota had a long bed and a tailgate and hit just the right note a hot newly single dad might want to hit. I had begun flirting with the possibility that I might soon be making out with any number of single moms in coastal Georgia.

"Man, you look great!" everybody said at church. "How are you losing so much weight?"

"Grief just melts the pounds away," I said, to confused looks. Nobody knew a thing.

In the days before her surgery, our mornings and days and nights were rife with stage-whispered fights behind closed doors, agonizing snatches and fragments that carried into kitchens and bathrooms and hallways. Coco had to know. She was now fourteen. She was no fool.

"She doesn't know," Lauren said. "They don't know."

One morning before school, all five of us were in the kitchen when Pippi and Ginsburg piled out the door to walk to class.

Coco stopped at the door and turned to us. "I had the weirdest dream last night."

"Tell us about it," I said.

"I dreamed that Mom was having an affair with a dad from another school." Coco had a funny look. "It was so weird."

"That is weird," I said, looking at Lauren, who'd lost all the blood in her face.

Comedy was all I had left. In the New Testament, Paul passionately exhorts his readers, "Watch ye, stand fast in the faith, quit you like men, be strong!" Then he says, as if in rejoinder to himself, quiet, calming, "Let all your things be done with charity."

Comedy, so often acidic, was a charity in this dark season. You had to appreciate the little ironies, the incongruities of it all. My devoted Christian wife, who worked at a sweet little Christian school, was trapped in a torrid love affair and was now about to have her uterus permanently removed, which would require me—the villain of her story—to care for the villain of my story, which was her: to bring her trays of soup, help her shuffle to the toilet, place additional pillows behind her to allow her to sit up in bed and tell me she wanted me to die, just like David wanted Uriah to die. She hated me with all her being and admitted she had often prayed for my death.

"I always hoped you would get hit by a car. You know, on your bike."

"Hope springs eternal," I said.

A few days before the surgery, we had what I was sure would be our last date, if you can call it that. We needed to do some Christmas shopping for the girls. At one department store, she looked at rings.

"If we stay together, I want a new wedding ring," she said.

"We'll see."

What balls on this woman, to suggest the possibility of loving me again. Later, we ordered takeout and sat in the car eating gyros and split a bottle of red from Whole Foods. We had some of the best conversation we'd had since the first year of our marriage. It was almost romantic. This is what they don't tell you about infidelity. Unless you separate and never see each other again, you end up sharing so many intimacies. You Christmas shop for your kids and drink out of the same bottle and see each other naked stepping out of the shower. You want to hate but you cannot. The nakedness, literal and otherwise, won't let you.

The day of the surgery, in the black of dawn on the morning of December 11, 2020, I drove Lauren to the hospital a few blocks from the house. I was not allowed inside, due to the pandemic, and so walked her to the door of the intake and stood there watching vapor rise up from her mouth and mine. She was afraid. She clutched her favorite pillow and overnight bag.

"I'll be in the truck. Don't you go dying on me."

I did not try to hug her or take advantage of this tender moment, when she was afraid and had plenty of reason to be—the unknowable future, the imminent removal of her motherhood from her body, the perfect symbolism of it all.

"Can I have a kiss?" she said, fearful as the girl she'd once been. I kissed her on the cheek.

"On the lips?" she said.

"Fine."

It was the kiss of an old friend for another, I guess. There was love in it, but mostly there was comfort. It felt like it would be our last kiss, forever.

Six hours later, I was allowed inside, to sit with her in recovery. She was weepy in the bed. She reached for my hand, fell asleep, woke up, fell asleep. I considered ending this love story by suffocating her with one of the stiff hospital pillows.

"Thank you for being here." She was being sweet, but she was high.

Back home the next day, we got her squared away in bed, a garden of pill bottles and juice glasses on the nightstand. Our church—still clueless about the affair—lined up meals every other night through Christmas Eve.

"Sleep in here with me," she said.

She was always so afraid of being alone. I'd been on my office couch for weeks already and didn't mind a real bed. I slept beside her, in case she woke in the night bleeding, dying. She held my hand as she drifted away into a dreamless prescription coma.

Chapter 25

NOTES ON CHAD, REVISITED: A *DATELINE* EXCLUSIVE

2020

When the very architecture of being is called into question, when the most important structures of your life turn out to have been constructed over marshland and the tide of suffering rolls in and sweeps everything away, it becomes nearly impossible to reply warmly to emails. The very concept of Microsoft Outlook becomes a cruel joke. Zoom transmutes into a muted nightmare. Oh, you want to brainstorm ideas with the team? Sorry, I'm currently experiencing a soul tsunami. Can we reschedule?

Fortunately, the towering and hateful storm of my wife's infidelity featured the silver lining of her hysterectomy and, hiding somewhere behind the clouds, the warm glow of medical leave required to care for her. My request was granted by HR, and Lauren was bedridden and the kids were occupied with school for a few more days before the holiday. It seemed the perfect time to begin the waterboarding. I would make her talk. Lauren was stove-up in the bed like James Caan in *Misery* and I was Kathy Bates with a sledgehammer of questions.

"Time to wake up," I'd say, handing her a glass of apple juice and her first round of pills. "How's my little nightmare this morning?"

Her convalescence made it harder to hate her, which helped, too, as did the drugs. She was hopped up on a little of everything and too high to protest. I was a good nurse, brought her ginger ale and soups and muffins and heating pads and more questions.

"When do you and Chad talk? How does all this work? It sounds exhausting."

"It is. We don't really talk. We text. But we had to stop doing that, too, when Lane found out a few months ago."

"So how have you been communicating since?"

"LinkedIn, mostly."

How humiliating, to communicate with your lover via LinkedIn messenger, the lowest form of communication developed by humankind. That ghostly digital wood haunted by robotic sales leeches. It wasn't tawdry. It was pitiful.

"Why do you love him?"

"I don't know."

"What do you do? Like, when you're together?"

"I don't know. We talk. Watch YouTube."

"So you watch YouTube. That's pretty hot."

"His house is filthy. I do the dishes. Sometimes I fold laundry."

"So now you have two houses to clean? I thought he was helpful."

The man didn't even have the courtesy to do his own laundry. Sounded like a real fairy tale. Could she not see the comedy here?

She threw me a few bones. In addition to telling me she wished I were dead, she also told me I was a good father. It had taken me years to learn how, she admitted, but I had grown, though perhaps the growing had come too late, at least where the marriage was concerned. She sounded like a woman on her deathbed. She also told me that, despite my maddening flaws, she felt I had always loved her better than she had loved me and that she believed I would have a happier life without her.

"I know you think he's an idiot," she said, "but he can sometimes be funny."

"He's got a funny haircut. I'll give you that."

Why was she still here? It was possible she wanted to stay for all the best reasons: hope, love, a conscious choice to honor her promises. It was possible she remained in our bed for all the wrong ones: shame, exhaustion, the cowardly perversions of domestic security. I formulated theories. I shared them with her.

"Maybe this is all about your dad. Maybe it's one big Father Quest."

After all, Lauren and her father were kindred spirits, attentive caregivers, vaguely hypochondriacal neurotics. She was a daddy's girl, and his betrayal and abandonment had devastated her adolescent sense of security, weakened her faith, abstracted her inherited biological paranoia into a generalized terror, hadn't it? Hadn't his leaving set her on a lifelong quest for a reasonable facsimile of the man who might make the hurt go away? Hadn't the death of her mother a decade later detonated a thermonuclear bomb, obliterating what remained in her of hope?

"When my mom died," she said, "I was pretty sure God didn't want me to be happy. I became a different person."

Maybe what happened was, Lauren's abandonment by her father transformed her into a strong woman, master of control, feeler of no feelings. Lauren is an alpha, and for better and worse, so am I, which was not ideal. You can't both be in charge. We were two betta fish in the same tank, fighting for the alpha role. Chad, however, was "helpful," though she ended up doing his dishes, too.

"I hated you. I resented you," she said. "I needed help with the girls, with the house. With pickups and drop-offs. You were always too busy."

"I've had two jobs since we got married. One that pays the bills and another one that pays the other bills. There was a time when I was a ghost in our house, I know that, you know that, but somebody had to pay for the house. Plus, I helped. A lot. Maybe you had to convince yourself I wasn't helping, just to make leaving easier."

Lauren isn't bossy, but she is a great boss. She carries within her a vision of how things should be and go, especially with our children, or any children—and she's usually right—which is why, over the years, so many parents have paid her money to realize this vision as a babysitter, nanny, nursery coordinator, teacher, school administrator. I think Lauren must have resented, privately, the fact that the birth of children requires a whole other person to be involved and contribute genetic material to the proto-humans, such that their two visions (of how things should be and go with the tiny humans) be unified. It struck me, there in the bed during her recovery, as she unpacked the pros of Chad and the cons of me, that she did not so much want a husband as an employee—and that I had been, in her eyes, a bad hire.

Back on the cul-de-sac, before his downward spiral of poor life choices, Chad's property had always been well-kept. He checked on elderly neighbors. He treated my daughters like his own. He treated my wife like his own, too. A great guy.

A life with Chad would give her a compliant partner who let her run the show.

"He worships me," she said.

"Just like your dad did."

"He thinks I'm perfect."

"I believe he may be incorrect on this point."

Maybe this was no father quest. Maybe it was just another love story, *Titanic II: Jack Is a Merman.* Maybe she truly believed she was Kate Winslet and Chad was Leo and I was Billy Zane, the cruel villain.

"When they moved away a few years ago, it was like something from a movie," she said. "I cried for days. I sat in the truck and cried. I'd lost my best friend."

He was her best friend. It couldn't be denied. He shouldn't have been, shouldn't have been allowed to be, it should never have come to this, but it had, and they were. They had so much in common: they'd both lost parents, both felt bereft of happiness and hope for so long, both wanted simpler lives than the ones they'd ended up with. When he came roaring back into our lives in 2017, it was every romantic story all in one, if Lauren could only jump off the back of the boat. But this theory, too, would not suffice. Last I checked, your soulmate doesn't compel you to abandon your family and burn down a beautiful, if imperfect, life. Their story had plenteous romantic twists and turns, sure, but Chad was no Jack, Lauren no Rose. And me, well, I can be an assface, but I was no Billy Zane. I felt more like the floating door.

A week after her surgery, I went back to sleeping on my office floor, unrolling my body onto a squalid futon mattress to stare into the endless abyss and feel such terrific pain that it made me understand the Psalms and the music of Adele in a whole new way. Imagining your wife in the embrace of another man—and knowing this image was very real and had happened in your own home, in your bed, in your car—is enough to send you down the chute of hell.

I lay there in the dark and heaved and moaned, my body

buckling with pain. I imagined her running to him, being held by him. I have never felt pain so bottomless.

"Everything is so dark," Lauren said, as I set a small cube of lasagna on her lap.

"Yeah." I looked at the pills on her nightstand.

"I'm too chicken," she said.

"We could both die. Murder-suicide. We could be on *Dateline*."

"If I die, he'll kill himself, too."

"No, it's okay, I'll murder him first. *Dateline* will love that."

"Murder-murder-suicide," she said, snotty, laughing a little. When you get to the end of hope, comedy is all you have left.

Three days before Christmas, I felt a highly specific pain in my abdomen and discovered the next day that my gallbladder was trying to murder me and had to be removed.

"I'm like Job," I said to her one night. "God is taking everything I have, even my organs."

"I'm going to end it with him," Lauren said to me, the same day I learned about my need for gallbladder surgery. "I'll go over there and end it."

"Cool. Whatever."

The doctor said she was okay to drive now. It had been two weeks. I went in for another diagnostic scan, and she hobbled out of bed and over to his house to end it forever.

"I did it," she said, that night. "It's over."

"You said that last time, too."

When I suggested she get a new phone number and new email address and cut avenues for communication with Chad, she lost her shit, really lost it, angry as a cat in a closed box. A blind man could see she hadn't ended it. Christmas hovered like a happy ghost looking for some other family.

"You haven't really ended it."

"I can't. I don't know how."

Christmas night I slept alone on my office floor, and when I woke up on December 26, I stopped waiting for her to make up her unmakeable mind.

"If you really want to be with him, nobody's stopping you but you."

"I don't want to leave the girls."

"You've already left them. All you have to do now is pack your things."

I pulled her suitcase out of the closet and set it on the bed. "Go talk to him. Start your life together. Because you can't have a boyfriend and a husband. We're not European. There are rules."

We could split custody fifty-fifty if she and Chad legalized their attachment pathologies with a marriage certificate. I would not fight her in court for anything, I explained. I had let go of my thirst for justice. God could handle that on his own cosmic schedule.

"Go see him tonight. You should find out where all his skeletons are buried before you pack your own skeletons and carry them over there."

"He's about to be evicted by the sheriff."

"That's always a good sign. You two could always live in a box. We'll be here, in our prison of a house, with all this hateful indoor plumbing."

Chapter 26

THE GALL

2020

The next morning, something happened. That's the madness of all this: somethings kept happening. The somethings couldn't be stopped. The warring powers inside Lauren would, any minute, rend all her body's atoms into a trillion exploding nanoparticles, which I was anxious to see. The detonation was imminent. It might be the thing that saved her from hell. You could see it all happening inside her, the cosmic fight: She loved this other man, but could not make herself leave us for him, even though I now stood in the doorway with her suitcase and a loaf of banana bread to wish her well. I'd vowed to love and honor this woman in times of plenty and want, and here was the want you hear so much about. My stubbornness, which had made my wife hate me for so many good reasons over the years, had finally found its moment. I would not force her out the door. I wanted her to feel the full weight of her abandonment of her daughters, who still had no idea of the hellish pit that had opened under our home.

The something that happened, two days after Christmas, was this: she texted me to come into our bedroom, where she slept. I sat on the couch writing, while Gary snored at my feet. It was still dark out, a time of morning when I was typically the only one awake.

"Can you come in here?" she texted.

I went into the bedroom.

"I can't do it," she said.

"Do what?"

"Be with him. I can't."

She looked terrible, dying, like an alcoholic with the DTs: a woman made of glass with great cracks widening across her body and face.

"I wrote him an email. I can't send it. I can't hit the button." She handed her laptop to me, barely able to hold it up. "Can you hit the button?"

I took the laptop. I hit the button. She grabbed the machine and slammed it shut and threw it across the bed as if evil spirits might crawl right out and pull us both in. But I wasn't convinced. Addicts quit all the time and still shoot up.

I left the bedroom and wrote a text I'd been waiting six weeks to send. It was time to tell my friends—again. I'd told them in 2017, and here I was with new news, which was old news. I fully expected them to tell me I was a fool. And I was.

Jimbo and Jason and Soren came into the backyard one by one that night, in silence. Jimbo and Jason knew about 2017, and now they heard about the exciting sequel. Soren heard the tale for the first time. I told them everything, and they sat there as the flames of the fire burned long into the night.

"I'm so sorry, man," Soren said.

As a pastor of a small church where everybody was so obviously broken—doubters, disbelievers, desperadoes, the perpetually displaced, each family limping into our community with wounds—Soren knew too well of crushing sorrow. My story did not shock him. He is young, with all the brio of a hooligan, but listened with the curiosity and empathy of a wizened old veteran of the wars of being, expressing grief and understanding far beyond his years. Unlike Hairshirt, Soren did not propose genial threats of banishment to get my wife back into the fetters of good behavior and docile submission. He did, however, explain that I had every right to cut Lauren loose, should I desire to.

"Jesus says you can," he said. "Adultery and all. I hate to say it."

"I know," I said.

"But there may be another way."

"A harder way."

"Yes."

He didn't know what that way was, he admitted. Neither did I.

Jason and Jimbo could scarcely believe this had happened all over again.

"You guys seemed so much better," Jason said.

"I'm stunned," Jimbo said. "I'm just stunned."

We talked for a good two hours about everything: the sad state of matrimony today, their marriages, mine. Jason asked me not to shoot myself.

"I'm not sure it's me I want to shoot."

"Don't bang your secretary," Soren said.

"I don't have a secretary."

"Good."

Long into that long midwinter's night, which filled up my heart and reminded me there were still people in the world who loved me, the fire burned to embers, and Soren stood to leave and said

something that would've freaked me out a few years before, but
not then.

"I love you."

That's what he said.

Not "You're a fool."

Not "Fuck this bitch."

I love you.

Most men don't say this, unless they're drunk. His words spread
their wings across my backyard, over the fire, a cosmic envelopment
against death and destruction. I felt it. It felt as if God himself had
laid in my hands a coat of mail. *Here, wear this. This is love.*

Soren threw himself to the earth and put his head on the gravel
of my backyard and prayed like a man in the Bible. I cried so much
as he prayed that I felt my body would burst. He prayed for revelation, apocalypse, miracles. This was no Calvinist prayer of highborn
abstraction. This prayer named names. As he prayed, Jason reached
over and put his great big bear paw on my knee. Jimbo cried almost
more than I did. All three men prayed and then left, and I sat there
in the dark alone, the light of the dying embers of the fire refracted
by the prisms of my tears. I was so sad I listened to Bob Dylan, which
always makes me sad, because the man just cannot sing, but his songs
can tear open a heart and let it bleed good blood. I cried some more.
I sat there in my lawn chair in the dark and wondered if Lauren was
awake in the room that had once been ours. I reached my hand toward the embers, to feel them. Could she? Where God was sending
the both of us, I could not say.

The days blur. Word was out. Our friends knew everything now.
They texted daily with encouragement, offers of food, invitations
for driveway beers to steady my sanity and help with the girls and
empty the recycle bin of my heart. Nobody called Lauren, as far as

I could tell. She had nobody but Chad and she'd just cut him loose, theoretically.

A few weeks before, I'd called Lauren's cousin Julie—they had once been close as sisters—and told her, you know, Lauren could probably use someone to talk to about all this besides just me. Julie's father, a pastor, had officiated at our wedding. Julie knew our story.

Julie came and stayed with us for a few days. I hoped the presence of family would wake Lauren from her zombie stupor. I think it helped, a little. Julie's a sweet woman, funny and kind. They had coffee. They sat on the porch. Lauren talked. Julie listened.

"How's she doing?" I asked Julie, when Lauren was in the shower.

"Not good. She's not herself. It scares me."

"I don't know who she is."

"Neither does she."

Next I called Julie's brother, Stephen, who'd gone through something similar a decade before, and his words comforted me.

"I would kick her out," he said, of Lauren, his cousin. "That may be what it takes."

He'd kicked out his wife, and they'd stayed separated for a year before reconciliation. They now had three children and what looked like a healed marriage.

"She'll just go right to this guy," I said.

"I get it. Everybody's going to tell you what to do. Only you can know."

Stephen hooked me up with his mother-in-law, Deb, who had also gone through something similar many years ago. Deb was a marriage whisperer. She didn't give me answers so much as ask questions.

Did I want to save the marriage?

Had I considered an in-home separation?

How was I taking care of myself in all of this?

Good questions. I didn't know the answers.

One afternoon I drove to my mom's apartment. It was time to tell her, too. I sat her down and narrated the whole horrible epic poem of the last three years. Mom was floored.

"I don't want you telling all your friends," I said. "Only a few people know."

"Of course."

She texted me daily for updates, naturally. We were her only family for a thousand miles. Our fate would be hers, too.

"You haven't said anything to anyone, have you?" I asked.

"I haven't told a soul. Except Vicki. And Sandra. And your brother."

"Mom."

She was as busted up now as the rest of us, Lauren most of all. My wife was not well. We sat in my office, her and Julie and me, on New Year's Day.

"You have to block his number," I said. "He's still out there."

"I can't," Lauren said. "I tried. My phone won't let me."

"That's not true."

He was still a ghost in the house of her heart. Julie left, and then it was just us again, Lauren and me and the ghost and the not knowing.

The next day, Soren called. "You think Lauren would mind if I reached out?"

"Go for it," I said.

Over the next few weeks, he and Lauren met privately. Soren

did not reveal much about their conversations: he was in counselor mode. I did not pry. I did ask him, after their third or fourth meeting, how their talks were going.

"Anything I should know about?" I said.

"I asked her what it was like to be married to you."

"Oh no."

"Yeah."

"Not great, is my guess."

"Yeah, no."

A week later, and it was now my turn to have an organ removed. I allowed Lauren to drive me to the hospital but didn't want her coming in. Lauren dropped me off at the intake before dawn, as I had for her a month before, and drove away.

Back in pre-op, a nice lady with a mouthful of gum laid me down flat and wordlessly shaved me from my nipples down to the top of the pubic triangle. She trimmed with great tenderness: the closest thing to physical affection I'd received from a woman in more than a year.

"Who you got in the lobby? We need a phone number," she said.

They were going to put me under for a few hours, and when they put you under, you have to have somebody in the lobby, in case you never wake up.

"I don't have anybody here. My mom might come later."

"Who brought you here?"

"The woman who brought me here is gone."

The lady continued to shave me and I wept the saddest, most silent tears that have ever crawled out of my face, in there under the whitest lights, about to go into the dark, utterly alone. The lowest low keeps getting lower.

"You got somebody here," the lady said, minutes later. "Says she's your wife."

Lauren came into the pre-op room. She'd come back.

"I'm a terrible wife, but I can be an okay friend." She tried to smile.

God, it was like a Noah Baumbach movie.

"Thanks, I guess."

She moved out a week later.

Chapter 27

THE WOMAN WHO
BROUGHT ME
HERE IS GONE

2021

The day before she moved out, we told the girls. We'd kept this nightmare hidden from them, as best we could, for two months. If you'd have told me, on some happier day in the distant past, that I would learn of my wife's love for, and desire to marry, another man, and that she would live in my home for two months, all the while furtively communicating with this man daily, I would have believed you insane. You yourself would never allow it, you say. But when catastrophe comes calling, you don't know what in the hell you'd do. Because hell is what it is, and hell runs by different laws. Down is up and up has flown to regions unseen.

Rage is the natural response, but not perhaps the supernatural, which is what you need in hell, I was learning: patience, for example, and kindness, and self-control, though these fruits come hard even when life is good. They come hardest of all in hell, and hell is what it felt like to sit down with the girls and tell them their mother was moving out.

"You ready?" I said to Lauren, that Sunday night, my sutures still fresh. She would be moving out the next day.

"I guess."

We called the girls into the living room.

Lauren's new apartment, a one-room carriage house, was three streets over. She had been incommunicado with Chad, she claimed, ever since the sending of that email two days after Christmas. We agreed to give this plan a month, not quite forty days and nights but close: a wilderness, time for God to work some kind of desert magic on both of us as he did for the Israelites. She felt she needed to go away into a cave and "work things out." I did not resist. She was no prisoner. She'd get the girls every other weekend and two nights a week for dinner. She'd see them after school and leave before I got home, a ghost in her own house.

The girls gathered, sadness already in their eyes.

These precious girls. Good kids. Terrific with children. They play together. They do their homework. They hot glue things to other things. They cook. They draw. They read. They win championship trophies and sportsmanship awards. They feed the dog and empty the dishwasher and the garbage. They're funny. They're smart. They make uncouth jokes using words like *adjacent* and *malodorous*. They're sweet. They love sleepovers and long baths and the pool and the beach and broccoli and milkshakes and brownies. They ask for brussels sprouts and eat them all. They beg to stick their heads out of the sunroof and to ride in the back of the truck, and against their mother's wishes I let them do it. They are endless sources of divine light. Lauren and I had gotten so much wrong in this life, but when you look at these three girls—their unfettered joy, quiet diligence, strong friendships, spirited play on courts and fields— we'd clearly gotten some of the most important things right. When we called them into the living room to tell them that Lauren was leaving the next day, it was nothing short of a nightmare.

Coco, the quiet, conscientious child who possesses the most assiduous insight, threw a plate and spoon at the wall and screamed.

Pippi, the wildly expressive child who loves to give gifts and make breakfast for her sisters, stood up and told Lauren she was not allowed to move out and then ran to her room and climbed under her bed, where she wept for an hour.

Ginsburg, the baby, ran upstairs and surrounded herself with every stuffed animal and asked to be alone.

If Lauren truly was the author of this moment, the agent of action, then I wanted her to see the fullness of what she'd done to these children, her stripping away of their most essential instantiations of cosmic and material stability. What can drive a parent, a mother, a heroic mother, even, for so many years, the one who dragged us to church all those Sundays when none but her wanted to go, the Good Cop of this marriage, to leave her children in the plain light of day, other than madness, sickness, an invisible terror others cannot see? I had plumbed the heights and depths of my crimes against her and came up with nothing that could merit the exposing of our children on the mountainside of existential dread.

"You're doing to them exactly what your father did to you," I said, later that night, her last night at home, the children holed up in their rooms.

"His life turned out okay," she said, deadpan.

"He hasn't spoken to his children in a decade. He doesn't even know his own grandchildren. Sounds like a great life."

"I know. I'm so evil."

"You're a monster."

She filled a cup with apple juice and retreated to our bedroom for what might be her last night in our house, forever. You don't imagine monsters loving apple juice, but some do. Maybe she wanted me to think her a monster, just so I'd let her go.

Chapter 28

THERE WAS A MAN IN THE LAND OF UZ

2021

There was a man in the land of Uz, whose name was H.; and there were born unto him three daughters. His substance also was three bicycles, one drum kit, many lawn chairs, a thousand books, five of his dead father's guns, a cat named Joan Rivers, an African tortoise named Bootsie, and a chocolate Lab called Gary. H. had been blessed beyond measure with beloved friendships, a strong community, an enormous round head, low cholesterol, and many diversified investments whose rates of return he pretended to understand. And H. prayed for his children and sacrificed much to build up for them long and happy lives, even when he forgot to lock the bathroom door. Thus H. did continually.

And Satan said to the LORD, "He's happy because things have gone okay for him."

And the LORD said to Satan, "Maybe."

And Satan said to the LORD, "Watch this."

And Satan did take from H. his wife, and also his gallbladder.

And so H. stood alone with his three young daughters, who could not locate their school uniforms, and H. did weep and gnash. And H. did prepare school lunches, and his daughters opened their lunch boxes and gnashed in return, for H. had given them foodstuffs they found most repulsive.

"Father, you have put too much mayonnaise on it," they screamed.

"Father, I am forbidden by law to consume tomatoes," they cried.

"Mama is better at this," they wept.

H. desired greatly to explain to his children that their mother was the author of their pain, but he knew this was somehow against the rules, and so he did not slander the name of his wife, though he did explain that the home was under new management and many policies would be altered to reflect the values of the new regime.

"Mama cuts the crust off my sandwich!" they declared.

"I'm going to eat the crust off myself, how about that?" said H., biting into the bread.

And when H. folded the laundry, his eyes could not discern whose panties were whose, and, lo, many panties went into the wrong drawers, and his daughters did moan with horror at the incorrect panties, and H. did rage.

It came to pass that H. became the kind of man who drank boxed wine out of Solo cups and lost track of everyone's underwear.

"If you're old enough to read Latin," said H., "you're old enough to fold your own shit-covered panties!"

"May we utter curses, too?" they implored.

"Hell, why not."

And, lo, the children uttered such foul curses into the air, crying and laughing, that his home seemed full of crazed peoples. And in that day was much weeping and laughing and cursing and hair that did not look right.

"Mama does our hair in the mornings," they said.

"Where is Mama?" they said.

"You have no hair, and you do not know its ways," they said.

"It's not fair!" they said, endlessly, day and night.

"Life is not fair," said H. "Some people have no chin, while others have two or even three chins. This is the word of the LORD."

In those days, the LORD allowed Satan to reveal to H. the depths of his own monstrous failures as a father and his own shame that for so long his wife had done the hair and the school lunches and the laundry, and that this, too, might be why she was now in a desolate desert cavern three streets over. H. was exceedingly vexed when, at the chiropractor, he found himself indicating "Marital Status: Separated."

H. opened his mouth and cursed the day and said, "What hath my vertebrae to do with my marital status? Wherefore shall the bonesetter careth for the location of my wife?" H. cursed the day of his birth and drank White Claw in the driveway in the rain.

The LORD sent H. to a therapist, J.

And J. asked H., "How do you feel?"

And H. said he felt sad about his dead marriage and grateful for his church and his many friends who loved him and he felt exhilarated about the adventure of single parenting and the possibility of dating beautiful women one day very soon, for he received frequent messages from any number of hot single moms who just loved his books and didn't seem like they would leave him for a man who can't even grow a beard, and J. said, "You sound angry."

And H. did say, "I am very angry."

And J. inquired, "Where in your body do you feel it?"

And H. said, "I feel it in my mouth. In my jaw. In my face. In my words."

In the dark of darkest night, when his children were at church youth-group activities, H. did drive his truck far to the home of the beardless man, who did attempt to steal his wife, to see if his wife's car was there, and, lo, it was not.

But he felt, you know, it was possible.

H. felt his rage might be channeled to increase the suffering of the villain, but he did not. He did not consider pouring gasoline on the villain's run-down truck and setting it afire. He did not consider spray-painting COUNTRY RAP SUCKS on the villain's garage door. He did not fantasize about releasing asps into the villain's home through a cracked window, nor did he hire him, through a false name, to perform some odd job at a random address where he could be slain by hired goons, nor did H. even consider placing a case of cold beer on his doorstep after infecting the cans with COVID-19, nor, for example, posting about this man on the neighborhood Facebook page as having exposed himself to children at the park near their home, nor did H. watch and rewatch the scene in *Casino* where Mafia thugs pound Joe Pesci's character with steel pipes and aluminum bats and drag him into a rectangular hole in a cornfield and pitch dry silt onto his dying face with shovels, no, H. did not imagine doing that to Chad, not at all, not even a little, though H. did give Chad's name and number to telemarketers selling funeral insurance, but H. did not do all those other things, for vengeance belongs to the LORD and also to the sheriff, who would soon be evicting the beardless man from his home.

And H. did find this demonic rage coursing through his body with terrific speed and so H. drove home and raged against his daughters for disposing of sanitary napkins in the nonapproved way and for failing to locate and dispose of the animal waste in the yard, as requested, and for refusing to consume even half of the school lunch H. had prepared with diligence and at great expense, and H. did erupt again as the children did scream and weep and moan and slam many doors, and H. did feel shame at his erupting, seeing that for so long he'd derived so much strength from all that had been removed from his life, emboldened to act courageously only because his wife had made it possible until she could no longer make it possible.

And, lo, H. did weep.

Then H. arose and bought another carton of cigarettes to assuage his pain and sat in the driveway in the cold of a winter's night and prayed for the ending of the rage and the rising of the sun. In all this, H. ate hardly any victuals, but did not charge God foolishly.

"Let the day perish wherein I said, 'Will you marry me?'" said H.

For H. did regard the day of his marriage as a hateful day. "Why is light given to a man whose way is hid, and whom God hath hedged in? For my sighing cometh before I eat, and my roarings are poured out like the waters. For the thing which I greatly feared is come upon me, and that which I was afraid of is come unto me. I was not in safety, neither had I rest, neither was I quiet; yet trouble came."

Now when H.'s friends heard of all this evil that was come upon him, they called to him each from their own places, and they wept, and mourned, and did try to lift his spirits and give him many grievous counsels.

"Unforgivable," they said.

"If she wants to be with this loser, let her."

"She doesn't love you anymore."

"She may never have loved you."

"Cut her off."

"It's over."

"Date not a stripper."

"Hurt not thyself with pills or guns."

"People will think you're nuts, no matter what you decide."

"God will work on you in this wilderness."

"Want to go to his house and kick his ass?" said Sam. "I'll help."

"Want me to come down?" said Mark. "I shall bring my guitar."

"Pray without ceasing," said Soren.

And, lo, H. did google without ceasing.

"How to win back your ex."

"How to reconcile after an affair."

"How to plan a romantic encounter with someone who wants you dead."

H. watched many YouTube videos about how to make a woman want you and these videos turned him crazy, suggesting he post sexy, cool images of himself online to encourage a healthy lust and envy in his wife, though he could not imagine she would be getting hot and bothered by a shirtless man with visible sutures. And the voice of the LORD thundereth marvelously from the whirlwind and said, "Stop googling."

And H. hated the thing he saw in the mirror, for he was broken and hideous. He had many regrets about the past. He wanted to change. He wanted to be a new man. Naked he came from his mother's womb, and naked shall he return thither: the LORD gives, and the LORD hath taken away, and sometimes the LORD wants you not to be naked in the house, not with children old enough to be horrified by it; blessed be the name of the LORD.

And his daughters asked, "When is Mama coming home?"

And H. said, "I don't know."

And H. did pray with his children at night.

And, lo, many nights, H. drove past the tumbledown cavern where his wife did lie in the dark. From the outside, as he drove by casually, not at all like a weirdo, the place looked like garage apartments he'd rented in his twenties, the sort of sagging hovel where you might see a rat smoking a bowl on the roof. What was she doing in there? Two nights a week, she was in a real estate class. Two other nights, she had the girls. The other three nights a week, God presumably worked on her. H. hoped it was God. It might be the Beardless Devil, who could be creeping into her apartment in the witching hour, a little gremlin in flip-flops.

And H. asketh the LORD, "If I see his heap parked on the street, what should I do, after slicing his tires with the knife I keep in my truck?"

And the LORD saith, "You have another devil to fight."

For Job did battle with the tragedy of senseless suffering and friends who give bad and occasionally good advice, and Jesus did battle with Satan, and Elijah did battle with the prophets of Baal, and David did battle with Goliath, and in these sad days of desolation and single parenthood, H. did battle with the devil in his living room, and its name was GARY.

Chapter 29

SINNERS IN THE HANDS
OF AN ANGRY DOG

2021

The beast ate everything in the house: razors, soap, loofahs, jewelry, aspirin, syringes, bones, cloth napkins, Band-Aids, sticks of butter, a beloved pencil sharpener, dining room chairs, scrap lumber, the doors, the baseboards, tea sets, crown molding, Apple products. If it wasn't nailed to the wall, he ate it, and if it was, he ate the wall. I watched him lap up a puddle of dishwashing detergent and turn to me and ask for more. He slept in a crate filled with blankets, which he shredded into strips and consumed like beef jerky.

I soon became a connoisseur of "indestructible" dog beds and would wake to find that Gary had upcycled his indestructible bed into a wearable poncho. I soon launched my training plan, which consisted of buying training books and allowing Gary to eat these books.

He was not yet a year old and we'd been lied to about what he was. He was no dog. He was now a small omnivorous horse. I was the only human in the house large enough to walk him. The demons of my marriage gave way to the demons inside Gary: prong collars, praise, pats, prayers, nothing worked. I got him fixed, hoping this would ease his passion for playful violence, but fixing him did not fix him. Feedback from dog-sitters read more like police reports:

"Fears nothing."

"Unresponsive to commands."

"Vigorous nonstop humping."

At home, with only one adult in the house, we could do little to control him.

"Gary, no!" I said continually.

"Gary's got my pillow!" Pippi said.

"Gary's in the bathtub!" Ginsburg said. "He's licking shampoo off my face! I can't see!"

Looking back, I think maybe it was God who possessed Gary. To give us all something to do together. To invite us to scream at the ceiling.

"Gary's eating the cat food!"

"He's eating the cat litter!"

"He's eating the chair!"

"He's eating the chair?"

Then, later: "He's throwing up the chair!"

"Yeah! Good boy!"

I cried and screamed at the girls for unfinished chores, who cried and screamed at me for an incomplete marriage, who cried and screamed at Gary for eating a Bible, because Satan was his master now. "It's fine," I said to the girls, trying to keep Gary from eating the couch. "Your mom hates this couch."

"What a big puppy!" everybody said on our walks, as Gary threw himself on the ground, prostrate, wagging his tail, hoping to taste their pants.

"He's a therapy dog," I said. "His owner requires it."

·   ·   ·

Lauren came to the house almost every day, crept in like a burglar while I was still at work. I found signs and evidence everywhere.

A load of towels neatly folded.

A toilet purple with Fabuloso.

A kitchen floor mopped and still wet.

School lunches, packed and stacked in the fridge for the morrow.

Was all this cleaning some perverse apology? Swiffering has always been her love language. She speaks in the poetry of shining surfaces, writes in the prose of warm bedsheets. I appreciated the help, God knows I did, but also wanted her to leave or come home. None of this halfway business. Go clean your own foul carriage house. This home was my project now. It would take a miracle to make it hers again. God would have to wave that big wand of his. One of us would have to get hit by a bus and almost die and wake up from a coma months later for this thing to turn around.

Sometimes, when I came home from work, I saw other signs, less comforting clues to what Lauren was thinking and feeling.

A small wall mirror disappeared.

A favorite pillow, a blanket, missing.

A colander, a serving spoon, vanished.

What need had she of a serving spoon? Was she throwing dinner parties over there? For whom? The rats? I couldn't think about it.

One night soon after, the girls and I prepared to go to dinner at Jimbo's with his family and a few other friends. If this sort of nightmare ever assaults your family, you're going to need friends who nurse you back to health with mac and cheese.

The weather that evening was wet and foul. I instructed Ginsburg to take Gary out into the backyard to relieve himself, but Gary got away and would not come back in.

"Somebody please come help me get Gary!" she screamed, on the verge of tears.

"I'm coming!" I ran outside into the rain to help.

We were maxed out, emotionally, spiritually. The girls' grades had begun to plummet; their teachers, noticing changes in behavior, meanness or malaise, sent regular emails to this effect. My own work had begun to falter and spit, my brain an engine with water in the tank.

I ran onto the side porch and into the backyard, eager to murder the dog who had made everything that much harder in the hardest season of our lives. Gary frolicked in the rain with exquisite, demonic joy. We could not catch him. He ran through shrubberies, leaped over the firepit, over Ginsburg. I threw myself into the gravel and mud and weeds and straw to catch him, over and over, but could not. Soon, Coco and Pippi were in the yard, too, all of us befouled and sodden and barking at one another and Gary. Ginsburg looked into the sky, and I don't know if you have ever seen a fourth grader scream at God, but I have. God screamed back with lightning and thunder and more rain, which frightened Gary back into the house.

In the truck, on the way to Jimbo's for dinner, we sat in silence, wet and angry.

"I have so much anger," I said.

"Me, too," Ginsburg said.

"Me, too," Pippi said.

"Do you guys want to scream some more?" I said.

"Yeah," Ginsburg said.

"Let me introduce you to Rage Against the Machine," I said. I rolled down the windows and we stuck our arms into sheets of rain and laughed and cried.

•   •   •

We had a good meal at Jimbo's. Others were there. My mom was there. We laughed and told stories and it seemed like everybody knew my wife was gone forever, but nobody said anything. Even people who didn't know, knew.

"How are you?" people said, looking into my eyes with the pathos of Oprah. Not "How are you these days?"; not "How are things?"; but "How are you?"

"Oh, you know," I said. "Staying alive."

"Yeah," they said.

"Nobody's dead, yet," I said.

And they laughed, and I laughed, and the girls and I said our goodbyes and got in the truck, full of love and carbs. The rain had passed. I played quieter music on the ride home and the girls were silent, and I was silent. It felt like we might just pull through this. Part of me expected to pull into the driveway and find Lauren's car. She'd be there, finally, maybe, frightened back into the house by the lightning and thunder of her own choices. She was ready to do the hard work of rebuilding our marriage. She couldn't stand the alone-ness of the sad little carriage house, the deprivation of the love of her family.

"When is Mama coming home?" Ginsburg asked.

"Soon," I said.

I can't say why I believed it, but I believed it.

When we arrived, there was no car. But I did not let go of my hope just yet, not until I walked into the bedroom. The photos from our walls were missing, all except those with me in the picture. She'd come in and taken them all.

Chapter 30

LOVE AT THE LONE WOLF LOUNGE

2021

That night, I took off my wedding ring and dropped it in the little pewter cup on the chest of drawers in my office, a creaking tower of furniture passed down from my mom's mom, whose first husband—my grandfather, Harry—cheated on her back in Mississippi a hundred lifetimes ago in Rolling Fork, Mississippi. Granny had taken my mom, who was six, and left town, moved up to Greenwood, where she got a job doing hair at Shirley's, joined the Greenwood Business and Professional Women's Association, bought herself a little house on Baird Street, and filled it with new furniture, including this tall chest.

A woman had to be made of pretty strong stuff to sue for divorce during the Truman administration, back when single moms were as rare and shunned as lepers. Mom says Granny hadn't blinked an eye when word of Harry's infidelity got out, putting seventy miles of alluvial farmland between her and him. She never looked back. Looking back was all I could do. But now it was time to pull a page from Granny's playbook and look ahead. The ring sat in its shallow cup now, where it sank out of memory.

My left hand was lighter now. It felt odd for a day or two, and then all it felt was naked and free, just like the rest of me. I studied my naked self in the bathroom mirror and found my abdomen's four surgical scars, little fleshy slots sized for a dime, were healing up just fine. Who would be the next woman to see them, touch them, lick them? I very much wished to be licked by some animal other than a quadruped.

Yet, even as God dismantled my ego one proud truss at a time, two or three new beams of confidence were added whenever I received supportive, suggestive DMs from some new woman. Many in our community had learned of our separation, including compassionate single women across the city, who were, you know, just checking in on me.

"We should catch up," they texted.

"Let's grab a drink!" they messaged.

"How are you these days?" they asked.

"We haven't spoken in forever!" they exclaimed.

"Here's a Bible verse that made me think of you," they whispered sensually.

Many of these financially independent women with great hair and marathon bodies pretended to know nothing of the separation, though they could hardly hide their zeal for drinks and deep conversation that might or might not end with a little light licking.

A good deal of the messages were from women who'd been cheated on, and I learned that the experience of infidelity inducts you into a secret club of others like yourself, likewise betrayed, who emerge like mushrooms after a summer rain to tell you of their anger and their loneliness and their healing yoga practice, which has made their bodies stretchy. Some of these women were still healing and some were healed and most were probably very stretchy.

"You need a good lay," said a cougar at the Lone Wolf Lounge, which I'd begun wandering to on nights when Lauren had the girls. I'd spilled my story, and she, I believe, felt these words would encourage me to stop wallowing in the sorrow of it all.

"Maybe," I said.

"It will do so much for your energy," the cougar said.

None of my church friends suggested a good lay with a stranger, or even a satisfactory lay with a family friend. I didn't want to have sex with anyone in particular. I wanted to have sex with everyone. I was lonely and hungry and needy and unclear about the wisdom of throwing myself in the sack with some new woman, even ones with interesting birthmarks worthy of close study. I had no illusions about the wisdom of sex outside the bounds of love-ratifying covenants, but it might, as the cougar said, do wonders for my energy.

If this sounds like a bad idea to you, please consider that I was not in the clearest of mental states. Entertaining the possibility of new love gave me hope. The sky felt brighter, possibilities swarmed around me like bluebirds of a new happiness.

At the grocery store, I flirted with the lady slicing the deli meat. At the liquor store, I flirted with the lady handing out masks. On the sidewalk, I flirted with the lady walking her wiener dog. I tried not to get weird. Sometimes I just smiled. Smiling was a revelation. Every woman smiled back. I played a game with myself called Could I Marry Her? Could I marry the lady selling hemp anklets in the park? The nurse practitioner who gently fondled my abdomen? The handsome lady in the Tremfya advertisement with moderate to severe plaque psoriasis? Yes, please! When you're on the rebound, everyone's sexy as hell.

On weekends, I drove to the various parks of our city to blast music from the truck and throw the ball with Gary. By some divine blessing, he suddenly began obeying my commands, retrieving and sitting and staying and retrieving again with surprising reliability. Others stared admiringly as my enormous puppy, bigger than most adult dogs by then, performed how all men wish their dogs to perform. The ball was the trick. A ball could control Gary's mind. All else fell away. His breeding was superb in this respect. Remove the ball from the equation and he was once again a dragon of chaos. The ball turned him to obedient putty. Women loved this dog.

"How handsome!" they said, walking over. "So well-behaved!"

"Thank you," I said, studying their ring fingers.

"Is he friendly?" they asked, walking closer with their own friendly dogs.

"So friendly." Would they consider petting me, too?

We would get to talking and talking and before long we'd be walking together and pretty soon we'd be finding out what friends we had in common and how we'd once been to the same party and how funny it was to live in a small town and then they'd say something like "I think I saw your TED talk!"

And I'd say, "Fun!"

And they'd say, "The stuff you said about your wife was so sweet!"

And I'd say, "Funny story about that."

Then I'd tell them I was separated.

And they'd say, "Oh my gosh, I'm so sorry."

And then they'd reveal their own sad story, because every single woman over thirty walking a rescue dog has a sad story, and before long I'd be saying, "Oh my gosh, I'm so sorry."

And they'd say, "Would you like to see my tattoos?"

And I'd say, "I love body art."

And none of this happened, quite like that. But I did meet

plenty of women who seemed capable of nursing me back to emotional health after a series of jointly therapeutic showers. Was my soulmate somewhere out there, in this tiny seaside town, waiting for me to not ask about her tattoos?

I don't believe in the idea of soulmates, not because I am unromantic, but because I am unstupid. Lauren, in one of her many convalescent confessions, said Chad was very into their being soulmates, to such an extent that, according to him, they'd both lived many lives, incarnated and reincarnated, searching for each other across history until fate joined their property lines and slowly they awoke to the cosmic truth of their journeys toward each other across the universe. They were born in the same year, the same month. This particular detail served as Exhibit A in the case of their destiny. Who knew this cargo-shorted Hobbit possessed such devotion to romance?

"He's convinced we will be together," she once said. "Nothing can stop it."

"I could stop it by running over him in his driveway," I said.

Lauren spoke with condescension of Chad's poetic attachment to destiny. Clearly, he'd used this argument in a bid to compel her to end our marriage. According to him, she only stayed with me because she was fearful, weak, habituated to the idea of living in a house where the bills got paid. Couldn't she see that the universe wanted them to be together? That he was the other half of the friendship necklace she'd been carrying all her life, the left shoe to her right? He did his best to stoke the fires of romance in her heart, but the tinder was sodden. All the romance had been stamped out of her soul over the years. The only destiny she believed in was darkness, it seemed. And now she was gone, off in the dark of her garage apartment, and Chad might be over there right now, squirting all the lighter fluid he could find.

• • •

I don't believe in soulmates but I do believe in sneakers. Maybe the dog destroyed one of your Jordans. You can find another in that size. The world is full of Jordans. Used, and with minor defects, just like me. My new lover, who would she be? What if she was out there, somewhere, not quite a soulmate, but close?

She would have swimmer's arms and broad shoulders and be tall. Could be short. She'd love parties. We'd have much in common: both divorced with beautiful children to whom we gave just enough trauma to make funny. She'd probably run, but not marathons. She's not a monster. She wouldn't be a writer, God no. She'd have a more stable career, like painting or event planning. Could be one of those sexy farmers you hear about, raising bean sprouts. She might have a little land out from town, with a miniature donkey named Ellen. She would ask me to read my work aloud in bed, and she'd put her head in my lap and wrinkle her nose when something didn't sound right. She would laugh at the funny parts, after which we'd have lots of exploratory sex.

Maybe her husband cheated on her with some vacuous, barely legal Coachella succubus and she burned his collection of concert T-shirts in the yard. She refuses to listen to any of his favorite bands anymore because, like me, she's petty. She sends me favorite songs and makes playlists and wears a lot of jangly bracelets and overalls. She has a loom somewhere, a studio of some kind, featuring many candles and skulls. She wears my old oxfords while she makes whatever it is she makes. She's probably religious, but not a fanatic. She's got her own trauma, I don't know, maybe she was given up for adoption by an addict, which turned her not cold and hopeless but funny and hot. She'd be from somewhere exotic, like Sweden or Baltimore.

She prays with her children but can't stop talking about Mercury being in retrograde, and when I tell her she's nuts, we fight.

Good fighting. Loud and emotional, followed by lots of nudity that ends with laughter and a bike ride downtown to lie in the grass and do edibles and read Baudelaire. She's tempestuous and demanding and fears nothing, and when she does, she talks about it. She talks all the time. She never stops talking, not even during sex. Sometimes I wish she would stop. We're best friends, even though she probably doesn't exist. Probably.

"I think I'm going to start seeing other women," I said to my best friend, Mark, one day, over the phone, updating him on the magical adventure of my marital separation.

"Are you sure that's a good idea?"

"No. But I need some way to get Lauren off my mind."

"Have you tried alcoholism?"

There was one woman in particular, a cutie with the most endearing laugh. I'll call her Mary. I'd seen her at the bar after work on days when Lauren had the girls. We'd had a drink or two, talked, laughed, made butterfly-inducing eye contact. She didn't seem like the type to own a donkey or skulls, but she smelled like cookies and flowers and this was enough.

"She's cute," Mark said, when I sent him her profile photo. "Are you smitten?"

"I would be open to a smiting."

Mary and I knew each other from around town, art shows, cocktail things. I had zero evidence she felt about me the way I was open to feeling about her, but I'd made her laugh enough to know it was worth a shot. She had swimmer's arms. Maybe the shoe would fit. One night I called her up and we talked and laughed for two hours.

We made plans to meet up for a drink at a bar on a hotel roof when Lauren had the girls, and I was pretty sure I knew how the night would end. I even put a few condoms in my jacket like a teenage boy and could hardly believe I was doing it. The condoms were spares from the happier days of my marriage, when Lauren, wracked with migraines, stopped taking birth control. Now those condoms were coming with me to the bar. I felt both hope and shame. I know some of you reading this believe, like the cougar, that I needed a good lay. Others will be horrified that I would treat my heart like a plaything.

That night at the Peregrin, overlooking the spires and canopied squares of Savannah under a clear and cool winter sky, Mary and I talked for hours. I could already smell the fragrant cleanliness of her apartment in my imagination, the inviting softness of her bed-clothes, the thrill of seeing a new body naked, all the candles she would surely have arrayed in strategic locations. Did she know of Lauren's affair and her leaving? My guess was yes, though I hadn't come right out with it. Savannah's a small town and I knew she knew. She didn't seem like the kind of woman who goes looking to bed married men. I just came right out and told her everything.

"Oh my God," she said. "I am so sorry."

Nothing turns the ladies on like a man weeping at the bar. Mary got a frightened and pitying look in her eyes. I was a sad, lonely, broken husk. I saw the look and she saw me see the look and that was it. No candles. No bedclothes. No cookies. I might have thrown myself from the rooftop bar had I not felt it might further ruin Mary's night. We hugged goodbye and I drove home alone and sat in the driveway and felt like the world's largest piece of shit, that I would toy with another woman's heart to salve a hurt that could never be healed by anything but space and time.

Chapter 31

ASEXUAL HEALING

2021

"How'd it go?" Mark asked later.

"Not great," I said. "I'm still a virgin."

"That's probably good."

I invited Mark to come down and keep me from whoring myself out like a runaway. Mark and I spent the weekend cleaning toilets and sweeping up enough of Gary's hair to make three or four hearth rugs. We swiffered the floors and cleaned out the pantry and the fridge and made a fire in the backyard and he played me some new songs on his guitar and I read him a new story and we laughed about the absurdity of our marriages and the desolation that lurks around the corner of every life. This is what I needed. I needed love, but not from naked bodies. Women at parks did not want to lick me. They wanted only to pet Gary.

Another weekend when Lauren had the girls, Jimbo and Chip took me out to Tybee Island for a couple of days to cut loose. They found us a cheap condo and we ate baskets of fried shrimp and emptied bottles of bourbon and played darts in bars where you could smoke, because Tybee is where dreams go to die of tuberculosis. We ran into old friends and made new ones and boogied at Doc's to a band who played Skynyrd and Eddie Money like it was 1977 and danced with gravelly voiced grandmothers long into the night. I found myself on the subfreezing sidewalk with a tawny, sun-chafed local who bummed a light and looked me dead in the eye.

"You've got pain," he said.

"I do."

"Your wife has run off."

"She has."

"You're feeling about as low as a man can feel."

"I am."

"You're wanting to put the business end of a shotgun in your mouth."

"Not really."

"You're waiting to pull the trigger and let it all go dark."

"Nope."

He grabbed me by the coat and shook me violently. "Don't do it, brother!"

"I'm not."

"Don't give in to the darkness!"

"I don't plan to."

"Don't lie to me!"

He punched me in the gut and I punched him back and we wrestled for a bit and I couldn't stop laughing and then we stopped and smoked another cigarette and later Jimbo and Chip apologized for leaving me alone with the demented man. But it made me feel loved, that even this tormented soul had seen pain in me and wanted to help.

• • •

When I got back home the next day, the house felt empty of ghosts. I bought small dry-erase boards for the fridge door, where I wrote out meal plans for the week and chore assignments for the girls. I got myself an app to keep track of grocery lists. I revolutionized the production of school lunches and set aside time on Wednesdays and Saturdays for laundry. I bought opulent new laundry baskets. I pampered myself with luxurious, affordable new lotions. I purchased barrels of detergent, bar soap by the gross, enough paper towels to soak up the world's tears, but not mine. I stopped crying the day I saw those pictures missing from the walls. In their place, I hung hooks. Lauren always mocked my lust for hooks and hangers of every kind, and so I hung hooks in the dining room, hooks in the garage, hooks in my office, great rows of assorted hooks everywhere, for backpacks and raincoats and brooms and dog leashes. This was a House of Hooks now. Welcome.

I wanted to walk the Camino de Santiago. I wanted to ride my bike across the Yukon and fight off Kodiak bears. I wanted to buy a condo downtown, big enough for the girls and me, somewhere along the St. Patrick's Day Parade route. I stopped eyeballing area women and eyeballed Zillow instead. I got the number of a reliable, conscientious divorce attorney from an attorney friend and opened new bank accounts.

The girls and I started eating dinner together every night, even though this felt a wicked challenge with everything going on in our lives. But we did it. We sat there, and I felt so destroyed, shattered, and expended after twelve hours of unending emotional and literal labor, but there we sat, Coco to my right, her mother through and through. They look alike, beautiful introverts trapped in a family of outed freaks. Coco often looked at her sisters and me as if we'd escaped an institution. She'd begun threatening to go to college somewhere far away, where her sisters could not find her. She missed her mother terribly. They'd always been best friends.

There's Ginsburg, at the far end, the baby, chewing and praying for a hedge of protection against inclement weather, as liable to leap up from the dinner table and perform an improvised tap solo as disappear into her room to hide from storms. She's a born performer, as comfortable under a spotlight as under a reading lamp. Like her mother, she is a ballet dancer. Like her father, she believes the world wants to know everything about her.

Then there's Pippi, who calls me her "evil twin." Our resemblance is upsetting to her, which I get. I don't want to look like me, either. She is endlessly expressive, always crocheting, drawing, painting, cooking, crying, hissing, taping charcoal self-portraits to the bathroom walls, leaving ghostly handprints on the toilet like a crime scene dusted for evidence. Like her mother, she never met a baby who does not love her. Like both her parents, she has issues with authority, which is why she refused to close her eyes during our prayers before dinner. I'd catch her slowly disappearing a noodle while making direct eye contact with me, like a psychopath. If any of my children murder me, it will be her. If only one cries at my funeral, it will be her.

We missed Lauren at the table, missed her so much that Pippi took to sitting in Lauren's usual spot, to my left, so we wouldn't have to look at the empty chair. We laughed. We talked of our days. We cleaned our plates as best we could and cleared the table together. After dinner, we began watching movies again. I introduced them to *Raising Arizona* and *Seinfeld* and they introduced me to *Gilmore Girls*, and we even watched torturous episodes of manic children's shows where every episode is like the fever dream of a dying clown. It was nice. Ginsburg snuggled up next to me in the big chair and

Pippi lay on Gary and Coco kissed me on the head when she shuffled off to her room to write essays on *The Social Contract*. This
felt healthy. We were figuring it out. We were learning how to live
without Lauren.

In a final flourish of beautification, I turned to the kitchen, where
I now spent most of my waking hours. A wide, bare wall above the
breakfast nook shouted for attention. You see this wall as soon as
you enter the back door. It would be the wall Lauren saw every
afternoon when she came into the house to remove more photographs and pillows.

If Lauren could denude my walls of photographs, then I could
clothe them again in even more photographs. Thousands of 35 mm
Kodak moments lived in the storage boxes under our bed. I dug
them out one night after the girls were asleep, so that I could get
good and drunk first. I knew these bins held clues and barbs of
memory that would require anesthetic to behold.

I found photos of Lauren's mother (in a car, young, pretty, shy,
hair in rollers, looking away from the camera), my parents (Pop
laughing and clutching Mom, pretending to escape), photos of me
as a youngster (silly faces, nonstop) and Lauren, too (pensive, in a
Sunday dress, waiting to see *The Nutcracker*), me with friends in
college (wild, booted, full bluegrass), her with friends (leggy, pixie
cut), photos of our courtship (making coffee for her at our camp-
site, laughing on a hotel bed before a concert, hugging at a football game, fondling each other's faces with oven mitts). I found a
surprising number of photos of our kissing, in public, like a pair
of degenerate pervs. There was the photo on a fat little sofa, in a
one-bedroom apartment, the night we were engaged. I noted with
some sadness that every item in the photograph was now gone: the
painting, the couch, my wife.

The next day I strung up all these happy photos to fill that emptiness above the nook to remind the girls and me of all the joy our
family had seen and felt over the years, photographs of our life together: with children, daughters on beaches, daughters at carnivals,
daughters on rope swings, daughters holding sparklers and Pop-
sicles and little sisters, toothless grins, smocked onesies, first days
of preschool, endless leotards and first positions, babies just home
from the hospital. There were photographs of all five of us at parties, dinners, cookouts, in the backyard for Lauren's fortieth birthday party, mere weeks after the end of her first affair with Chad,
and all of us on book tour together, in cities across the nation, and a
photo from our honeymoon, Lauren sitting on the bed in the cutest
brindled sundress, ankles crossed, leaning back, glowing, smiling,
prettiest girl on the planet. And I found the curled image of a baby,
in black and white, a sonogram: the only photo anybody ever got.

One photo was even more poignant, from our wedding day, a
photo as astounding and bathed in heartbreak as any picture I've
ever owned. In many ways, this photo held the only real answer to
all the whys I'd been asking all this time. In the photo, my wife looks
like a being from a more perfect world, despite what had happened
in that same church a week before, despite all the hurt hidden in her
smile. This picture said everything. My wife would never think of
our wedding without thinking of death.

The events of that winter of 2003, to which I have only vaguely
hinted in this book, cast a dreadful pall over our entire marriage,
as well as a strange and beautiful light, when Lauren's reality detonated like a hydrogen bomb, burning shadows that have never
faded. Something changed in her that winter so long ago, a seed of
something that grew hateful. She fought it, suppressed it, pressed it
down, locked it up, but it grew big and ugly until it flew across the
countryside, burning homes and eating up all the livestock.

. . .

"It is a miracle that we married at all" is what I want to say whenever anybody asks to hear the story of our wedding, which they always do, when they see the photo. It is no ordinary wedding photo. They hold the picture in their hands and say, "Wow!" or "Is this real?" They can hardly believe it. Their eyes go wide and they smile and say, "Fun!"

Fun is when the Messiah shows up to your reception with a dozen kegs of hooch, as he does at the Wedding Feast of Cana in the book of John, his very first miracle. But Jesus brought no wine to our wedding. Only a fool would have described it as fun.

What the extraordinary photo truly depicts is a miracle, which is funny, because I don't believe in miracles, or I didn't, not until the day of my wedding. I always laughed a little at rods morphing into serpents, suns refusing to set, dead men rising up and just walking around at cocktail parties, scenes that outstrip the limits of the rational mind and rival anything in science fiction. Healing the blind and the sick, okay, I get that; who doesn't at least want to believe in the fairy tale of a sick child made well again through divine magic, but all this nonsense about water and wine. Surely the Savior of Humankind had more important tasks than getting everyone drunk at a reception.

I will tell you about our miracle, which crashed upon our lives like a thunderstorm that spread out over our lives and covered everything in astonishment and disbelief. It has taken me nearly twenty years to understand exactly what happened at that wedding. I will tell you the story.

Chapter 32

WHAT HAPPENED
BEFORE THE WEDDING

2002–3

Six months after our first date, on a Sunday afternoon just before Christmas, I called Lauren's mother, Trudy, and asked if I might come see her that night, and she knew why. Moms always know. The day was cool and clear and I drove up Highway 49 to Yazoo as the lowering sun splintered through naked trees. For three years, I'd been living in Illinois for grad school, trying to grow up a little and finish a terminal degree that would make me seem as smart and sexy as possible to English- or theater-department hiring committees. The bleak Delta landscape of Mississippi looked not unlike the dismal winter prairies of the Midwest, I thought, as dull and endless as the plays of Samuel Beckett or a good Calvinist sermon. Sometimes I could hardly tell the difference between the two.

Trudy opened the door, smiling. These past few months, this woman had been loving and gentle with me and laughed at my jokes and made me feel welcome in her home, but that day she seemed different, more than human. It is easy to beatify survivors of cancer. I thought of her marriage, the betrayal, the desertion, the disease. All of it shone through our every word like light through a hand on a bulb.

"Can I see the ring?" she said. I pulled it out of my pocket—two diamonds from her own deconstructed engagement ring, two of my grandmother's, and one purchased with an assist from Citibank. The ring felt heavy with enchantment.

"It's perfect," she said.

We stood, walked to the door, talked of marriage and the children her daughter and I might one day have. She asked if she could pray for us. She held my hands and prayed for both of her daughters and our imminent weddings and unknowable futures. The older sister, Shelby, had just gotten engaged to a med student named Hudson. Shelby and Hudson would marry first, in May. We would marry in June, at the First Presbyterian Church of Yazoo City, just up the street, the same church where Lauren had been baptized as a baby. It was a perfect fairy tale, all this wedded bliss, two weddings and two sisters on two different Saturdays in late spring.

"Tell me you will be a good man to her," Trudy said, taking my hand.

I didn't have the courage to tell her I didn't know what a good man was but felt certain I wasn't one, at least not yet. I was still a child. I sat in my dented Volvo wagon for a few minutes, studying the ring. Trudy waved from the stoop and gave me a thumbs-up. I smiled and drove away. It was the second day of winter. She would be dead by spring.

I got myself back to Jackson and proposed to Lauren that night, on the front porch. The ring didn't fit, so we shoved it on with brute force and kissed and showed everyone and said nothing about how the ring hadn't fit.

It seemed a miracle, this ring, the stories in its stones now wedded to my own story, and I thought about my future mother-in-law
and how ten years before, the medical community had given her
six months to live. What I know now is that when they say "six
months," they don't mean it. They mean "soon." They mean "now."
But a decade on, she was alive. For her to have made it this far, that
seemed a miracle, too, though I did not believe in miracles, not even
a little. I especially didn't believe in miracles when Lauren called me
one night that January, after I was back up in Illinois, to tell me her
mother was in the hospital again. The cancer was back.

"It's all over her," Lauren said, crying. "It's everywhere."

"What are they going to do?"

"They gave her six months."

Our wedding was in five.

Family members soon descended on the hospital in Jackson,
every day a new development, lucidity, morphine, sleeping rotations
in a hospital room.

"You need me there," I said.

"What I need is sleep. Finish your dissertation."

The new idea was to do the two weddings during the same
weekend, maybe in April. Trudy could make it to April, the doctors
said. They were sure of it, until they weren't.

"The doctors don't think she can make it that long," Lauren
said in early February, frantic.

"March?" I said.

"I guess."

"That's in a month."

"It's in three weeks."

Had we even planned a wedding? Much less two?

By mid-February, it was decided we would marry in early March,
all of us, two grooms, two brides, two bridal parties, one minister, and

that we would then go to the hospital and see Trudy and do it all again right there in the oncology wing. But that plan would change, too, when Lauren called again to say that her mother was gone forever.

"I love you," I said. "You're not alone."

"You have to come get me. Can you be here with me right now?"

"Yes," I said, though I would have to drive through pieces of Illinois, Missouri, Arkansas, Tennessee, and more than half of Mississippi to get there.

"You have to come now. Hurry."

I dropped everything and shoved a month's worth of clothes into the largest duffel I could find and bought a cheap suit on credit and drove all day to the church through snow, rain, and darkness and changed in a truck-stop toilet and arrived smelling like cigarettes and a truck-stop toilet. For the first time in my life, it seemed, I was hurling toward something and not away.

I entered the small church with the full parking lot and fell into a roiling sea of heads and arms and eyes and hands, looking desperately for Lauren in the downhearted fray, everyone chatting and sobbing and nodding and doing it all so respectfully, mournfully, gravely, even the chuckling. Presbyterians are expert chucklers.

Everyone was so attractive, all the cousins and aunts and uncles, a sea of Brooks Brothers and Chanel and loafers and pearls. These were not hillbillies. I did not belong here, in my woolen watch cap and workmanlike leather shoes and a long naval peacoat wide enough to warm a team of oxen. I felt like a second mate on my way from the galleys to the longshoremen's winter ball, an actor in costume, unsure of my lines or even my role. My parents were here, somewhere. Mom would be consoling people she didn't know and Pop discussing the seasonal rut of woodland game with some pastor's wife near the cheese tray.

I found Lauren in a corner, smiling, eyes shining, listening to a heartwarming story about her mother that would make nothing better.

At the graveside service early the next morning, the wind and rain whipped as from the prow of a North Atlantic whaling ship, bitter and cruel, numbing. Immediate family only. I was there, too, lumbering across a cemetery hillside with Lauren, and could not shake the feeling of a man in a dream, a third-party observer to the grief of this family and Trudy's three children, Lauren and Shelby and Jeremy, their younger brother, still in college, all three in various states of disbelief. Their lives had once been perfect, or seemed so, this happy family of five blown apart by betrayal and abandonment and disease and death, a ten-year tragedy now in its sad denouement. Lauren's father, Jeff, was absent.

Later that morning, we gathered for the memorial service in the First Presbyterian Church, the whole town having come to mourn in this old and dreamlike temple, a castellated Gothic puzzle, battlements and segments in Romanesque red brick, with two aisles and stained glass and dark wood abounding and a defilade of golden organ pipes behind the raised pulpit. Sadness hung like black bunting from every face in the sanctuary, as we all countenanced the woeful end of this woman's woeful life. We sat down front and you could feel the press of eyes behind us, silent exclamations of dread.

"Those poor children" is what they were thinking. Those poor girls. About to marry.

That night, after the winter rain had sopped the soft earth of the grave, and the church was quiet and dark, and kin had driven back into the night to hotels and homes, and the Pyrex dishes of other families sat gelid in the fridge, the four of us remained in the small living room in Trudy's cottage on a quiet Yazoo street: Lauren, Shelby, Jeremy, and me. The mood was grim but peaceful. Their mother, as they say, no longer suffered. So many questions had now been answered. Her brutal and hopeful life of the last decade, during which her children became young adults, that suffering was now finished. Only the children remained, to sit and wonder and try, with the assistance of borrowed medication, not to think too much about a future without a mother or a father.

The fairy-tale double wedding, which everyone had forgotten to plan, due to the unstoppable grief, was a week away. I braced for the breakup that would be all too easy to understand. Her sister, her little brother, needed her. I was willing to give her anything she needed. Stability? Hugs? Distraction? I was a child. I knew more of Greek comedy than death or love. Maybe what she needed most was for me to walk away and let her grieve. The miracle for which everyone had prayed did not come. Not yet.

Chapter 33

THIS IS HOW IT ENDS

2021

Eighteen Februarys later, I thought of the hurt we might have avoided had I been the one to walk away, quietly, the week her mother died. And now I awaited a sign, something, anything, to cue the curtain and bring down the lights on this sad little comedy.

Some would say I had all the signs I needed, a thousand of them, that my unwillingness to pull the plug and let us die was a bald refusal to acknowledge the truth: we were already dead. I cannot say why I did not lose hope. "Now faith is the substance of things hoped for," says the book of Hebrews, "the evidence of things not seen."

But I could not unsee the sign I saw that morning.

"Oh, wow," I said, when I saw it.

If this was not a sign, nothing was, for I now beheld the indisputable, laughable evidence that it was time to call the divorce attorney and finalize the papers. My mouth fell open. My brain fell out. "Holy fucking shit," said my mouth, laughing.

I laughed at my foolishness, to have clung to the tattered banner of hope for so long. I laughed at the size of my wife's balls—and
Chad's.

Like a good American author, I have a range of Google Alerts programmed to notify me when my name appears online, in news arti-
cles, book reviews, literary roundups. I also have alerts for the names
of people who owe me money and people from my past who've gone
off the grid. I have alerts for Lauren and the girls and my mother,
should she ever be named in a lawsuit for stalking one or more of
the actors of *Downton Abbey*, which seems likelier with every passing day. A few months prior, I set alerts for Chad, too. I would not
waste my days stalking this man. I would let the trolls of Silicon
Valley do it for me.

And, lo, there it was, in my inbox: a Chad Alert. The link took
me to a page devoted to freelance home repair, where he and other
local handymen could be hired to caulk bathtubs while casing
your home for pawnshop fodder, or in this case to build bathroom
shelves. The page I saw before my eyes read:

CARRIAGE HOUSE BATHROOM SHELVING

He'd posted photos of his handiwork, for curious prospective
clients. On the finished shelves of stained pine were: a hairbrush,
shampoo, toilet paper, and a pale yellow makeup bag that belonged
to my wife.

This was the same small bag I'd seen on every trip and vacation
for half of my life, the capacious pouch where I went digging for
Neosporin and Q-tips when none could be found elsewhere, the
same bag she'd brought on our honeymoon, and which now accom-
panied her on what I suppose was a kind of honeymoon with Chad.

He had built her some shelves, which meant he had been inside her new apartment, which meant he obviously lived there.

So it was true. My worst fears. She was not over there in the carriage house practicing mindfulness meditation or reading *Streams in the Desert*. She was not engaged in any cleansing fasts or spiritual quests. My wife was living with the world's smallest handyman.

My only comfort, in having discovered his website, featuring photos and reviews of Chad's multifarious skills—ceiling fan installation, trampoline assembly, light carpentry—was in reading client reviews. My favorite was from "Deedee S.", who explained, in her turbulent summation of minor kitchen repairs Chad had been hired to complete, that he had "destroyed the breakfast nook" and had "asked to borrow my tools." At some point during the repairs, things had fallen out between Chad and Deedee S. "He asked me not to write this review, as he was fleeing my home."

I found some reassurance in this review, a third-party validation that my assessment of Chad was not without merit. He had wrecked many homes, it seemed. But my pain soon flooded back, with the knowledge that Lauren was no longer pining for Chad, but rooming with him, too, and I knew what must happen next. So often in this story I have not known what should happen next, but no longer. I pulled out my phone to call her and say goodbye and to settle the terms of our disunion, at least until the attorneys got involved, which was now unavoidable.

"Hey," I said.

"Hey."

I hadn't heard her voice in a hundred lifetimes. A curious thing, to hear a voice every day of your life for almost two decades and then to be deprived of it and then to hear it again in a rush of water through a thirsty pipe.

"How are you?" I said. "How are things?"

"Okay." A thinness was in her words, stretched emptiness underneath.

"Does he live with you now?"

"Yes."

"I guess this is how it ends."

I knew that I should've said it three months ago, or three years ago. I could've saved us all so much heartache. Our girls had gone to the carriage house twice a week for dinner and even spent the night there a handful of times, sleeping on air mattresses, eating Hamburger Helper like hurricane refugees. Had they been there with him? Had our children known this secret?

"He leaves when they come over," she said.

Where did he go, when they came over? I wondered. The library? Did he sleep in his truck? On a park bench?

She'd wanted to live her truth but hid this man like a pint of vodka under the driver's seat. My anger was not violent and it was not loud. Had my children not seen his clothes in the closet, his Speed Stick on the shelves he'd built? Rage welled up inside from the deep places, that my children had been sleeping under a roof where this man lived. I touched the hilt of the sword in my heart and knew it was time to defend my home from anything and anyone, even my poor, changed wife.

"I can't have you back in the house. And no more sleepovers with the girls at your place. This is it. This is how it all ends."

So much to do now. Lawyers. Phone calls. We had to tell the girls everything—or at least the Disney+ film treatment of everything.

Remember our old neighbor? Your mom's living with him now in a shed above a stash of garden tools and rat poison on the other side of the park. You can't go over there anymore. I'm so sorry, girls. We're getting a divorce.

All hope of a happy ending to the story of this marriage was now vacated, swept away. We'd bottomed out and discovered the floor of this thing, 100 million miles down, a long and stupid journey into the abyss that had changed us all and consumed the last four years of our lives, really the last decade, every nod, look, lie, text, touch, tryst, kiss, secret LinkedIn message, dragging us down to this sad and hopeless place. We'd found the depth of depths, and the only thing to do now was climb out. I started with a visit to my new divorce attorney, a Catholic woman who they said was the bane of bastard landlords and abusive foster parents.

I noted with some concern that her office was above a liquor store. Not quite the sort of thing you want to see, but they said she was a cur and I suppose this setting made a kind of sense. I climbed the stairs and found the door along a hallway lined in rank motel carpet.

"Come in!" she said, opening the door. I'll call her Janet. She had long and wild gray hair, like an ancient high school art teacher. There was no receptionist, nor even a lobby: just a single room blanketed in—well, there's no other way to say it—stuffed animals.

I sat at the table and she sat across.

"Let's hear it."

"My wife is holed up in a lovers' nest with a homeless man."

"Oh, boy!"

I told her the whole sad story. She took copious notes. She said "Oh, boy" a lot.

"What now?" I said, after an hour.

"I'll write up the papers."

·   ·   ·

I called Lauren that afternoon to confirm the address where she might be served. I stood in the driveway and dialed her number. It was warm, the sun out, spring doing its best to work its way out of the deadness. It was almost eighteen years, to the day, of her mother's death.

I don't remember the first hour of the conversation, just a sad rehash of the life we'd lived that was now forever dead. I do remember saying, "So you're married, and you're living with a man who is also married, and our girls are about to learn all this."

She said nothing.

Did she really mean to teach our daughters this twisted story of love?

"What are you doing, Lauren?"

Again, she said nothing.

I said again, "What are you doing?"

Minutes went by. All my words were finished. God stopped me. Should I speak now? No. A minute. Five minutes. Ten. I could hear her breathing. The earth quivered. The concrete of the driveway hummed and buckled. Birds hushed. Traffic vanished. Planes stuck themselves fast in the sky.

"Everything is so dark," she said. "I can't control it."

She began to weep, her voice deepened, coarse, ground into dust. She began to howl with the truest, saddest pain I've ever heard through a phone. If you've ever heard someone cry out from the darkness, from the absolute terror of hell, this was it, as though I stood at the gates of a city and could hear her being slaughtered by a beast just beyond the edge of darkness. More silence: frightening silence, helpless, weak, dying, trapped, prey to be devoured.

"I can't stay here." Her words were urgent, grasping, gasping, desperate. "He's on his way. You have to come now. Hurry."

Chapter 34

A MIRACLE IN YAZOO

2003

"L et's elope," I said, the day after the funeral.

"Okay," Lauren said.

"Let's go somewhere warm and get arrested for public indecency."

I made jokes. This is what I do. This is all I've ever really done.

Weddings are the bread and butter of comedy. This is the first thing you learn about Shakespeare—tragedies end with eulogies and comedies with wedding toasts and ribald intimations of procreation, the heroes married off and sent into a bedchamber with a bawdy joke. It's as much about life as sex, the deadness of tragedy reborn as young love and the promise of babies. Even the Bible comes to a wild and raucous conclusion in what's called "the marriage supper of the Lamb," where Jesus marries the Church. That's how you know there's sex in heaven. There has to be. You don't end your book with a wedding and not have sex after.

Not that any of us were thinking about sex or love or weddings

or miracles. Lauren and Shelby and Jeremy wandered through that
week as through a haze, addled by antidepressants, antianxiety
meds, gin, wine, casks of grief. They slept at Trudy's house, the two
sisters and the brother, orphans all, not yet grown. I stayed in Lauren's apartment in Jackson. We talked every day. I would drive up
and see her. She seemed untethered to the earth, about to float away.
How do you hold on to a thing like that? How do you love in times
of want, when you fail even to love during times of plenty?

"What can I do?" I asked.

"I don't know," Lauren said.

"Somebody's got to be doing something."

"The aunts are trying to figure it out."

My mom hosted a shower for Lauren and Shelby. Lauren
brought the gifts back to her apartment, unopened. I stacked them
in a corner and wondered when they would be returned.

Would this wedding happen? We'd need a cake, I knew that. I knew
that weddings were planned months, years, in advance. I knew that
everyone in this family was in no condition to plan a thing, due to
the gut-wrenching death of the brides' one real parent, and I knew
there was no money. Trudy's modest income entirely vanished due
to the treatments and surgeries.

"Is there a rehearsal dinner?" I asked Mom. "Nobody's telling
me anything."

"Maybe. Your father says he'll pay for it."

Pop had suggested buying a hundred buckets of fried chicken
and having the dinner at a deserted Kmart that had been transformed by voodoo into a skating rink.

"What can I do?" I asked Lauren again, on the phone.

"Keep your dad from having our rehearsal dinner at a Kmart."

"It's not the worst idea."

"It is. It's the worst idea."

"I love you."

"I love you, too."

She was right. It was the worst idea. Everything was the worst idea. The wedding was the worst idea. My panic and bafflement gave way to anger, not at God but at the person who authored all this sadness: Lauren's absentee father. Trudy's cancer had gone undetected for so long because Jeff hadn't provided health insurance, before he'd had the affair and walked out, which meant Trudy hadn't gone to a doctor for years. Lauren said her mother felt the unmistakable bulge of tumor long before she ever saw a doctor. No money for it. Evil wears a lot of masks: violence, murder, shootings, rapes, arson. But the evil I have seen, evil done by human hands and human agency, is slower and crueler than arson. It moves like a darkened river of magma down the hillside of a family and rends lives and digests goodness in slow motion until nothing remains but ash and rock. When you got right down to it, as far as I could tell, Jeff's dereliction had resulted in Trudy's death and endless heartache and seeds of bitter heartache in the woman I would or would not marry, who could know but God.

I did what I was told and picked up a rental tuxedo and on the appointed day crawled into the basement kitchen of the church and waited. The wedding would happen after all. My groomsmen showed up in their tuxedos, and none of us were sure how any of this was happening so soon or why. After an hour or two, the groomsmen departed and I was alone with Hudson, the other groom, the two of us in slightly different tuxedos, originally intended for two different weddings.

"Well," I said.

"Here we are," Hudson said.

We'd not even had time for proper invitations to go out, much less find flowers or a cake. Would there be a reception? Would anybody even come? Everyone in the family had gone back to Alabama, North Carolina, Missouri, Florida. Did Lauren even have a dress?

Hudson was as confused as I was about it all, as gray and wan as the rest of us, though he did look nice in his bow tie. I should've gotten a bow tie. I wore a necktie, stiff and black. Funeral clothes. It didn't drape right. I made one last trip to the toilet to retie the tie. They say you don't remember much from your wedding day, but I remember the great red pimple right between my eyes, exactly where a sniper would place the crosshairs. I remember a tuxedo that fit about as comfortably as a sandwich board. I felt hideous and puffy, a Twinkie in the rain. I remember the feeling of being an enormous sodden sandwich-board-wearing Twinkie about to bungee jump into an abyss of love and pain. I remember being led to a small room behind the pulpit, a lamb led to the slaughter of his own ego, and I remember stepping out onto the stage with Hudson and the minister, Bill, Lauren's uncle.

What I saw in the sanctuary was unexpected: four hundred people, smiling and weeping already and the thing had not even begun, and you could feel the room vibrate with feeling, a spiritual inversion of the funeral that had taken place here just days ago. Bridesmaids and groomsmen marched in down both aisles, pouring into the sanctuary to hymns and soaring sonatas, all these beautiful cousins and childhood friends and brothers and blood brothers. Everyone had come back.

And that's when I saw the flowers, green and white and yellow and pink and violet, flowers with no name and every name, everywhere, around us, up and down the aisles. Where had they come from? Who'd found them, bought them, placed them? The music turned, and the congregation quieted and stirred and then stood.

Shelby, the older sister, entered first, gliding down the aisle in a borrowed dress, escorted by her little brother.

The church has two aisles and two sets of sanctuary doors. Shelby had gone down the right aisle. Lauren would come down the left. I looked at the closed doors behind which Lauren stood, waiting. I hadn't seen her since the night before. I wanted to be surprised. The church seemed a thousand yards deep. Shelby made it to the stage, opposite Hudson. I could not peel my eyes away from the door. I could not imagine what might come through it. I wanted to run up the aisle and tear open the door and hold her, but I had to wait. It would be her coming to me, now. Later, it would be me going to her.

Lauren, I later learned, wore the bodice of her cousin Susanna's wedding gown, stitched at the last minute to a skirt from some other dress, but all I saw was that radiance gliding toward me to "Trumpet Voluntary in D Major," until there she stood before me, this princess of Denmark. The officiant, her sweet uncle Bill, made me repeat some vows, and I couldn't tell you what I promised. Lauren's glow scrambled my language centers. Bill could've had me recite the Port Huron Statement and promise to lasso a bison and fashion a coverlet from its hide and I'd have said, "Sure." The next thing I remember, we were married.

I do not recall how we got to the reception nor how there was a reception at all, so grand was it, flowers in the chandeliers, the most stunning Frank Gehry–ish wedding cake blanketed in a coat of shaved white-chocolate spirals, long tables of food, little baby crab cakes and fried catfish hors d'oeuvres plucked from the fry basket of God. I remember faceless names and nameless faces and hugs and handshakes and Sunday school teachers from my childhood and big bearlike men pawing my biceps and women weeping into my boutonniere. I remember driving away with a basket of food in the car.

Mostly what I remember is not knowing how any of it happened, which is how I knew it had been a miracle, all of it, a thousand miracles tethered up in one blinding illumination. How else do you describe a $50,000 wedding that nobody planned? Because nobody planned it. To this day, nobody knows how it happened.

But we do know some things. We learned, later, that the chandeliers full of flowers, like something from Titania's bower, came from every yard in Yazoo. A lady who made cakes made ours. Somebody, we were told, slipped her cash for the ingredients. The food was made and brought by ladies from the church, they said. Someone owned a catfish farm. All these people have names. Just pick up a Yazoo phone book and choose one. Call Lauren's aunts. They'll tell you. They'll drive you around and show you the yards where the flowers grew. They'll show you the catfish farm and the home of the lady who made all the cakes.

What happens when you see a miracle? Do you throw yourself on the carpet before the Almighty? Give away all your possessions? Maybe you think you'd join a religious order or be one of those grateful survivors on the local news after a twister spares the family hog, found cradled in a distant sweet-gum tree, compelling you to look right into the TV cameras and testify to the mighty love of Jesus. But if you read closely, when people see Jesus work a miracle, they don't usually testify into cameras. Many fear what they see and run away. Others think the man freakish. Many believe Jesus might be doing the work of Satan, because, honestly, people with no health insurance don't deserve to be not blind. What business had this Palestinian redneck healing lepers? What's a leper without leprosy? And how dare he tell the weather what to do?

"Weather ought not to be controlled," I can hear people saying. "It's unnatural."

"I heard he walked on water," they said.

"Who cares? What this country needs are decent public toilets."

It would be years before I fully understood the meaning of the miracle in Yazoo, which wasn't about the sudden, unexpected materializing of a double wedding that nobody had paid for because an entire town pulled it out of their hearts, but rather about what becomes possible when people run toward one another and not away. I'd always thought churches were for preaching, a way to make you behave, a bridle on freedom, a way to sing you into submission. I'd always thought families were for sucking you back down into the gutter of history and genetics, but maybe I'd been all wrong about everything. God doesn't answer every prayer in the affirmative, but some wishes he does grant. The rehearsal dinner ended up being held at a country club after all, despite my father's plan to have us all eating chicken wings at a skating rink in the haunted shell of an abandoned department store.

I often think of our wedding day, driving away from the reception through those cool, late-winter woods and into the rest of our lives. Lauren's mother was dead and her father was a ghost and she seemed so tender and delicate and strong all at once. She was an orphan, terribly alone, despite being my wife. Now, a trillion lifetimes later, a photo sits in my home, telling the story of a double ceremony and a wedding party large enough to storm the gates of Cinderella's castle: two stunned and luminous brides, two bewildered grooms, a platoon of groomsmen and bridesmaids fanning out left and right, an optical illusion of organza and satin, everyone gloriously radiant.

"A double wedding!" people say when they see the photo. "Wow!"

It was always hard to tell the story. There's too much *wow* in the photo to explain.

The memory of our wedding, which has grown in my heart from a touching cocktail anecdote into a story that has changed the way I see the world, has made me believe in magic again. All of life is a miracle—I believe this now—and maybe to see this fact, maybe you have to have everything burned away. Maybe the only people who believe in miracles are the people who have no other option. And now a thousand hurtful and glorious lifetimes later, I held the phone, through which came the shattered, shaking voice of the woman who was through some miracle still my wife. Perhaps I would have to storm a castle after all.

"Hurry," she said.

"I'm on my way." I hung up.

Chapter 35

THE CARRIAGE HOUSE

2021

The distance between our home and the carriage house seemed cosmic, boundless, three streets over in a whole other dimension. I raced the blocks at light speed. What would I find when I arrived? A dead body? A murder-suicide? Why had I brought this gun?

You wake up in the morning, you never know what the day will bring. Three months ago, I was a man with an exceptionally normal life, walking my dog and riding my blue bicycle to work every day and mowing my little postage stamp of lawn, and now I was a single dad with a gun in his pants on his way to the O.K. Corral. I texted Soren for backup.

Find a church where your pastor texts back, "On my way."

I'd like to say that I took pause, to weigh everything, to reckon and judge, to place on one side of the ledger everything horrid and hurtful my wife had done to us, and to write on the other all the goodness she'd given us across time and history, the decisive acts of love she'd performed heroically for so many years until the moment she could no longer be the hero. Maybe it was all a test, a dare, a wicked wager by a weakened spirit, to see what would happen, to see if one man walked the earth who would not make her suffer more than she had, even at her worst. But I didn't think about all that. I didn't think at all.

"For my thoughts are not your thoughts," says the book of Isaiah, "neither are your ways my ways, saith the LORD."

I came to a stop in front of the carriage house driveway and left the gun in the truck and took a knife instead, bounding up the carriage house stairs like a one-man SEAL Team Six. I came to the door, over which hung a single, solitary, ridiculous horseshoe. It was entirely possible Chad was already there, waiting for me on the other side of this door with a gun of his own. Anything was possible.

"Jesus," I said, in prayer or expletive, and opened the door, and then, even though you know it's coming, you always know, but when it happens, you feel like God is in the room, because the door opened and there she was.

The squalid little apartment stank with signs of Chad: the sad tuneless guitar he could not play, his ridiculous seashell collection, the truck-stop art, marijuana pipes tossed about like toys, a decorative installation of cordless power tools in the corner.

"Where is he?" I said.

"I don't know. I don't know what to do."

We began throwing clothes on the bed. Their clothes, their underwear comingled and spilled out of drawers and closets. We raked photographs and trinkets off shelves, grabbed unopened bottles of rosé, tableware, the yellow makeup bag. A lime-colored monstrosity of a sport coat hung on a closet door. Would Lauren object to my urinating on it?

I ran down and up and down the stairs again, sweating now, the knife so heavy it nearly pulled my pants right off me, great piles of clothing and pillows and tableware and a nice new rug and framed photographs in my arms. Maybe this is why God made me buy a pickup truck.

Soren now stood in the driveway. "What do you want me to do?"

I half expected him to be wearing his clerical collar, like Father Damien in *The Exorcist*, but he wore jeans and a T-shirt.

"Just stand right where you're standing," I said. "If he shows up, do something."

Soren stood in the driveway, a man of God at the mouth of hell, and probably laughed to himself that his seminary training had not required any courses on martial arts.

In minutes, we were finished loading. I walked through the two rooms one last time.

"Is that your phone charger?" I said.

"That's his," she said.

I considered stomping on the neck of his guitar, but pocketed the phone charger instead. I am a practical man. We locked the door and Lauren ran down the stairs and I stopped on the landing and, in a poetic flourish, turned the horseshoe upside down. In the driveway, I thanked Soren for his services. He took off, and so did we.

"I can't stay here," Lauren said in our driveway, minutes later. "He'll find me."

I began unloading the truck with fury, throwing my wife's most valuable material possessions into a garbage heap of blouses and bedsheets in the garage, knowing that I had to get Lauren and her car far away from here, she could not be here, this was no longer her home and no longer a place of refuge. Lauren added to the pile, more and more, and before we were finished, she, her face drawn and aged, her voice quivering with horror, said, "I'm sorry, I'm so sorry," and collapsed in the driveway.

I ran to her, but could not pick her up, her body weighted with all the world's sorrow. She wept, belted out the gravest moans, the sound of all creation's howling in terror.

"I feel so alone, I feel so alone," she said, heaving, sobbing.

"You are not alone."

I laid my hands across her body and prayed for her like a battlefield chaplain as she lay heaving on the cracked concrete of the driveway. Have you ever seen a living creature die? I've seen many. To see the life force rattle out of a body is a powerful thing, holy and horrible. Sometimes you try to stop it, sometimes you try to hurry it along, but mostly you behold and shudder. I watched something die on that driveway. This woman was no longer my wife. I was no longer her husband. We were just two children of God. That's it. That's all anybody is, in the end.

Chapter 36

WHAT JUST HAPPENED

Two Months Later

"So, yeah," I said to Dr. Berman. "That's our story."

"Most of it," Lauren said.

"Classic rom-com," I said.

It was April now, the previous fall and winter like a half-remembered nightmare I kept having to remind myself was no nightmare, but had actually happened. How were we not all dead or catatonic with the horrors we'd seen and felt?

In therapy, I talked a lot at first. I don't even know what I think if my mouth doesn't give me a hint. But I had been talking for twenty years. It was her turn. So Lauren talked. And talked. And talked. I found every session exhilarating and gruesome, like a riveting new podcast about my own murder.

Dr. Berman taught me how to listen, and he taught Lauren how to share. The stifling noose, around her neck for a lifetime, worked loose, finally, and she began to breathe again, to let it all out: a mother she'd buried, a father she longed to know, friendships she'd lost, dreams that had died. So much had died and needed to be allowed to be dead: a baby, a mother, our marriage. We had to bury our love and roll the stone over the tomb and wait to see if it would come back to life.

Her noose loosened, and so did my blinders begin to fall. I began to see what I would not look at before: the young woman I married, wracked and bound by unspeakable grief; the young mother ensnared by the unceasing demands of maternity and childcare; the woman who set fire to the home in a bid to escape what felt to her like endless pain. The truth of what she could now say and what I could now see began in whispered words and grew and grew over many sessions into a great putrid mound of emotional wreckage. She added hers, I added mine. Dr. Berman helped us sift through the pile for salvageable gems of understanding and haul off the rest. She was not the same woman from before, flinty and hard. We were casualties of war. The betrayal had killed us both.

Dr. Berman gave me permission to ask painful questions and permission not to resent the silence when she stared into the middle distance for ten minutes before saying a word. You probably have questions, too. Did she move back in, just like that? Did Chad hunt her down?

She did come home, though the homecoming took some time. In the months between the carriage house and our first session with Dr. Berman, a lot happened. Cue the montage: a plaintive Iron & Wine track over scenes of quiet hope, Lauren carrying a duffel bag into Jason's and Louise's guest bedroom, where she would sleep for a few days. Shelby in her minivan, shooting down I-16, teary at the wheel. Mom on her apartment balcony, praying. Soren at the dinner table with his wife and sons, doing a shot of Jameson in wonder and exhaustion, grateful he'd not had to fight a man he'd never even met.

Cousin Julie at home in Montgomery, checking her phone, getting the news, crying in relief. Shelby and Lauren and our girls in a hotel, eating takeout. Chad trolling the streets of Savannah looking for her like an ex in a Lifetime movie. Lauren on a plane to St. Louis, to be with her cousin Stephen and his wife, Kate, a couple who possess much wisdom about how you can die and walk again. Me, sitting in the driveway with a cigarette and a gun. Lauren driving home from the airport a few days later with her bag and a wedding ring.

I say, "Do you want to be married to me?"

Lauren says, "I want to try."

This is how we came to Dr. Berman.

Once more, I slept in my office on the sofa, or sometimes on the little mattress, thin as a truck-stop sandwich. The girls took turns sleeping in the big bed with Lauren. Our home was a field hospital. Without provocation, one Sunday afternoon a few weeks after she came home, Lauren handed me all her new passwords to her new accounts, her laptop, her phone. She got an app that tracks everyone's location, which was her idea, not mine. An app would not restore my marriage. I had no illusions of that. Sure, I wanted the app long ago. You bet. She did not. As one might imagine. But now we had the app. It's just an app. It couldn't exactly mend busted hearts and resurrect the dead. But it could help. Rebuilding broken trust is a little like rebuilding someone's face after a disfiguring chain-saw accident. It can be done, but it'll look different for a while, maybe forever, until one day it looks mostly normal, or you stop noticing the scars, or caring much when you do.

Chad harassed her for months, stalked her, threatened reprisals, begged her for gas money through tears. He'd once had a lawn, a home, a career, a family. He'd lost everything. You had to feel for the guy on some level. I had to call him and explain that the romp was over, Six Flags was closing, it was time to go. I wished him luck and told him that if he ever contacted anyone in my family ever again, I'd break both his legs, and we ended the call.

He was eventually booted from the carriage house, where he squatted solo for months, never paying a penny of rent, though he did construct a small birdhouse for the owner out of scrap lumber, I am told, as a thank-you. They say he now lives in another state.

In the months after she came home, a new ritual commenced every morning around seven. Lauren would come into my office and we'd shamble outside together to sit in the driveway and smoke and warm ourselves in the morning sun. The tailgate of my truck makes a fine coffee table. Sometimes we talked of the girls or Gary or what we needed for dinner, but mostly we spoke about everything that had happened.

"Did he hit you?"

"No."

"Did you use with him?"

"No."

Quite often, after another impossible question, we sat in silence, the sounds of distant aircraft and nearer songbirds animating the brightening sky. Many of these mornings, Ginsburg, always the first kid awake, tiptoed outside wrapped in a blanket. As soon as we heard the back door open, Lauren would hand me her cigarette, so that I now appeared to be smoking two.

"Please don't smoke," Ginsburg said to both of us, one morning.

"This is how we heal," I said.

"You'll get cancer," she said. "You'll die and then you'll be dead."

"We've already died and come back," I said. "Run along."

And so it was that I asked every question, and she attempted to provide every answer. Why did she love him? Why did she stop loving me? Where did they meet up? Did they have a favorite song? A wedding plan? Did he have unsightly birthmarks?

"Why did you ask me to come get you that day?" I said.

"I couldn't do it alone. I felt trapped."

"By him?"

"By everything."

"But you loved him. That's what you said."

"I did. But it wasn't what I thought it would be. It felt like darkness."

This is how we spent most mornings for months, unpacking all this garbage together, flicking cigarette butts into the yard, working through the mystery of our marriage and the affair among the distant cawing of the crows.

Like a good writer, I searched for a skeleton key to our story that might unlock the truth of the whole sordid tale, though the truth was right in front of both of us: A long, long time ago, two idiots got married. Like all human beings ever to walk the planet, these two young people carried their own compulsions and demands into marriage: two happy childhoods, fraught by different modes of love and instability, and two wayward young adulthoods, charged with loss and discovery. We wed and quietly tormented each other with our unspoken pathologies: my proud independence and mulish aspirations of professional success and the need to be adored, her proud independence and mulish aspirations of domestic perfection and the need to be adored. I found a hundred thousand readers to adore me. She found a neighbor.

"Divorces happen all the time," Lauren said. "I didn't think you wanted me anymore. I thought I was doing you a favor."

Before he got famous for being a sexual degenerate, Louis C.K. said this dumb thing about marriage: "Divorce is always good news because no good marriage has ever ended in divorce." The reality is that every marriage is a partnership of two broken assholes with good intentions and varying degrees of ability to deliver. Marriage is as much a mystery to me now as the origins of the universe and the laws that govern the behavior of matter. What makes one work is just as strange as what makes one not. But I possess more information now than I had when all this began. We both do. Lauren has had to come to terms with some difficult truths, such as how her husband has grown a mustache, and I have had to grapple with other truths, such as how my wife left me for the human equivalent of Diet Mountain Dew.

It's easy to forgive Chad. The sickening truth, which I cannot deny, is that, despite my hateful proclivity to compare this man to Pepsi products, he showed her kindness. He was kind to her, not in the big and most important ways, but in the small and most important ways. He listened. He laughed. He was kind at exactly the right time, in exactly the right way, when our marriage was weakest, and his kindness fertilized a genuine friendship into a terrible infatuation that grew desperately unkind. Lauren probably made our marriage sound hellish to him. He must have convinced himself he was saving a woman from hell. But he was wrong. The hell they imagined became a real hell for all of us. It's easy to forgive someone you'll probably never again see.

Forgiving Lauren is much harder. I see this woman every day. She's right there in the bed next to me, a bed we once again share. I would like to forget all she did and said, but for some reason God is not allowing me to forget just yet. He wants me to listen. The memories do not dissolve. They cohere into captivating art films that play endlessly in the International Infidelity Film Festival of my mind. I have tried willing forgiveness from the deepest parts of me, pulling it out by the tail and handing it to Lauren, but this doesn't quite work. Letting go of the past is about as hard as Taylor

Swift says it will be. These last few years have been about as fun as giving your cat a haircut with garden shears. Our new church has helped us hold the cat.

When Lauren came back to Christ the King with us for the first time in many months, nobody got weird, although they got a little weird. Most didn't know. Many did.

"I know what everybody's thinking," Lauren said. "The wives especially."

"Those people love you."

"Not all of them."

Those first few Sundays, Lauren must have felt like Hester Prynne on the scaffold, her betrayal a fat, seething gorilla in the back pew.

"It just feels weird," she said.

"Everybody knows you left me twice for the same man. That feels pretty weird, too."

Things would be funky for a while, I told her. They would have to be. Every Sunday, it got a little less funky. She would talk to the other moms about school and work and the girls, and their stiff smiles softened. She opened up. She connected with Katie, one of those Christians with a nose ring and a trauma tattoo. They went out to dinner one night and stayed gone for hours.

"I told her everything," Lauren said. "I started at childhood and didn't stop."

"What did she do?"

"She cried a lot."

"Crying is good."

"She said we have to be friends now."

"Friends are good."

•   •   •

They say you can't feel the earth spinning, but the whole planet felt like one great carousel, every circling of the sun a reminder of the battles where we bled and died. In summer, I remembered that a year before, my wife was off at some fishy marina with another man. Fall reminded me of all the Sundays she slipped off to run mysterious errands. The smell of Thanksgiving dinner shot me down a Proustian chute of terror. Christmas held its own unwanted gifts, the air turned fragrant with death and change: the pungent bouquet of fabric-softened clothes emanating from the dryer exhaust, which always smells different in winter, reminded me of all those frigid mornings and nights I spent alone in the driveway, staring up at the stars and wondering where all this would end. The misting deodorizer I used on my truck the week I bought it carried me backward into the fog of the worst Christmas on record. The color of the light, the chill of the air, the crisp leaves underfoot, all of it was dizzying, the revisiting of a haunted battleground.

I still do not nap well on Sunday afternoons, especially when Lauren is out of the house, driving Coco to volleyball practice, getting her nails done. I can follow her on the little surveillance app if I choose to. Still I cannot nap. Whenever she looks cute for no apparent reason, I get that old sick feeling. I wish I didn't. I tell her she looks cute and don't say anything further. Maybe later, I say something. Maybe I don't.

"You know, this is your story, but it's mine, too," I said one morning that spring. "I think I have to write about all this."

"Oh, good," Lauren said.

"Don't worry. It will be funny."

"I'm funnier than you. Maybe I should write something."

"Maybe you should."

"Okay."

A few weeks later, she sent me a story.

Chapter 37

A WHORE IN CHURCH

1994–2022

BY LAUREN KEY

My marriage to Harrison died last year. In the ground, dirt on it, dead.

In my life, I've seen a lot of things die. Things you never thought would die.

I had a happy childhood, for a while. In many ways, we were a typical homeschool family, at least for the 1980s. Mom wore denim jumpers and made her own bread and yogurt. We had *Little House on the Prairie* Day. When my friends were at school learning algebra, I was at home churning imaginary butter.

Money was always an issue. Dad had been a pastor but left the ministry for a series of unstable jobs. He could be irresponsible with money but he was very involved as a parent, attending every soccer game, every ballet recital. He was highly attentive to ailments. When I got something in my eye, he'd grab a light and inspect it, very concerned, nodding his head like an internist. A little dramatic, but he made me feel seen and safe. I loved that about him.

One Sunday morning—this was the year I turned sixteen—he woke us up. I figured we were going to Six Flags as a surprise. We'd done this once before. He'd get a tiny bonus, and instead of paying the rent or buying groceries, we'd go to Six Flags. He loved those little surprises. He sat us down that morning and told us he'd asked Mom for a divorce. Surprise!

A complete blind side. Maybe I wasn't so seen and safe after all.

A few hours after he left, I called to tell him he forgot his pillow. We are lovers of our pillows and I knew he would miss his. I guess I was secretly hoping he'd come back for it and stay. He did come back for the pillow, but didn't stay. I was heartbroken. Jeremy, my little brother, got mad. Shelby, my big sister, got mad and stayed mad. I went numb.

A few months later, we heard of his plans to marry another woman. We heard she had great pillows. Younger pillows, I think, with less wear and tear. We also learned that he'd been cheating on Mom with this woman for many years. I hated him.

A year later, I headed to college. It was like the scene from *Are You My Mother?* Where the baby bird asks every tractor and dump truck she finds, "Are you my mother?"

For me, it was "Are you my father? Will you make me feel seen and safe?"

I asked and asked, sometimes just for a night. Dad was a ghost. A handful of phone calls or birthday cards. He did call once to tell me his new pillow was pregnant. He hoped I'd be excited. I was not. I was hurt all over again. He was replacing us, one pillow at a time.

While Dad was building his new life, ours fell to pieces. Mom struggled to pay bills, balance a checkbook, make big decisions. I didn't want to be like that. I did not want to be so dependent on any man that I couldn't function if he left. I felt a constant pull between independence and a deep need to be seen and known.

Cancer hit Mom my freshman year. It had its general cancer story. Good days with good news, bad days with bad news. It's gone, it's back. It'll be fine, it will not be fine. I was so angry at God. Hadn't my mom been through enough? Hadn't we all? The pain of all these questions made numbness feel the safest choice. Chemo, double mastectomy, experimental treatments, it's all a blur of hope and anger. Mom moved to Mississippi, to Yazoo City, to be closer to our college and her brother and his family. The years passed. Mississippi became home for all of us.

The year I turned twenty-four, I fell in love with an old acquaintance from college. I remember seeing Harrison at a wedding that summer. It was 2002. There he was in the church lobby: tan, slim, shaved head, pale blue linen shirt. I thought, "Damn. He looks good." This was a strange thing to think about Harrison. I mean, this is a guy I'd seen a million times before on campus and never looked twice at. It was love at ninety-fifth glance.

That night, he asked me out. We were a thing almost immediately. He was funny and smart. My mom described him as "an old shoe." She meant it in a nice way.

Six months later, Harrison proposed. The ring, which held two diamonds from my mom's old ring, was perfect—and a little tight. I forced that sucker on because, you know, it's bad luck if your ring doesn't fit. We would need all the luck we could get.

A few weeks into 2003, the cancer hit us again, harder this time. Like all mothers of brides, Mom dreamed of dress shopping, registries, showers. She kept saying, "I really need to find a dress. Maybe when I feel better." She would never feel better. She would never leave the hospital again.

I worked at a Greek restaurant right across the street and would bring Mom sweet tea but not stay long. I had to work, I told her. I was busy, I said. Busy pretending she wasn't dying. Busy pretending we didn't have two weddings to plan.

One night she called me at work and asked for tea. I lay in her hospital bed and she apologized for so much, moments she knew she would miss. Holidays. Birthdays. Babies. We shared a love of babies. She told me she knew I'd be a great mom.

We were taking shifts at the hospital, and my brother and I were staying the night. I was in an extra hospital bed and he slept in a chair. Her breathing was labored but steady. Then silence. We both sat up. He got the nurse, who confirmed: she was gone. We sobbed and hugged and made all the phone calls. Our sister, aunts, uncles, cousins, my dad. Dad. It was his birthday.

She died on his birthday.

You cheat on me? Fine, I'll die on your birthday.

I called him and told him.

"She said she forgives you," I told him. He cried.

We buried her on the little hill in the Yazoo City cemetery.

Ten days after the funeral, in the very same church, my sister and I and our two grooms got married. I was numb all over again and just putting one foot in front of the other as I walked down the aisle. I watched someone else get married in my body. People looked at us like wounded animals. *How are they holding up? How are they doing this?* A marriage should be born in hope and promise, but ours was born in shadow and grief. There was miraculous beauty in it—how the town came together to make it all happen—but the flowers and cakes were gone as quickly as they appeared, and sadness is what came after. My brother, sister, and I had been so close for so long. Our happy homeschooling *Little*

House on the Prairie life was forever gone and dead. No father. No mother. No home.

For years, I relived those last days of my mom's life. The first years of marriage are difficult for everyone, no matter how in love, and my loneliness made our marriage harder than it should have been. I couldn't let Harrison see how much hurt was there. Instead of telling him how sad I was, I did what I thought wives were supposed to do. I made our home beautiful. I made giant casseroles, pot roasts the size of carry-on luggage, enough food to feed two families, but it was just us. I was a terrible cook. I once put green beans in the beef stroganoff.

Harrison said, "This is weird."

I cried in front of him that time.

He got mad when I would dry his socks because, I don't know, I was under the impression socks could be dried. *The green beans are weird? You're weird.* I told him he failed to mention how weird he was before we got married. He insists he made this very clear.

If you've read Harrison's other books, you know how hard those early years were for him, too. He was under his own dark cloud, trying to become a writer and hating every sentence he wrote. He wanted a new career every day.

"What do you want to do?" I asked.

"I'd like to be an astronaut. Or a vet. Or a dentist."

This was quickly feeling the opposite of safe and stable, and that scared me.

During our fourth year of marriage, Harrison was hired at a prestigious school. Our first baby was six months old and we headed to beautiful Savannah, Georgia, the cobblestone streets, the history, the ocean. It was pretty. Maybe I could be happy here.

After three years in Savannah, we had three girls. I was drowning in diapers, sleep deprivation, mountains of laundry, mountains of dishes. I missed my sister and my brother. I missed my mom. I needed her. I needed help. I was so jealous of friends whose moms lived right around the corner or just an hour away or who, you know, were *alive*.

I loved being a stay-at-home mom but no one prepares you for how lonely it is. We couldn't afford babysitters so, for breaks, I went to Walmart by myself on Saturdays or stole a few minutes during naptime. I always felt guilty, though. Harrison had work to do and I should have just taken the girls with me to the grocery store and saved him the trouble. I was terrible at sharing my feelings, terrible at asking for a break or asking for help or saying when I was frustrated. This is what I wanted, after all. Babies and a home and homeschooling, my own little house on the prairie. We didn't have much but we had everything we needed, and yet I grew more miserable with every passing day. I felt so alone. Harrison, the old shoe, seemed about as miserable as I was.

They never tell you this, but being married to a funny person is hard. We constantly picked on each other.

"I feel another migraine coming on," I'd say.

"It's all in your head," he'd say.

But the thing was, my head really was killing me. Migraines. The worst kind. Deadly. You want to die. You have to lie down on the bed in the dark just to stay alive. I don't know, maybe this was my body's way of telling me that silence and numbness only work for so long. Anxiety, grief, family trauma, it's got to get out somehow. My skull could only hold so much. It tried to explode. It was hell.

I blamed Harrison. My bitterness about his constant writing grew, his nose always stuck in a book or a laptop or staring out the window looking for the next idea. He looked everywhere but at me. He had big dreams and I was pretty sure those dreams didn't include me. I felt so much bitterness. He was going to get his time, no matter what. His career, no matter what. His breaks, no matter what. I felt boring to him. I felt insignificant.

"Don't be such a killjoy," he'd say, whenever I would explain that I didn't think the babies should ride in the basket of his scooter. He put them in dangerous situations, places where they might get hurt. The opposite of numbness. He felt everything and felt it big and wanted others to feel big, too. He didn't want our girls to be wimps. I wanted them to keep their skulls in one piece. He loved tying ropes to one end of skateboards and one end to the bikes. He'd throw the kids as high as he could in the air. Why do dads do this? It's a global problem.

No one really talks about marriage struggles. Not Christians. Not the real struggles. Sex, pain, anger, loneliness. Not a word. You'd think they would. Christians love to talk about sin and struggle, but we look past the many nightmares of marriage like an army of the blind.

I didn't want to be like my dad. I didn't want to leave. But also, I did. I wanted to run, to walk away, to go somewhere happy, where I didn't have to feel numb anymore.

Those early years in Savannah, Dad and I reconnected, which was easier with Mom being gone. He came to Savannah and met his granddaughters. I softened toward him. Tried to understand him. He didn't set out to destroy us. No one sets out to destroy their family. But as a child of a broken home, divorce didn't scare me. I'd survived. It wasn't out of the realm of possibility and I didn't want to be miserable forever.

Our neighbors were miserable, too. Always discussing divorce. They had a young son and afternoons were spent playing outside or going to the park, all of us, mostly me and the other husband. I was home all day, every day, and so was Chad.

We became friends. We shared a love of kids and little house projects, silly jokes, simple lives. It was innocent flirting at first. Texts about TV shows or what the kids had done that day. I'd hand him nails while he was fixing something. He'd take out the trash and help me around the house. We'd run errands for each other, grab a gallon of milk at the store. You know, good neighbor stuff. Until it grew into bad neighbor stuff. Thinking about him consumed me. He was so kind to me. His marriage seemed destined for divorce. Mine did, too. I justified all the ways that Harrison had failed me.

One day, I told Chad I loved him and I knew I shouldn't.

Let me give you some advice: If you think you're in love with someone who's not your husband, don't tell him. Because once you do, it cannot be unsaid.

I tried to pray him away. I tried to will him away. I tried to stay inside more and send the girls outside without me. Nothing worked.

During all this, Dad emailed me one day and asked if he could stop paying the money owed us monthly after Mom died, as part of their divorce settlement. My siblings and I discussed it and agreed that Dad should honor the debt. It was the least he could do. Couldn't he keep this one promise to his first three children? We wrote him and asked him to honor the debt. We told him we loved him and wanted him in our lives. He did not see it that way. He replied with a short email and cut us off, forever. Said he wanted no further contact. He would not pay. He would no longer be our father. I felt abandoned all over again. Like Mom died, all over again. I wished it were him who'd died. We haven't spoken since. That was fifteen years ago.

· · ·

I realize many people reading this will have had much harder lives. Maybe you're a refugee, a victim of violent abuse, maybe you saw your parents murdered, maybe you never even knew your parents, I don't know. But what happened to me, my father, my mother, all of it, it killed me. Made me dead inside. My friendship with this man next door felt like the only bright spot in my life. I wanted to wipe away everything and start over. Harrison had no idea, none. He was clueless. I was living two lives.

And then in 2014, after nearly eight years as neighbors, Chad and his family moved away, to a new job in a new city. I knew it was for the best, but I was so sad and so tired of being sad. I resolved that my life was just sadness and that's how it was and would always be.

Everybody moved on. Harrison sold a book and got famous. I got the big new house. Everything seemed happy, but I was as numb as ever. Resigned to it. Trying to smile.

Three years later, Chad's family moved back to Savannah. No longer neighbors, but not far away.

One weekend the first summer they were back in town, his wife invited us for dinner. As weird as this sounds, she and I were friends. She was so sweet to the girls, just as sweet as he was. They were some of my only real friends. The day she asked us for dinner, Harrison was in France, out of the country for two weeks. I took the girls to their house and it was nice. After we left and went home, I got the text that shook me.

"You were beautiful tonight," Chad said.

He went on, about how he loved my hair long and how much he'd missed me and how glad he was they were back in Savannah. He said he wanted to tell me something but wouldn't tell me over text. He wanted to come over. I said okay. The next night, he walked in the back door, straight to where I stood in the kitchen. He scooped me up, kissed me, and said, "I love you. I've always loved you."

"I love you, too," I said.

I felt so guilty I threw up every morning for weeks. My stomach was in knots but something strange happened, too. I felt my numbness become less numb. It's like the affair uncorked a lifetime of feelings trapped inside, which felt so good, a relief, the way vomiting is a relief. But bad, the way vomiting is bad. Because now I had new feelings to trap inside.

The constant lying and sneaking around began. Deleting messages, changing my phone pass code, changing it again. Lying and saying I needed to run errands or work late or work early or go to the gym. It was shocking how good I was at keeping this secret life a secret. But then, I was good at keeping things inside. A pro. Been doing it all my life.

The affair was a high and a low all twisted together. Affair or not, when you start something new, it feels so good. A rush of heat. Butterflies. I hadn't felt like that in a long time. The low was obvious. *This is universally wrong. Evil. Horrible. Sinful. I'm going straight to hell. I'm just like my dad. Bad. Bad. Bad. Bad. Bad.*

So I did what I knew how to do best. "Numb it up, girl! We'll figure this out."

You know what happened next.

When we told our spouses we wanted divorces, I felt only numbness. Harrison fought it, fought for me, refused to kick me out. But I didn't feel flattered. I felt trapped. My sister drove across two states and drove me to a therapist. I'd barely talked to her in months but she showed up as all good big sisters do. I sat on the therapist's couch: T-shirt, shorts, no shoes. No shoes at the therapist. That's how you know it's bad. My arms were crossed and my heart was a block of ice that I did not ask for anyone to melt. I'd spent of a lot effort on the numbing and hardness and was not about to let someone soften all that now. You want me to feel feelings? You want me to deal with my dad leaving? You want me to deal with my mom's death? No, thank you.

Chad and I broke it off. Harrison and I picked up a big old rug and swept it all under and moved on. We changed churches. We tried to change habits. At counseling, I wore shoes and uncrossed my arms and knew all the right things to do and say. What you do is, you take a shower and put on your makeup and a smile and say "Jesus" and "God" and quote a few Bible verses and everybody will leave you alone. A year passed, then another. We got pregnant, we lost the baby. More blurring. More sadness.

God, if you're out there, maybe cut me a break?

The year after we lost the baby, that first summer of the pandemic, Chad and I reconnected. He'd sent an email, a shot across the bow to see if I would respond. I asked him to leave me alone, but he was persistent. And he'd been my best friend. And I was an idiot. I agreed to meet him in person and catch up. A little more advice: don't do this.

The cycle started again. Secret life, secret texts, secret secrets. A few months later, Harrison knew. He just knew. He asked. I told him. That's when the fun really began. By *fun*, I mean *nightmare*. All that had been safely under the rug was now unsafely out. This second confession made the first seem like child's play. This was war. The war was in me.

Two months into this hell, I told Harrison I needed to move out. I wanted to be on my own and see what it was like. He did not want me to go but knew one of us had to leave. He even offered to move out if I promised to end things with Chad. But I couldn't promise that. I couldn't promise anything. I needed to break out of the prison of myself and had to do it alone.

I found a carriage house just a few streets away. The girls asked why I was going. I told them I needed space. And I left. I left my family. I moved out. Left my children. Left my home. Left everything, pretty much, but the pillow. I did not forget my pillow.

The weight of my leaving is almost impossible for me to comprehend, even now. I'd hardly even left our girls to go to Walmart, for crying out loud. I'd always believed I was a good mom, the best, just like my own mom said I would be. Advice: maybe go to Walmart alone more often and it won't come to this.

The worst was watching the girls' silent tears fall down their faces the day we told them I was moving out. Our girls were so confused as to why I would go. I'm a lot of terrible things, but I've always been a good mom. The day I left, everything I thought I was, was no more.

After I left, I tried to make up for it. I wouldn't be like my dad. I would see the girls. I saw them almost every day after school, had them over, made fun meals. But it didn't matter. I wasn't there to kiss them good night or fix school lunches or brush their hair.

That first night alone was the worst. It was so quiet. I wanted to go home so badly. I wanted to be with the girls. I missed them so much. But I did not miss Harrison, and I knew I had to want to be with Harrison if I went home. I had to miss him, too. I had to figure that part out. I didn't want to just stay married for the kids, as so many do.

Our friends and family were as confused as our girls. Christians, who claim to be the best in these types of situations, are often the worst. Some leaned into me and tried to help. Others avoided me like a bomb that was about to explode. It was good gossip for many. A few invited me to lunch on their very high horses so they could say they would "pray" for me, when, really, they just wanted to see a real live whore up close. Lunch? *No thanks. I'm good down here in my whore trough.*

When I was growing up, my grandmother would often say, "I'm sweating like a whore in church." As a kid, I assumed this imaginary whore was sweating in church because she knew Jesus was watching her and scowling his disapproving scowl. But now I know. The whore is not sweating in church because of Jesus. She's sweating because of all the Christians.

I stopped going to our new church, which only had a few families at the time, which was tough. I've been in church my whole life. God, whom I'd so often hated, or wanted to hate, suddenly felt like someone I needed on my side. I wanted to feel God's hand on me. I knew he was still there. I didn't want to hate him. I wanted to feel my mom's hand on me, too. She was always there in those walls, in my memories. I could feel her shouting hymns from heaven.

I visited another church by myself. Bigger, more anonymous. This was not the kind of church you go to if you really want help. Too easy to hide. I sat there by myself and wondered, "Who knew? How much did they know?" I had an affair target on my head, but also an affair radar. I could see it in the eyes of others. I know what it looks like to hide things. We shared a secret code. Some wanted help. Some wanted out. I saw it all.

After a few weeks of loneliness that I couldn't bear, Chad found me. I'd tried to end things over and over, but he always came back. A text. A call. An email. His wife had left a few months before and they were officially divorced now and selling their house.

And just like that, he moved in. This had always been our plan, so why did I still feel dread in the pit of my stomach? Maybe it was that he would be gone for long hours, late at night, disappearing. Or staying up late when I wanted to go to sleep. Or not having a solid job. Asking me for money. Talking to his ex-wife. No. It was the undeniable truth that I was running as fast as I could down a path of death, with darkness at its end.

I don't know how to explain what happened next except to say that God's hand was on me. It was a supernatural experience. Harrison's grace and mercy to me, it was so shocking. Where before I thought only of Chad, now I was consumed only by the shock of that grace. It made me mad that I couldn't just walk away and have the life I thought I wanted. Why wouldn't Harrison just leave me or tell me to go? Why wouldn't he cut the final thread and let it be done? Why did he love me so much? It was annoying.

Harrison was making this difficult and my arms were crossed but my heart was not quite the solid block of ice it used to be.

That day at the carriage house, I remember lying on my bed—a bed I now shared with another man. Harrison and I were on the phone discussing child custody and insurance and money. He'd found out Chad lived here. Harrison was done. Chad knew I was on the phone with Harrison and was frantically calling and texting over and over.

"Are you okay?" Chad texted. "What is he saying? Why won't you answer me?"

It was like a scene from a Keanu Reeves movie. I knew a bomb was going to explode. People were going to die. I had to cut a wire, but which one? Green, blue, red, yellow? I didn't know which wire would save the world and which would kill us all.

Harrison drew one last line in the sand. He made me pick a wire, and I'd better do it fast. God picked a color and handed me the scissors and said, "Cut."

• • •

I left a lot of things at the carriage house that day. I left the strong Lauren. The independent Lauren. The numb Lauren. The Lauren who didn't want to feel things or talk about things or hurt. What we brought home was the broken Lauren. She was the only one left.

We had no plan. I lay on the floor of our garage on top of my pile of stuff and cried. I cried for my dad. I cried for my mom. I cried for my years of lying. I cried for our girls. I cried for Harrison's broken heart. I cried for Chad. I cried for me. I cried for my choices and how my choices had hurt so many people. All the hurt poured out.

I got a new phone number. New Facebook. New email. Rented a car. Stayed with friends. I even got a new job. I tried to cut ties as quickly as I could. That is not easy. It's not easy to start over. But it was so refreshing in so many ways, too. I cut ties to every high horse in town. If this was going to work with Harrison, it was going to have to be all new.

Harrison and I started the long road of putting up the bricks in our wall of trust. One brick at a time. Then trust would be broken again. A few weeks after leaving Chad, I caved and gave him my new number. I told myself it was just for closure or emergencies or whatever. Then he would call or text and the wall would crash back down. I told you it was not easy.

Harrison and I dug in our claws, determined to make it work. But I didn't want to just make it work. I wanted to find love and peace in our marriage. I wasn't going to just stay with him because it was the right thing. This had to be the real thing, too.

It took a year to know it was the real thing. A year free of this other man. A year repairing my relationships with my family. No one prepares you for all the relationships that will need to be repaired. It wasn't just about and Harrison and me. There was work to do.

Harrison made jokes about murdering Chad, then me, then killing himself. I made jokes about murdering Harrison, then Chad, then killing myself. Murder, murder, suicide. I confessed all the times I'd hoped Harrison's plane would crash or he'd get hit by a bus while riding his bike or maybe he'd eat contaminated chicken or get high-speed melanoma on his giant bald head.

"That's sweet," he'd say.

We didn't really want anyone dead, but it sure felt good to be honest and raw and laugh. We were always good at laughing.

That first year home, there were so many awkward and terrible moments. *Hey, so I was living with this other dude and now I'm back, so you want tacos for dinner?* There is no rule book. We would watch a movie together and someone would cheat on someone in the show and I would die all over again and I'm pretty sure Harrison would, too.

The big iceberg in my heart needed to melt and it's still melting. I still struggle with being vulnerable and kind. I love being a mystery of secrets. I've had to rethink romance. I've had to rethink love. It's romantic to steal away for forbidden kisses and text for hours into the night. But maybe love is more than that. Maybe love is loyalty. Forgiveness. Trust. Not running away.

I no longer feel trapped. I so often feel sad, but not hopeless. I feel a lasting love and peace for Harrison that I'm not sure I would have felt if we hadn't gone to all the dark places together. He could hold this over my head but somehow does not. Forgiveness in a supernatural way. That kind of forgiveness is definitely not normal. Little about my story, or my husband, is normal.

I have had so much death in my life. Actual death, emotional death. But I have had life, too. We have three amazing girls I love more than words can ever express. I'm so grateful that the story of my leaving will not define their lives, the way my dad's leaving almost defined mine. I almost killed them to get what I thought I wanted. Thanks be to God I did not. This is a line we say every Sunday during Communion. Soren hands us the bread and the wine and he says, "Body of Christ, broken for you."

We reply, "Thanks be to God."

I used to cringe when saying that. But now it feels different. Now it feels like (deep breath, exhale):

THANKS BE TO GOD
Body of Christ, broken.
My heart, broken.
My life, broken.

I think I had to let myself be broken, to be broken and die, to let the best parts of me live. These days, I'm okay with sweating in church. I'm home. Home with Harrison and our girls. Home in a church where I can tell people who I am, and they love me anyway. Home in a church where sweating is normal. It's not a cold sweat. It's not fearful. It's just real. Because the people are real. Because I'm no longer hiding.

Find those people. Thanks be to God I did.

Chapter 38

HOW TO STAY MARRIED

Fifteen Months Later

If you want to stay married, the first thing you're going to need is to be insane. Because staying married is insane. Getting married is not. Getting married is fun. In the weeks and months before the wedding, you're in passionate love with this glorious gift of a human: the ring, the announcement, the engagement photos where you hold hands and close your eyes and lean in and touch your foreheads together like a pair of telepathic freaks, that part is fun. Staying married is not fun. Staying married is like being kicked repeatedly in the head by a mule who loves you, and the mule is God.

This is not to say you should not marry. Plenty will read this book and say, "Lo, this is why I choose to remain single." Many do, and I lust for their disposable income. But somebody's got to populate the damned planet and make the people who will raise the cruelty-free chickens and overthrow despots and build space freighters, and the babies who will grow up to work all these wonders thrive best with two parents in the same house, we know this:

two people bound together by covenants not easily dissolved. Be offended at this simple truth if you like.

For a brief and harried season of my life, I was a single parent and just about died. The dishes alone were enough to make you deny the existence of a loving God. Parents are like arms. You can swing it with one but two work best and three would be weird.

Perhaps one day we will evolve ourselves into some better arrangement for the children, where benevolent armies of solar-powered robots raise children on expansive baby farms, but until Elon funds this nightmare, marriage is what we've got. It's good for us and it's good for the kids, even when it hurts like hell. I think often of our daughters and what they have learned of love in this strange season. I suppose we've given them enough trauma to turn all three into artists or writers, or at least law students. But we're here, all of us: a nuclear family, detonated but not destroyed. We won't be traumatizing our children with our divorce. We'll traumatize them with our marriage, as God intended.

I thought of ending this book with a heartwarming scene of new-found domestic tranquility, but it's spring now, as I write, the least domestically tranquil of seasons for parents of school-age children, with its comical abundance of finales: ballet recitals, art shows, awards ceremonies, the eighth-grade cookout, the fifth-grade pool fest, the soccer pizza party, a volleyball luncheon, and an annual athletics banquet that lasts approximately seventy-two hours (which, to my annual surprise, does not actually involve food), as well as an *Anne of Green Gables*–themed tea (for which Ginsburg will have to bake a pie and make fudge, because apparently the book features many important scenes involving pie and fudge), in addition to the spring choir concert, where all three of our daughters will perform. People who don't have children don't know that they're missing the pleasure of watching a concert where half of the children appear never to have heard of music at all. Many of the songs are beautiful and tender, whence I place a hand on Lauren's knee, and she places a hand on mine and squeezes, and we feel all the feelings all at once, while other songs, well. The middle school boys alone seem to be suffering from a collective trauma that prevents them from singing at a volume detectable by the human ear.

You say you won't be the kind of parents whose kids do all those things, but they won't be home forever. We are teaching them to be human: to win, to lose, to throw their bodies and hearts and voices into the wondrous fray of life. In addition to this dizzying array of events, Lauren and I have what are called "jobs," and attending every important moment is uniquely difficult. She goes to some events, I go to others, we go to some together. Parenting is tag-team wrestling. Tap in, tap out, stay alive. Our family is working again. It is a miracle, and anything but tranquil. So instead, I will end this story with a few closing words on how, exactly, one might stay married, according to my limited wisdom.

What I recommend is, when you stand there and speak vows, it's hard to imagine ever wanting to divorce this beautiful person, but you have to. You have to try to imagine it, just so you're not surprised when one day you find yourself imagining it, and when you do, in the dark of a bedroom where you're probably not the only one awake, you then have to imagine staying married, not just for the children and the house payment and the role you play in keeping the wall of civilization upright and strong but because you promised to, you sack of tumors. This is the joke and the surprise of marriage. You promise the impossible and then have the audacity to attempt it.

But sometimes you have to get divorced. Violence, or merely

the credible threat of physical harm, requires it. If your spouse has attempted to sever your head or another important body part, for example. Childlessness, too, makes divorce an easier and often more ideal option. If we didn't have children, and if my wife had attempted to sever my head, I probably would've divorced her. It would've made a funnier book.

If you want your marriage to survive, another thing you need to do is get help. Many people, men especially, resist therapy, because quite often men are idiots. Lauren and I are fortunate to have absurdly generous health insurance, which is how we can afford all those weekly appointments. Everybody likes to talk about how money can end a marriage. Nobody talks about how money can help save one. If you and your partner can't afford therapy, or you find yourself on a six-month wait list for the only good therapist in town, you still have options. Find wise people. They're everywhere if you know where to look. I had many phone calls with people I'd never even met in person, such as my wife's cousin's mother-in-law, Debbie, because I was told this angel of a human considers this sort of counsel her ministry. Debbie lives eight hundred miles away, and those and so many other phone calls with so many wise and caring people—Mark, Rachel, Stephen, and others—gave me breath of life when I was five fathoms deep. Find these people. They will keep you alive. Avoid the idiots if you can. The world is full of bad advice from bitter and hopeless wretches who don't even know they're not helping. Avoid those who urge you to vengeance or say you deserve better. The only thing you deserve is better advice from people who have a rudimentary grasp of the nightmare of marriage for both people in it. Run far and fast from those who say different.

Talk to at least three people you love who've gone through a divorce. Those folks have been through the fire. They've buried things they never wanted to bury. They are some of the wisest people I know. People who've died and come back usually are. You'll hear a different story every time, but mostly you'll hear about death: of egos, of illusions, of who you thought you were. One of your greatest misconceptions, the one you must jettison as soon as is convenient to you, is that you're easy to live with. You're not. You're a monster. Marriage reveals this to you, though you'd prefer to blame your partner, your parents, SCOTUS. Their monstrousness is so much easier to see.

And if you, like Lauren and me, can afford a little therapy, do it: solo therapy, marriage counseling, do it all. You don't have to go every week. But go when it gets hard. Go during the difficult years. Go before it gets as bad as it got for us. Go when you feel that distance. If you haven't had sex in three months, go. If your spouse demands sex nightly and you're experiencing unpleasant chafing and don't know how to explain this without sounding like you resent the sight of your spouse's nakedness, go.

Back in olden times, our ancestors didn't need so much therapy because when invading armies are burning your village, sexual chafing seems trivial. But now armies rarely burn villages, I am told, leaving more time for our egos to do the pillaging. Therapy and wise counsel from friends and the friends of friends can keep your village from being reduced to ash before it's too late.

As I write this, it's been well over a year since Lauren and I started seeing Dr. Berman, and by the time you read this, it will have been more than two. We were there every week, then every two weeks; now we're down to once a month. It's like going to the beach: a pain in the ass to get there, maybe you get burned a little or attacked by an unseen creature from the deep, but you're usually glad you went. In therapy, we don't talk about the affair anymore, though to be honest we never talked about the affair much at all. I mean, we did. But after we unloaded the story in that first session so long ago with Dr. Berman, he hardly ever asked about it again. He invited us to say anything and everything, but his questions tossed the affair aside like a dirty diaper. For our therapist, and eventually for Lauren and me, the affair was a MacGuffin, a brutal plot device that activated the real questions: Who are we? What is our duty to each other in this nasty and brutish life?

Dr. Berman asks about childhoods, fathers, mothers, how we don't fight, how we don't talk about not fighting, how we don't talk about not talking about not fighting, Lauren's long refusal to address her past, my refusal to let the dead bury the dead, my long insistence on justice over mercy. How easy it has been for me to fixate on the MacGuffin of the betrayal: the drama of its many salacious scenes, the sin, the secrets, the Taylor Swift–ness of it all. Many people, I know, will want to read this book because, as Lauren said, they want every lurid detail. People love to watch a marriage go up in flames, which affords the blessed opportunity to warm your ego by the fire. *We're not perfect, but look at these two.* It's a vicarious thrill, the itch to burn it all down and walk away, while proudly declaring, *We would never.*

If you think this could never happen to you, you're a fool. It's happening right now. Your wife is sending memes to your neighbor this very day. Does she send you memes, too? Your husband is a little drunk and texting an inside joke to a colleague whom he's so often imagined disrobing in a luxury hotel room that he could tell a police sketch artist what she looks like in the shower. What will you do about these thoughts? What will you do with the fact that one in four marriages experiences infidelity? If you're a man, you're more likely to commit infidelity than you are to play a musical instrument. If you're a woman, you're more likely to have an affair than you are to have bangs.

These odds are not great. All you can do is get your own heart in order. Ask God to help. If you don't believe in God, ask your therapist. Unbury the deadness in your past and reckon with it. Then give it a good funeral. Put out some flowers and get busy living. Buddha was right. The ego is your only real enemy, feeding off the hurt of your history. It is the adversary you must first slay before you can be of any real use to humankind.

Don't assume your partner is cheating. Assume your partner will, eventually. Assume you will, too. The world is full of Chads. Do something now. Ask for counseling. Ask for a long weekend. Snake the drains of your hearts together. If you're just going about your business, a nice couple in a good marriage, living your lives, raising your family, the drains will grow putrid and you won't even know. Go watch *Marriage Story* on Netflix. Imagine it's you. Read books on infidelity. On marriage. On love. On pride. On rekindling the fire. On sex positions that don't require too much stretching. No two marriages are the same. You will need help to determine how, exactly, to stoke the flame of love and burn away the deadfall of your own endless wanting. You pay pros to clean your teeth and replace your brake shoes. Why won't you pay someone to give your marriage a little more mileage, too? Therapy creates new intimacy, and not just for the sex. Go for a walk. Splurge for a sitter and go have a long breakfast somewhere. You must connect frequently, and not just via the reproductive organs.

Whatever your feelings about Christ being the bridegroom and the church being the bride, here's what I've come to see: Rome slaughtered Jesus, and that's what marriage will do. It will slay you, crucify and burn and behead you and everything you thought you knew about yourself. And the thing that is left, after all is burned and plucked away, that is the real you.

Marriage has changed over the millennia, and that's a beautiful thing, but the prophets of this present age would have us believe marriage should exist solely for the benefit of the people in it, for their emotional, psychological, and carnal empowerment, as though matrimony is merely an extended couple's spa experience featuring orgies and explosive self-actualizations that you can exit whensoever your heart desires. What if the prophets are wrong? Are we not freer than ever in human history, and sadder, and more anxious, more wretched? What if marriage, at its very best, exists to remake us into beautiful new creatures we scarcely recognize? What if, in some cosmically weird way, escaping a hard marriage is not how you change? What if staying married is?

None of our change has come easy. Our division of labor is now radically progressive, at least for the men in my family. I do a million times more housework than I once did, a trillion times more than my father. I now do most of the grocery shopping, most of the cooking, and most of the telling everybody to hush when they complain. It still takes threats of violence to get me to help with fitted sheets, but I now empty the dishwasher unprompted, which is a kind of miracle. The best thing about our new marriage is that my wife no longer has a boyfriend. In that sense, it's more traditional.

I am well aware, and I hope you are, too, that the mystery of the death and resurrection of my marriage is not solved by some complex algorithm involving the transactional distribution of housework. I'm not doing all this to keep my wife from having another affair. I'm doing it because I love her and she loves my help—and I know this (and this is key) because she finally found the words to tell me how much she loves my help, and I finally found ears to hear.

We're both new creatures, yet remain so very different. If I die tomorrow, she'll probably marry someone who does not sleep naked or make so many disgusting sounds, such as when I breathe, or speak, or have the audacity to drink water in front of her, before bed, while naked. Just as, if she dies, I'll probably marry someone who does not lose the ability to form sentences or express human love below 60 degrees Fahrenheit. We're not perfect for each other. We merely *are* each other.

One of my favorites, Alain de Botton, once wrote, "Compatibility is an achievement of love; it must not be its precondition." That is marriage, in the end: two of you, being you, warring against the worst parts of you, making space for the best to grow, and learning to see that some parts of your spouse are not your favorite, and letting those parts be anyway. Hating those parts is no grounds for divorce. The only thing worth divorcing, in most cases, is the hatred itself, and your inborn desire to shape the world to your will like some kind of Marvel villain.

Yet, to stay married, you will need more than therapy. You will need an entire community of people insane enough to love both of you, people to whom you cannot and will not lie about what is most real inside your wicked and wondrous heart. #VanLife sounds fun, but eventually you've got to park the Sprinter and find a village. Maybe it's a kickball team, maybe a book club, though you'll need more than a love for good novels to bind you together. For us, that community is our church. If church isn't your thing, I get it. It wasn't my thing for a long time. I once left the church of my childhood, lively and loving though it was, because I had more questions than they were prepared to answer. I found myself among other believers at big old churches who were fearless to take on the hardest questions ever posed by the human mind, but with cold and cruel answers.

They preached mercy but displayed little to my wife, when it mattered most. Somehow, by the grace of the thing we call God and
the everlasting mystery of the universe, my family ended up at the
weirdest, oddest little church you can imagine, with poor lighting
and broken windows.

It was this church of friends who showed us the third way I had
always hoped for: joyful, weird, curious, honest, fearless, and full of
reckless love for the broken and a willingness to enter darkness with
them. That's what Lauren and I are. Broken as hell. Our brokenness, it turns out, and our confession of that brokenness, and the
love we experienced from those around us, despite the brokenness,
or perhaps because of it, is what saved us.

What did our church do for us, exactly? They came when I
called. Handed children to their spouses and got in the car. They
listened to news nobody wants to hear. They sat with Lauren, too.
They did not tell her she was doing a bad thing and must now do
this or that good thing to fix it. She seemed plenty familiar with the
moral equations in play. They did not give answers, not at first. They
did the harder thing and asked questions. What does it feel like to
be her? And in the answering, her heart awoke to something. To
know people could see your inside and not revile you, this seemed a
surprising new variable of the equation.

And they texted me. "Checking in."

And "This bourbon won't drink itself."

And "You drank all of my bourbon."

And when Lauren left, they fed us. "Come eat."

And when Lauren came back, they fed us. "Come eat."

And they hugged me at church, knowing.

And even people who didn't know hugged me at church,
knowing.

And now they still hug me. And I wish they would stop. But it's fine.

"Can I hug you?" our friend Meredith said the other day at church, like a terrorist. "You look like you need a hug."

"Fine. I probably do."

They hug us. They feed us. We feed them. They feed our children and we feed theirs and they feed Gary when we're out of town and when they're out of town, we feed their cats. All we're doing is feeding each other, basically, with hymns and prayers and sermons thrown in there to remind us why.

Maybe you think me a fool for believing in a God that helped me stay married to a woman who gave me every good reason to let her go. Maybe I let bad things happen because for many years I had the emotional intelligence of a potted succulent. Maybe so. There are a lot of *maybe*s in this book. Sometimes *maybe* is all you have to hold on to. That's all faith is, an enthusiastic *maybe*. A passionate *probably*. A hopeful *hopefully*.

Was it God who saved my family? Does he dance in the wind, feeling good about my marriage, giving us the old thumbs-up? Is Jesus the literal, actual historical embodiment of that cosmic goodness, of love so amazing, so divine, love that begets love while melting your brain with its power, such that all I can do, when attempting to comprehend that love, is to show that love to others? What if God and Jesus are metaphors for something too impossible to fathom, which we attempt to fathom anyway? What if the endless fathoming is our duty? What if God and Jesus aren't metaphors at all? What if they're real? What if everything else is a metaphor for *them*?

Maybe some of these questions disqualify me from calling myself a Good American Christian, but I'm not worried about the approval of whitewashed tombs who can't tell the difference be-tween doubt and wonder. Those people are afraid to admit they don't know the answers to those questions, either. I take comfort in what Augustine once said, quoted by Soren in a sermon not long ago: "If you have understood God, then what you have understood is not God."

Audacity, therapy, honesty, intimacy, nudity, a belief in transcendent profundity, a loving community that does not bless the whims of your ego but loves you anyway: You need all these to stay married, and a thousand million other mercies besides, including perhaps the most obvious and impossible of virtues. You need comedy.

Our shared love of a good laugh was for Lauren and me the only way to express the unspeakable truths and impossible questions we've both faced without bursting our hearts in two. My wife has said many funny things in our life together, and one of the funniest is when she told me she was living with a man who probably cannot name the vice president. I've said some pretty ridiculous things, too, like when I told her I wanted to write this book.

Even now, at the end of this story, I don't precisely know how to reconcile my wife's love for another man with her love for me, her desire to burn it all down with her desire to care for everyone around her. I want the answers to be easy. I want perfect knowledge of all things in heaven and earth, because perfect knowledge is per-fect power and I would very much like to be omnipotent, which seems like it could help with chores. But comedy reminds me that while I may have many admirable qualities, my strength and intelli-gence are no match for reality. Laughter is often the only solution to insoluble questions. How can I, for example, continue to sleep next to a woman who wanted, for the better part of a decade, to attend my funeral, so that she could marry another? I don't know. I will never know. The human heart is a terrain that cannot be mapped by reason alone. Virtue cannot solve the riddle of marriage. All I really know is this: the most powerful force in the universe is love and the strangest is forgiveness. I will never fully understand either but then I still don't know exactly how elevators work and I enjoy elevators all the time.

All the yesterdays described in this book feel a million years in the past, each terrible flesh-eating moment now a fossil buried in memory—fossils that only occasionally get reanimated and try to eat us again. Not long ago, a friend who went through something similar said to me, "You forget. You move on. Everything is fine and great, and then in a flash, you remember all over again and the rage fills you like it once did."

This, too, has happened. It is not a calculated rage. It is not planned. It is not welcome. The feeling springs forth from the dark places in me, and sometimes I feel that this rage is only trying to help, to remind me, to make me vigilant, and sometimes I feel that the rage is evil, accusatory, telling me to walk away, to be the one to leave next. I feel it. It is not a good feeling. If I feel this darkness too much, I talk to Lauren. I bring it up in therapy. I go outside and hit the drums.

The good news: comedy is all about miracles, transformation, new understanding, mercy. That's the real miracle of comedy: forgiveness, the greatest LOL of them all. What is forgiveness but burying the dead and being okay with it? What can be more impossible and necessary in this life? They say God doesn't keep a grade book, and I'm trying to throw mine away. "Love keeps no record of wrongs," we hear so often in wedding ceremonies, and we smile like fools.

But there's another verse that seems much clearer to me. It's in the book of Proverbs, which says, "All the days of the afflicted are evil, but he that is of a merry heart hath a continual feast."

Our days have so often been evil. We have so often lived in utter affliction, you, me, Lauren, the lot of us. This cannot be denied. But the darkness has been overcome, is being overcome, by shining what light we have into the places where you don't always want to look and laughing at the absurdity, the audacity, of life, and our audacity to carry on. The merry heart so often seems ridiculous to the afflicted because it is a heart of flesh, not stone. Stone hearts cannot laugh. Only soft ones, loose and alive, do that.

The hard conversations have grown fewer, dreams of tomorrow more plenteous. We don't talk about the past much anymore. But sometimes, we do. A few weeks ago, we sat in the driveway, enjoying the last cool evening of spring, the girls inside, finishing their homework.

"I need to ask you something," I said. "I know it's traumatic for you, but I have to ask."

"What?" she said, dreading what might come out of my mouth.

I took a deep breath, summoned the courage, and after a suitably pregnant pause, placed my hand on her arm.

"What do you want for dinner?"

She laughed, then looked at me, studied my face. She had something to say, too. She says things all the time now. It's terrifying.

"I really hate that mustache," she said.

"It looks a lot better when I'm naked."

"I'm your wife, and I'm actually very attracted to you." She climbed into my lap like some kind of sex kitten. "Why would you fuck that up?"

"You talk dirty for a good Christian."

"Who says I'm good?"

Later, I shaved the mustache. What do I care? Love means letting some things go. They say tragedy is all about death, but things have to die in comedy, too. Sometimes what dies is your old marriage. Sometimes what dies is you. But God can make a valley of bones dance again. Your marriage can return from the dead. They say Jesus looked different after he came back. His buddies didn't even recognize him. If your marriage gets resurrected, you'll look different, too. Badly maimed, possibly. Limping, smiling, a sparkle in your one good eye. The world may look at you funny. Because heartache and love will transform you and your partner into new and better beings, if you will only get out of the way.

When I began this book, I said how enthusiastically people have always loved my wife.

"I want to be her friend!" they always said.

"Your wife is my new favorite person," they said.

"She's the best!"

And then my wife ran off with the neighbor, and nobody knew, and still they said nice things, even as the nightmare unfolded its dark wings across my home. *She is not my favorite person*, I wanted to say. *She is not even in my top five.*

But I refuse to allow the wounds of the recent unpleasantness to undo goodness that always was. I never knew her before, not fully, but I know her now—including the parts she was once too fearful to reveal and the parts I was so often too frightened to see. I now understand that to comprehend the immensity of someone's pain is to comprehend the full breadth of the soul. The beauty of my wife is more beautiful to me than I ever could have imagined, because I see the fullness of her now, and I can admit, without reserve, that she is definitely one of my favorite people, perhaps even among my top five. How can I not love this woman, for how deeply she has allowed herself to be seen?

Coco will be gone in less than two years and Pippi and Gins-burg not long after, and then it'll just be the two of us again and this weird-ass marriage. We dream now of vacation homes, pools, buying a farm somewhere, renewing our vows in a backyard ceremony where Gary will eat some of our closest friends.

If Jesus ever comes back again—I don't know, maybe he will, they say he will—then I think we'll have a good laugh. Laughter can sometimes feel impossible when you have so much hurt to remember. Finishing this book will, I think, help me do the forgetting. Here, take our memories. Take our story. Let it do in you what stories do. I want to be done with it. The corpse of the old me is just bones now, bleaching in the front yard. The birds carry them away, one at a time. Eventually, all that remains is this ridiculous heart, two of them, hers and mine. Beating, and laughing, and doing what true lovers do.

Laundry.

Acknowledgments

In some ways, this entire book is one long acknowledgment of the people, both alive and dead, without whom my wife would now be living elsewhere and I might now be married to a dermatologist who owns a second home in Ibiza, and for these people and their sacrifices and mercies, we are forever indebted. They are:

The Bass Family

The Bell Family

Dr. Harold Berman

Mark Blanton

The Cavnar Family

Joan Dane-Kellogg

The Finn-McCool Fellowship

The Hart Family

Debbie Holley

The Kornegay Family

Love Handles ("Savannah's Hottest All-Male Party Band")

The Mehl Family

The Roberts Family

The Remington Families

The Segrest Family

Katherine Sandoz

Additionally, I want to thank all those at SCAD who extended to me profound mercies and brought food and threatened to do my laundry (Paula Wallace, Lesley Hanak, Carmen Stowers, and so many others), as well as all the people of all the churches of my life (for all of them taught me something of love), especially the people of Christ the King Savannah, a community of angels who can fly because they know how to take themselves lightly. Thanks be to God.

Thank you to Debbie Grosvenor who, in the midst of the events described here, became not only my agent, but also my friend. Her compassion and wisdom have made me a better man. And thank you to my editor Jofie Ferrari-Adler and his crew at Avid Reader Press and Simon & Schuster for publishing this horror novel masquerading as a comedy. Jofie's vibe is just what this story needed. His calming voice and easy laugh should be bottled and prescribed. When my blood pressure spikes, I relisten to his old voice mails.

Thank you to my parents, Lanny and Emily Key, for making me so amazing, talented, handsome, and delusional. And thanks be to God for Coco, Pippi, and Ginsburg, the wind beneath the wings of my Greater Prairie-Chicken, and for Lauren, without whom this book would most definitely not exist. Thank you for not begging me not to write this. You could have. I would not have listened.

And thank you to God for helping us stay married.

About the Author

HARRISON SCOTT KEY is the author of three books, including *The World's Largest Man* (winner of the Thurber Prize for American Humor) and *Congratulations, Who Are You Again?*, the inspiration for his popular TEDx talk, "The Funny Thing About the American Dream," featured at TED.com. He is executive dean at the Savannah College of Art and Design (SCAD) in Savannah, Georgia. Readers can find him at one of the links below:

www.HarrisonScottKey.com
www.facebook.com/HarrisonScottKey
www.instagram.com/HarrisonScottKey
www.twitter.com/HarrisonKey